'ABOVE PARTIES':

THE POLITICAL ATTITUDES
OF THE GERMAN
PROTESTANT CHURCH
LEADERSHIP
1918–1933

BY

J. R. C. WRIGHT

OXFORD UNIVERSITY PRESS
1974

Oxford University Press, Ely House, London W.1

GLASGOW   NEW YORK   TORONTO   MELBOURNE   WELLINGTON
CAPE TOWN   IBADAN   NAIROBI   DAR ES SALAAM   LUSAKA   ADDIS ABABA
DELHI   BOMBAY   CALCUTTA   MADRAS   KARACHI   LAHORE   DACCA
KUALA LUMPUR   SINGAPORE   HONG KONG   TOKYO

ISBN 0 19 821856 7
© J. R. C. WRIGHT 1974

Printed in Great Britain
by William Clowes & Sons Limited
London, Colchester and Beccles

PREFACE

This book is a study of the German Protestant church leadership between the revolution of 1918 which brought down the German Empire and resulted in a democratic Republic and the second revolution of 1933 when Hitler assumed power and proclaimed the triumph of the Third Reich. The Protestant leadership was a conservative group: it had been closely identified with the Empire and it was naturally hostile to the Republic and susceptible to the appeal of the Republic's enemies including the Nazi party. The story of the Protestant leadership in this period is thus in miniature one of the central themes of modern German history—how the German conservative and national liberal traditions became, at least for a time, submerged by the Nazi movement.

The scope of this book is similar to existing studies of other conservative institutions, such as the army, the Prussian civil service, and conservative political parties.[1] The most interesting question with all groups of this kind is whether there was any alternative to the way things turned out. In particular, could the German upper and middle classes have come to accept the Republic if the economic recovery of the years 1925-9 had continued? Or were they incapable of reconciliation with the Republic and should the economic crisis of the early 1930s be seen as simply the occasion of their desertion to the anti-Republican Right and not as an important cause of it? A second and related question is how close was the sympathy between German conservatives and the Nazi movement? Were the differences between them matters of principle or simply of temperament? In short, was there within the German Right what conservative opponents

1. F. L. Carsten, *The Reichswehr and Politics 1918–1933* (Oxford, 1966); W. Runge, *Politik und Beamtentum im Parteienstaa* 1965); H. A. Turner, *Stresemann and the Politics of the Weimar Republic* (Princeton, 1963); E. Jonas, *Die Volkskonservativen 1928–1933* (Düsseldorf, 1965).

of Nazism during the Third Reich called the 'other Germany'?[2]

The Protestant leadership represented a large community. The total nominal membership of the Protestant church during the Republic was almost 40,000,000—over 60 per cent of the German population. However, this included many members of the working class who did not go to church although they did not formally leave it. Those Protestants who went to church—about 11,000,000 or 18 per cent of the total population—came mainly from the middle and upper classes and it was this group of 'active' Protestants which gave the church its political tone.[3] The Protestant leadership had a mixed membership of lawyers, clergymen, and laymen. Some of its members were directly elected by the church synods and major decisions were referred to the synods. This ensured that the leadership remained sensitive to the feelings of active church members.

No comprehensive study of the Protestant church under the Republic has yet been made. Most work has been concerned with the part played by the church during the Third Reich. However, some aspects of the subject have been opened up in a series of important monographs. They deal with the political attitudes of the church in the First World War and the revolution of 1918, the social position and political outlook of Protestant clergy during the Republic, the political content of Protestant literature and the Protestant press, and the behaviour of the church in the crisis of 1933.[4] All these are based on a selection of printed sources. They depict the Protestant church as monarchist, nationalist, and authoritarian, as predominantly hostile to the Republic and ambivalent or openly enthusiastic towards Nazism. This

---

2. H. C. Deutsch, *The Conspiracy against Hitler in the twilight war* (Minnesota and London, 1968), p. 15.

3. Figures for the 1925 census and for communicants from *Kirchliches Jahrbuch für die evangelischen Landeskirchen Deutschlands* 54. Jg. (1927), 144-5, 223.

4. G. Mehnert, *Evangelische Kirche und Politik 1917-1919* (Düsseldorf, 1959); K-W. Dahm, *Pfarrer und Politik* (Cologne, 1965); H. Christ, *Der politische Protestantismus in der Weimarer Republik* (Diss. Phil., Bonn, 1967); G. van Norden, *Kirche in der Krise: Die Stellung der evangelischen Kirche zum nationalsozialistischen Staat im Jahre 1933* (Düsseldorf, 1963).

picture contains no surprises and, within limits, is an accurate one. It does not, however, do justice to the variety of its subject. No one could guess from it that the church made considerable progress towards coming to terms with the Republic, nor yet that a desperate, though unsuccessful, attempt was made to resist Nazi control in 1933.

One difficulty in writing about the German Protestant church is that it was not a single organization. It was—and is—divided into a number of separate provincial churches known as *Landeskirchen*. During the Weimar Republic there were twenty-eight independent Landeskirchen. However one of these, the church of the Old Prussian Union, stood out in size and importance from the rest and its leadership was able to exert a powerful influence over the whole Protestant leadership. The main emphasis of this book is, therefore, upon its attitudes and policy. Secondly all the Landeskirchen were represented in a federal organization known as the *Kirchenbund* and where there were important differences between them, they were discussed at its meetings. The records of the Old Prussian Union and of the Kirchenbund, taken together, give a reasonably full picture of the church leadership as a whole. On the one important occasion when the attitude of a few of the smaller churches was decisive—on the question of what policy the church should adopt towards attempts by Nazi Protestants to assume control in 1933—the records of the individual Landeskirchen chiefly concerned have also been consulted.

The following study can be divided into three parts. The first two chapters explain how, from being closely dependent on the Empire, the church was made secure under the Republic. Whatever their formal or emotional objections to the Republican regime, church leaders were prepared to strike a bargain with it. In fact the development of their political ideas can only be understood against the background of their negotiations with Republican governments on matters which directly concerned the church. The second part of the book describes the stand taken by the Protestant leadership in domestic politics and in foreign policy, its relations with the Republic's enemies, particularly the Nazi party, and its attitude during the final crisis of the Republic.

The last chapter relates how the church leadership was confronted by the challenge of Nazism in 1933 and was broken by it.

ACKNOWLEDGEMENTS

I should like to thank the Warden and Fellows of St. Antony's College, Oxford, the Alexander von Humboldt Foundation, and the Warden and Fellows of Merton College, Oxford, for their generous support. I should also like to thank the staff of the archives and libraries I consulted in Oxford, the German Federal Republic, West Berlin, and the German Democratic Republic. I received great help from individuals, in particular Anthony Nicholls who supervised my work for a D.Phil. and Jeremy Noakes with whom I shared several periods in Germany. My father, Dr. F. J. Wright, gave me encouragement. My wife, Susan, advised me on the revision of the manuscript. I am also grateful to Miss Jini Hetherington and Mrs. S. Harrold for their secretarial assistance.

CONTENTS

ILLUSTRATIONS AND DIAGRAMS   xiii

ABBREVIATIONS   xiv

GLOSSARY   xvi

Introduction   The Church before 1918   1

1. The Revolution Settlement   11

    i. The Prussian *Land* and the Old Prussian Union   12
       a. *The provisional government*   12
       b. *The Weimar constitution*   17
       c. *The church constitution*   20

    ii. The other Protestant *Landeskirchen*   26
    iii. The formation of the *Kirchenbund*   28

2. The Prussian Church Treaty   32

3. Domestic Politics during the Republic   49

4. Foreign Policy   66

5. The 'National Opposition'   74

    i. The 'national movement'   74
    ii. The NSDAP   77
    iii. The German Christians   91

6. The Crisis of the Republic   99

7. The 'National Revolution'   110

    i. The new state   111
    ii. Revolution in the church   117
    iii. The revolution victorious   137

Appendix: The appointment of the *Staatskommissar*   143

Conclusion   145

Epilogue   The Third Reich   148
 i. Nazi policy   148
ii. The reaction of the Protestant church   156
    a. *Conflict within the church*   156
    b. *Conflict with the state*   163
iii. Conclusion   171

Bibliographical Note   174

BIBLIOGRAPHY   175

INDEX   191

ILLUSTRATIONS

Plate 1 The Protestants demand a treaty   *facing page*   47

Plate 2 Socialist satire on monarchism in the church
facing page   53

Plate 3 Nazi satire on restrictions on the attendance of
uniformed groups in church   *facing page* 102

DIAGRAMS

A. The Old Prussian Union
Landeskirche   *page*   22

B. The *Kirchenbund*   *page*   29

ABBREVIATIONS

Archives

A.A.	Politisches Archiv des Auswärtigen Amtes
A.k.A.	Archiv des kirchlichen Außenamts
Bundesarchiv	Bundesarchiv, Koblenz
D.Z.A.	Deutsches Zentralarchiv
E.K.D.	Evangelische Kirche in Deutschland
E.K.U.	Evangelische Kirche der Union
G.St.A.	Geheimes Staatsarchiv
Lk.A.	Landeskirchliches Archiv

Parties

BVP	Bayerische Volkspartei
	Bavarian People's Party
DDP	Deutsche Demokratische Partei
	German Democratic Party
DVP	Deutsche Volkspartei
	German People's Party
DNVP	Deutschnationale Volkspartei
	German National People's Party
KPD	Kommunistische Partei Deutschlands
	German Communist Party
NSDAP	Nationalsozialistische Deutsche Arbeiterpartei
	National Socialist Party
SPD	Sozialdemokratische Partei Deutschlands
	Social Democratic Party
USPD	Unabhängige Sozialdemokratische Partei Deutschlands
	Independent Social Democratic Party

Journals

AELKZ	*Allgemeine Evangelisch-Lutherische Kirchenzeitung*
AKfdED	*Allgemeines Kirchenblatt für das evangelische Deutschland*

Other
Diss.   Dissertation
RGG   *Religion in Geschichte und Gegenwart*

GLOSSARY

Beamte   civil servant

Evangelischer Bund   independent, anti-Roman Catholic Protestant association

Evangelischer Oberkirchenrat   see *Oberkirchenrat*

Generalsuperintendent   senior Protestant clergyman in a Prussian province

General Synod   church assembly of the Old Prussian Union

Kirchenausschuß   executive committee of the *Kirchenbund*

Kirchenbund   federal organization of the Protestant *Landeskirchen*

Kirchenbundesamt   *Kirchenbund* office

Kirchenbundesrat   federal committee of the *Kirchenbund*

Kirchensenat   executive committee of the church of the Old Prussian Union

Kirchentag   public meeting of the *Kirchenbund*

Körperschaft des öffentlichen Rechts   corporation with a special legal status

Konsistorium   administrative authority of a *Landeskirche* or province of a *Landeskirche*

Kulturkampf   conflict between church and state

Kultusminister (Kultusministerium)   Minister (Ministry) with responsibility for church and school affairs

Kundgebung   public declaration

Land (plural, *Länder*)   German state or province

Landesbischof   bishop of a *Landeskirche*

Landesherr   ruler of a *Land*

landesherrliches Kirchenregiment   ruler's ecclesiastical prerogative

Landeskirche   provincial church

Landtag   provincial parliament

Ministerialdirektor   senior civil servant

Oberkirchenrat   central administrative authority of the *Landeskirche*, especially of the Old Prussian Union

Oberpräsident   senior official in the provincial (state) administration

Pastor   Protestant clergyman (also, *Pfarrer*)

Reichsbanner   Republican para-military organization

Staatshoheitsrechte   rights of the state over the church

Staatskommissar (also *Kirchenkommissar*)   State Commissioner, i.e. state official appointed to administer the church

Stahlhelm   anti-Republican ex-servicemen's association

Summus Episcopus   ruler's position as Head of the Protestant church

Vertrauensrat   joint committee of the *Oberkirchenrat*, General Synod representatives and other advisers in the Old Prussian Union 1918–19

INTRODUCTION

THE CHURCH BEFORE 1918

The German Protestant church had a complicated structure.
Following the great division within the Reformation in
Europe it was divided first into Lutheran and Reformed
(Calvinist) churches. There were important differences of
theology and organization between the two. •Lutherans
attached prime importance to the doctrine of justification by
faith (not works) and this corresponded with a certain
passiveness in secular affairs; Lutherans depended on the
state even for their church organization. 'Calvinism was
distinguished by the doctrine of the elect and belief in active
participation in the world; the Reformed churches had their
own system of church self-government.[1] By the end of the
seventeenth century the Lutheran church was the major
denomination in the central, north, and east German states
and in Württemberg, Ansbach, and Nuremberg in the south.
The Reformed church was important in the Rhine Palatinate
and Nassau and as a Protestant minority in the north-west.
The Roman Catholic church was dominant along the Main, in
the Upper Palatinate and Bavaria, and strong in the north-
west and south-west.[2]

During the eighteenth century there was a reaction against
the divisions of the Reformation period reflected in the
Pietist movement which stressed the devotional side of
Christianity. In the early nineteenth century attempts were
made to unite the Lutheran and Reformed churches into a
single Protestant denomination. In 1817, the third centenary
of the Reformation, Frederick William III of Prussia issued a
decree for a United Prussian Church. The King met strong
resistance both from the Reformed churches in the new
provinces of Rhineland and Westphalia and from Lutherans

1. F. Fischer, 'Der deutsche Protestantismus und die Politik im 19.
Jahrhundert', *Historische Zeitschrift*, 171 (1951), 474–6.
2. *Westermanns Atlas zur Weltgeschichte* (Berlin, 1956), iii, 104–5.

in the east, some of whom broke away to found a separate
Old Lutheran Church. The attempt to create a new denomination was abandoned but the United Prussian Church
survived as an administrative union; the Lutheran and
Reformed parishes of Prussia continued to follow their own
traditions but they were known as the United Prussian
Church and were treated by the Prussian state in most
respects as a single entity. The Prussian example was followed
in Hessen, Anhalt, and elsewhere and in Baden and the Rhine
Palatinate the original intention of Frederick William III was
carried out and a new united creed established.[3]

⌐ Apart from the division into three main types of church—
Lutheran, Reformed, and United—the Protestant church in
Germany was also divided by the frontiers of individual
German states, known as *Länder*. Each *Land* had its own
Landeskirche and sometimes, as in Hanover, both a Lutheran
and a Reformed one. In some cases separate Landeskirchen
survived after the *Länder* with which they had originally been
identified had been taken over by more powerful rivals. Thus
Bavaria contained two Protestant Landeskirchen, one
belonging to the Palatinate which had originally been
independent. The same was true of Prussia after its conquest
of the other north-German states in 1866, since Bismarck
decided to leave the Landeskirchen of the new provinces
intact. As a result the United Prussian Church became known
as the Old Prussian Union to distinguish it from the
Landeskirchen in the new provinces of Schleswig-Holstein,
Hanover, and the Prussian parts of Hessen. During the
Weimar Republic there were still twenty-eight separate
Protestant Landeskirchen in Germany. Of these the Old
Prussian Union, which contained about half the total number
of German Protestants, was the most important.

The idea of a single national German Protestant church
was discussed during the nineteenth century but the strength
of the different traditions of belief and of local loyalties
made it impracticable. It was not until the Third Reich that a
serious attempt was made to carry it out. However there was

3. W. Elliger, *Die Evangelische Kirche der Union* (Witten, 1967),
pp. 23–65. K. Kupisch, *Die deutschen Landeskirchen im 19. und 20.
Jahrhundert* (Göttingen, 1966), pp. 53–4.

progress towards creating a federal organization to represent the common interests of the Landeskirchen on national issues.[4] In 1848 a conference of leading Protestants (a *Kirchentag*) met in Wittenberg to discuss the formation of a Kirchenbund. This initiative petered out, but with the encouragement of Frederick William IV of Prussia regular meetings of the leaders of the Landeskirchen were held in Eisenach from 1852, known as the *Eisenacher Kirchenkonferenz*. At the same time a church newspaper for the whole of German Protestantism was founded. The Kirchenkonferenz remained restricted to senior church lawyers and clergymen until 1918; it was not widened to include members of the elected church assemblies (synods) which had been introduced into most Landeskirchen by the end of the nineteenth century. This restriction was due to the opposition of some Lutheran Landeskirchen who suspected the Kirchenkonferenz of being an instrument of the United Church and of Prussian hegemony. Nevertheless the Kirchenkonferenz grew in importance. In 1903 a standing committee, the *Kirchenausschuß*, was formed with its seat in Berlin, and from 1908 its Presidency was given to the senior official of the Old Prussian Union. This established a strong link between the central organization of all the Landeskirchen and the strongest single Landeskirche. The President's joint position gave considerable authority to a skilful man. Because of the federal basis of the central organization, however, there was no means of coercing Landeskirchen that rejected the policy of the majority.

The Landeskirche remained the basic unit of German Protestantism until 1933. This was natural as church affairs were a *Land* matter in which the Reich did not interfere directly before 1919 and subsequently only to enforce certain basic provisions of the Weimar constitution. Before 1919 most Landeskirchen were closely dependent on the state. The state guaranteed the Landeskirche certain

---

4. W. Delius, 'Altpreußische Kirche und kirchliche Einheit des deutschen Protestantismus', in O. Söhngen, *Hundert Jahre Evangelischer Oberkirchenrat der Altpreußischen Union* (Berlin, 1950), pp. 86–113. T. Karg, *Von der Eisenacher Kirchenkonferenz zum Deutschen Evangelischen Kirchenbund* (Diss. Recht, Freiburg, 1961).

privileges and in return retained control over it. The Landeskirche was administered like a governmental department by the appropriate *Land* Ministry, the *Kultusministerium*, and at a provincial level by the local government authorities for church and school affairs. There were, however, some qualifications to this general picture of dependence on the state. In Prussia both Frederick William III and IV thought that as a religious institution the Protestant church required a distinct organization. As a result the departments responsible for ecclesiastical affairs in the state administration were gradually separated from the rest. Later the development towards a secular system in educational and ecclesiastical matters gave rise to the desire for the separation of church and state. Synods which had been a distinctive feature of the Reformed Landeskirchen were adopted in most United and Lutheran Landeskirchen as well and given some control over internal church matters.

The process of separation had not advanced very far, however, before the collapse of the Empire.[5] Until 1918 throughout Germany the normal conditions of a Christian state were observed: freedom of worship, protection of the Sabbath, a state guarantee of church property, theological faculties in universities, religious education in schools, chaplains in the armed forces, hospitals, and prisons—all maintained by the state. In theory freedom of belief was allowed but in practice there was discrimination against agnostics in public appointments. Protestant Landeskirchen and the Roman Catholic church enjoyed the especially privileged status of a *Körperschaft des öffentlichen Rechts* (corporation with a special legal status). This was ill defined and the rights it gave varied from *Land* to *Land*, but in general it meant that the Landeskirchen were raised above the level of a private club and enjoyed some of the privileges of a government department.[6] Church officials had the status

5. W. Kahl, *Lehrsystem des Kirchenrechts und der Kirchenpolitik* (Freiburg, 1894).

6. Friedrich Naumann, a liberal Protestant politician and writer, asked for a definition of the *Körperschaftsrecht* during the committee work for the new constitution of the Republic in 1919. He was told that an official of the Ministry of Justice when asked to give a definition had replied, 'That is one thing I will not do'. *Verhandlungen der verfassunggebenden Nationalversammlung* (Berlin, 1920), vol. 336, p. 198.

of *Beamten* (civil servants) and the churches were allowed to tax their members and even to make use of the state administration to enforce collection of the tax.[7]

By giving the Landeskirchen its protection and exceptional privileges the state demonstrated its belief in the national importance of the Christian churches. In return the churches had to submit to state supervision to ensure that their privileges were not abused and that the national interest was served. The rights of the state (*Staatshoheitsrechte*) also varied between different *Länder*. They included the supervision of church finance and property administration, protection of church members against excessive church-tax burdens, the right to approve important church appointments and to confirm that church laws did not conflict with state ones.

The Protestant Landeskirchen were also subject to the crown in certain other respects known as the *landesherrliches Kirchenregiment,* which included the right to summon the synods, to approve synod legislation, and to appoint to senior positions in the church.[8] After the revolution of 1918 it was disputed whether these royal powers belonged to the crown as head of the Protestant Landeskirchen (*Summus Episcopus*) or as head of state, but eventually the state acknowledged that the powers had been purely ecclesiastical and were quite distinct from the Staatshoheitsrechte.

Despite these close ties with the state and the crown the Protestant Landeskirchen made some progress towards a system of self-government before 1918. The most important example was the church of the Old Prussian Union, where from 1815 internal church affairs in the provinces had been delegated by the government to a special body known as the *Konsistorium.*[9] There was one Konsistorium to each province and lay administrators and clergymen served on it. In 1829 a system of *Generalsuperintendenten* was revived with responsibility for the spiritual welfare of the provinces: the

---

7. F. Giese, *Deutsches Kirchensteuerrecht* (Stuttgart, 1910).

8. This applied equally to Protestant Landeskirchen in *Länder* with Roman Catholic rulers like Saxony, where the king delegated his powers to three Protestant members of his government. In the city states, Hamburg, Bremen, and Lübeck, the senates exercised the rights. Kahl, *Lehrsystem des Kirchenrechts*, pp. 169–235.

9. Elliger, *Die Evangelische Kirche der Union*, pp. 37–9, 58–9, 72–84, 96–9.

Generalsuperintendent was the leading provincial clergyman, comparable in status to a bishop. In 1848 at the suggestion of the Generalsuperintendenten a central *Oberkonsistorium* was created separate from the state *Kultusministerium*, though still retaining the *Kultusminister* as its chairman. The Prussian constitution of 1850 laid down that the church should administer its own affairs and, as a result, a further step towards independence was taken with the creation of the *Evangelischer Oberkirchenrat* in Berlin, a central authority at least in theory independent of the Kultusminister and responsible to the crown alone.

There was some doubt as to whether the creation of the Berlin Oberkirchenrat marked the completion of the new church organization or whether it was the prelude to further change. In fact no more progress was made until 1874–6 when, under Kultusminister Falk, synods were adopted in all provinces (they already existed in the Rhineland and Westphalia) and a General Synod was created to represent the whole church.[10] The General Synod had the right to give its consent to all church laws and to propose legislation of its own: where church laws were not in conflict with state law and did not concern any part of the Staatshoheitsrechte they were decreed by the crown; if the Staatshoheitsrechte were concerned a state law was necessary in addition to the church law.

This remained the position in the Old Prussian Union until 1918. The main features of the system, in which the administration of church affairs was shared by church officials and the synods with rights reserved to the crown and the Kultusminister, were common to most of the larger Protestant Landeskirchen.[11] Despite gradual progress towards self-government the emphasis remained on close ties with state and crown. The Landeskirchen did not achieve financial independence; the state paid all important expenses not covered by church tax, including the salaries of church

10. E. Förster, *Adalbert Falk* (Gotha, 1927), pp. 174–209, 302–36.
11. Kahl, *Lehrsystem des Kirchenrechts*, p. 169. The Oberkirchenrat of the Old Prussian Union was, however, exceptional. The other Prussian Landeskirchen had no equivalent institution and remained under the Kultusministerium. This was true in most *Länder* but in Baden after 1860 the Landeskirche also had an independent Oberkirchenrat. Ibid., pp. 215–217.

officials.[12] In many Landeskirchen the clergy were directly
employed by the state to supervise local schools, a duty
which led to the accusation that the church was the moral
police force of the government and made the church hated
by many teachers.[13] The church seemed to have no policy of
its own: for instance, in the question of social reform it
simply mirrored official attitudes, changing its mind with the
Kaiser between 1890 and 1895.[14] The initiative in social
questions passed to Protestant bodies acting independently of
the Landeskirchen like the Inner Mission.

Church members were divided into 'church parties' by
different traditions of belief related to political attitudes. The
church of the Old Prussian Union again serves as a model.
Within the General Synod there were four important church
parties.[15] At one extreme were the Confessional Lutherans,
who had never been reconciled to the existence of a United
Church, even in name, and jealously guarded the separate
Lutheran tradition. A little to their left stood the main
conservative party, the *Positive Union*, which accepted the
United Church but remained strictly orthodox in theology
and resisted the growth of liberalism in church and state.
They opposed the introduction of synods although they soon
became the dominant party within them. The centre was
represented by the *Evangelische Vereinigung*. It was the party
most strongly in favour of the United Church and contained
both orthodox and liberal members. On the left was a small
group of liberals represented after 1918 by the *Freie
Volkskirche* party which drew their main strength from
intellectuals and had an influential journal in the *Christliche
Welt* edited by Martin Rade.[16] Their primary concern was to
protect pastors who had been trained in one of the schools of
'modern theology' from the anger of their parishioners and
sometimes of the crown and the Landeskirche authorities as

12. J. Niedner, *Die Ausgaben des preußischen Staats für die evangelische
Landeskirche der älteren Provinzen* (Stuttgart, 1904).

13. E. von Bremen, *Die preußische Volksschule* (Stuttgart, 1905), p. 190. O.
Dibelius, *Das Jahrhundert der Kirche* (1st edn., Berlin, 1927), p. 67.

14. Elliger, *Die Evangelische Kirche der Union*, p. 102–5.

15. H. G. Oxenius, *Die Entstehung der Verfassung der Evangelischen Kirche
der altpreußischen Union von 1922* (Diss. Phil., Cologne, 1959), pp. 32–87.

16. J. Rathje, *Die Welt des freien Protestantismus* (Stuttgart, 1952).

well.[17] The liberals were also critical of the Landeskirche system, which they described as a *Staatskirche* (a state church), but they were less clear about the alternative they would prefer. One group wanted the separation of church and state, another was attracted by the ideal of the fusion of church and state with the disappearance of the church as a separate institution; the slogan of a *Volkskirche* (a people's church), to replace the so-called Staatskirche, covered both notions.

Conservative groups retained a clear majority in the synods even after 1918 when the restricted franchise in most churches was widened. Their ideal was a Christian state in which crown, government, and people shared the same creed (preferably Lutheran) and from which liberalism and unbelief were excluded. In this situation they would gladly have seen church and state closely united but as the state developed first towards constitutional government and parity in denominational matters (equal treatment of the Roman Catholic and Protestant Landeskirchen) and then further towards a secular system which protected citizens who had no religious belief, they became increasingly alienated. Despite their undoubted loyalty to the crown and the Reich they began to feel that as the actual state had moved so far from their ideal the church should be more independent. During the *Kulturkampf* in Prussia (the conflict between Bismarck and the Roman Catholic church), Protestants found that their church was also affected.[18] Their reaction is indicated by a motion in the Prussian *Landtag* (parliament) in 1886 demanding that the Protestant church should have more independence.[19]

The senior officials and clergy who held the leading executive positions in most Landeskirchen, while sharing the

17. Rathje, *Die Welt des freien Protestantismus*, pp. 64-74, 179-94, 201-10. The most important figures in the theological revolution were Albrecht Ritschl (1822-89), professor at Bonn 1859-64 and Göttingen 1864-89, and Adolf von Harnack (1851-1930), professor at Gießen 1879-86, Marburg 1886-9, and Berlin 1889-1921.

18. Dibelius, *Das Jahrhundert der Kirche*, p. 68.

19. This was a more extreme gesture than most Protestants were prepared to support before 1918; the motion received only 43 votes from the 123 Conservative deputies and was contemptuously dismissed by Bismarck. W. Frank, *Hofprediger Adolf Stoecker* (2nd. edn., Hamburg, 1935), pp. 158-9.

basic convictions of the conservative synod deputies, tended in practice to co-operate more readily with the state administration. This was particularly true of the Oberkirchenrat of the Old Prussian Union in Berlin which had great influence, both because it represented the largest Landeskirche and because its President was also automatically President of the federal Kirchenausschuß. A lawyer, trained in state administration, he was neither a clergyman nor the leader of a church party, but a Beamte.[20]

The Oberkirchenrat was criticized by liberal Protestants as a symbol of the Staatskirche and by conservatives for its readiness to introduce reform with the Kultusministerium. Though closely linked in law with the crown it was prepared to offer resistance even here, in the interests of the church.[21] It shared the values of the Beamte—above all his *Sachlichkeit* (impartiality). When, in 1917, the Kaiser asked for the Oberkirchenrat's opinion on the introduction of episcopacy the reply was that as bishops would take over the duties of the Oberkirchenrat and of the crown, this would be a further stage towards the separation of church and state. Although this might be the direction in which the church should go, they did not feel that it would be right for them to accelerate the process. The letter suggests that the Oberkirchenrat expected that in time the church would be made independent.[22]

Less than a year later, in November 1918, the separation of church and state was proclaimed in Prussia. The shock of Germany's defeat and the revolution initially threw the Protestant leadership on to the defensive but later it recognized that the Republic only continued the changes which had started in the nineteenth century. In 1926 an

---

20. There was no formal rule excluding a clergyman, however, and occasionally one was a candidate for election. One of the two vice-presidents was always a clergyman, known as the 'spiritual' vice-president; the other was called the 'secular' vice-president.

21. For instance in 1889 it refused to take disciplinary action against the famous court preacher, Adolf Stoecker, after he had fallen from royal favour and William II wanted him accused of insulting the crown. Elliger, *Die Evangelische Kirche der Union*, p. 105.

22. It is dated 8 Dec. 1917 and printed in Söhngen, *Hundert Jahre Oberkirchenrat*, pp. 196–208.

ex-President of the Oberkirchenrat described the Weimar constitution as decisive in giving the Protestant church independence, but,

It was at the same time . . . the conclusion of a slow but irresistible process since the transformation of the Prussian state first into a constitutional state, then into a state observing religious parity with an ever stronger and more decisive element of the inter-denominational Landtag which was basically neutral, not to say indifferent, to the church and religion. After the collapse of the check which still obtained earlier in the *landesherrliches Kirchenregiment*, the so-called 'separation of church and state' was the only solution.[23]

Protestant leaders might regard this development as no more than a necessary evil but they had been prepared for it before 1918 and, having accepted it, the way was open to finding a *modus vivendi* with the Republic.

23. E.K.U., Gen. XII, 63/Beiheft (vertrauliches Material): Moeller Denkschrift, 22 Dec. 1926.

1

THE REVOLUTION SETTLEMENT

The revolution of 9 November 1918 destroyed the Empire with which the Protestant church had been closely identified and brought to power the Social Democrats whose programme declared that religion was a private matter and that support for the churches from public funds should be stopped.[1] Church leaders feared that the separation of church and state would be carried out abruptly and in a form damaging to the church, on the model of the Third Republic in France. The abdication of the ruling dynasties created an awkward legal situation for the Protestant church which the Republic could exploit by claiming the former royal powers over the church for itself. There was also the possibility that liberal church members might seize the opportunity of the revolution to carry out a reform of the Landeskirchen regardless of the former church leadership.

Each of these fears had some justification, but in the end the Landeskirchen emerged unscathed and in some ways stronger than they had been before 1918. In this the example of the Protestant church follows the general pattern of the German revolution and, in particular, its failure to bring about a reform of German society which alone could have provided the new political system with strong support.[2] If the revolutionary government had possessed the will, and had not been faced by other immediate and formidable problems it might, for instance, have created a Republican army and civil service by legislation and political appointments. But it is more difficult to see how the ethos of the Protestant church could have been changed by government action. The

1. Clause 6 of the Erfurt programme of 1891; W. Treue, *Deutsche Parteiprogramme 1861–1961* (3rd. edn., Göttingen, 1961), p. 76.
2. W. Elben, *Das Problem der Kontinuität in der deutschen Revolution* (Düsseldorf, 1965); S. Miller, *Die Regierung der Volksbeauftragten 1918/19* (Düsseldorf, 1969).

Protestant church was too large an institution and too dependent on individual church members—the majority of whom were strongly conservative—for reform imposed by the government to have much effect, except over a long period of time. The *modus vivendi* which emerged from the revolution settlement was far from an ideal solution for the Republic but it was not a hopeless one, and even a stronger government might not have been able to impose a better one.

i. The Prussian *Land* and the Old Prussian Union

a. *The provisional government*

On 12 November 1918 the new government of the Reich, which was to hold power until elections to a National Constituent Assembly, issued a declaration guaranteeing freedom of worship and forbidding enforcement of religious observance.[3] The following day a declaration was issued by the similarly constituted provisional Prussian government. Its tone was sharper: it included the phrases, 'liberation of education from ecclesiastical tutelage' and 'separation of church and state'.[4]

Two ministers were appointed to the Prussian Kultusministerium, Adolf Hoffmann (USPD) and Konrad Haenisch (SPD).[5] Hoffmann, who was already well known for his hostility to the church, at once attempted to carry out reform by administrative decree overriding Haenisch who also believed in reform but did not want to force the pace. Hoffman left no record of his ultimate intensions, but they were probably similar to those of a socialist novelist, Alfred Dieterich, employed by the Kultusministerium.[6]

3. E.K.U., Gen. II, 32/1: *Staatsanzeiger*, No. 269, 13 Nov. 1918.

4. Ibid.: *Staatsanzeiger*, No. 270, 14 Nov. 1918.

5. On Hoffmann, see F. Thimme, 'Das Verhältnis der revolutionären Gewalten zur Religion und den Kirchen' in F. Thimme and E. Rolffs, *Revolution und Kirche* (Berlin, 1919), pp. 15–16, 25. For Haenisch's account of his tenure of the Kultusministerium see *Kulturpolitische Aufgaben* ed. by the *Arbeitsgemeinschaft für staatsbürgerliche und wirtschaftliche Bildung* (Berlin, 1919) and K. Haenisch, *Neue Bahnen der Kulturpolitik* (Stuttgart and Berlin, 1921).

6. D.Z.A. Merseburg, Rep. 76, III Sekt. 1, Abt. XVII, 212/Beiheft 1. Despite official denials a remark made by Haenisch in a letter to Heine (Prussian Minister of the Interior) on 27 Sept. 1919 shows that Dieterich's programme had been the policy of the governing parties. Haenisch wrote, 'The policy originally represented by the Social Democrats as expressed in the memorandum by Dieterich has become impracticable'; D.Z.A. Merseburg, Rep. 77, Tit. 123, 157/1. See also Thimme, *Revolution and Kirche*, pp. 30–3.

Dieterich proposed a programme in two stages. First a series of reforms should be implemented at once by ministerial decree under the authority of the previous Prussian constitution which guaranteed freedom of belief. These would end compulsory religious education and financial state support for the churches. The second stage, which would depend on the new Reich and Prussian constitutions, would aim at the complete subjection of the churches to the state. Churches would be treated as private associations under direct state supervision. Their assets would be expropriated or taxed.

On 16 November 1918 Hoffmann told the officials of the Kultusministerium that the separation of church and state was to be carried out without delay and that state subsidies should end at the latest on 1 April 1919.[7] The previous day he had decreed that children of dissenters should be freed from religious education and on 27 November the supervision of Prussian schools by clergymen was ended.[8] On 29 November the most ambitious decree, forbidding religious ceremonies in schools and making religious education voluntary, was issued.[9]

On 18 November the Oberkirchenrat and the standing committee of the General Synod set up a special council of advisers.[10] These three bodies, known jointly as the *Vertrauensrat*, made a formal protest to the Prussian government against the use of administrative decrees to make legal changes and demanded that the state should not interfere in the internal life of the church.[11] At the same time they issued a statement to the parishes, appealing to church members for their support and asserting both that they were not afraid of separation of church and state and that the government did not possess the legal authority to carry it out.[12]

7. D.Z.A. Merseburg, Rep. 76, III Sekt. 1, Abt. XVII, 214/1: Die geistliche Abteilung (Kultusministerium) to Prussian government, 21 Dec. 1918.

8. *Zentralblatt für die gesamte Unterrichtsverwaltung in Preußen, 1918* (Berlin, 1918), pp. 708–9, 757–8.

9. Ibid., pp. 719–21.

10. E.K.U., Gen. II, 21/1: minutes of the meeting.

11. G. St. A., Rep. 90, 2380: President of the Oberkirchenrat to Prussian government, 2 Dec., sending the legal protest of 30 Nov. 1918.

12. *Verhandlungen der außerordentlichen Versammlung der siebenten Generalsynode der evangelischen Landeskirche Preußens* (Berlin, 1920), ii. 79–80.

The unity of the church had, however, already been broken when, on 18 November 1918, a liberal pastor, Ludwig Wessel, told a meeting of 250 of his Berlin colleagues that separation of church and state was desirable because a free church would enjoy much more confidence. He outlined a programme of democratic church reform with less power for lawyers and more for synods and asked the clergy to co-operate with the government. A resolution along the lines of his speech was supported by an overwhelming majority of the meeting and sent to the Kultusministerium.[13] The government responded by authorizing Wessel to supervise Oberkirchenrat decisions and to chair its meetings, explaining that Wessel had been appointed as a mediator between the Kultusministerium and the church.[14] The Oberkirchenrat declared that his appointment was illegal.[15]

One motive for the appointment of Wessel was to show the workers' and soldiers' councils, which had been set up at the revolution and which still claimed some authority, that the government had matters under control and that there was no need for the councils to intervene.[16] In fact, there were no serious clashes between the church and the councils.[17] Several incidents were reported to the Oberkirchenrat but these included trivialities like public criticism of a senior clergyman for not saying 'Good morning'. There was one instance of a council ordering that church bells should be rung in honour of Rosa Luxemburg and Karl Liebknecht. Some cases of rough handling of clergymen were reported

13. D.Z.A. Potsdam, Reich Min. f. d. kirchl. Angelegenheiten, 22166. Ludwig Wessel was the father of Horst Wessel; G. Köhler, *Die Auswirkungen der Novemberrevolution von 1918 auf die altpreußische evangelische Landeskirche* (Diss. theol., Berlin, 1967), p. 44.

14. E.K.U., Gen. II, 27/1: Kultusministerium to Oberkirchenrat, 5 Dec. 1918. D.Z.A. Merseburg, Rep. 76, III Sekt. 1, Abt. XVII, 212/Beiheft 1: draft of the statement. The published version is in the *Deutscher Reichsanzeiger und Preußischer Staatsanzeiger,* 9 Dec. 1918, No. 290.

15. E.K.U., Gen. II, 27/1: Oberkirchenrat to Kultusministerium, 13 Dec. 1918. *Kirchliches Gesetz-und-Verordnungsblatt,* 1918 (Berlin, 1918), pp. 61–5.

16. Wessel believed this was one of the main reasons for his appointment. D.Z.A. Merseburg, Rep. 76, III Sekt. 1, Abt. XVII, 212/Beiheft 1: Wessel to Haenisch, 10 Jan. 1919.

17. The Kultusministerium kept a file on intervention by the councils in church affairs but it has disappeared. The Oberkirchenrat record is contained in E.K.U., Gen. II, 30/1.

and one senior clergyman was suspended for a short time. In general, government directives against local disturbances of this sort seem to have been effective.[18]

Wessel's appointment was probably also intended to put pressure on the Oberkirchenrat and to encourage church liberals. Haenisch, in particular, was anxious at the same time to reassure the Protestant population that the government did not intend to force through extreme measures. Given these conflicting objectives, it was not surprising that Wessel achieved very little. He never entered the Oberkirchenrat building and had no influence on its policy. On 13 January Haenisch allowed him to resign at his own request.[19]

Wessel's only action had been the organization of two conferences between representatives of the Kultus-ministerium and the churches.[20] These were chiefly important for a statement by Haenisch which revealed his fear of the opposition that had been aroused by the November decrees and the appointment of Wessel. He said that he believed separation of church and state was a historical necessity, but that the decision should be left to the National Assembly. He asked church leaders to dispel the impression that the Kultusministerium was ruled by a 'clergy-devouring, shallow Enlightenment, iconoclastic, sectarian spirit'. With their terrible difficulties, the government could not afford further unrest.

In the following weeks the provisional government abandoned its programme of reform by ministerial decree. On 18 December the decree on religious education was modified. On the 28th it was suspended wherever it encountered difficulties.[21] On 9 January 1919 the government officially confirmed that its policy was to defer reform to the constituent assembly.[22] There were two main reasons for this change. First Haenisch had always been more cautious

18. See E. Kolb, *Die Arbeiterräte in der deutschen Innenpolitik 1918–1919* (Düsseldorf, 1962), pp. 262–81; cf. *Kirchliches Jahrbuch*, 46. Jg. (1919), 334–5.

19. E.K.U., Gen. II, 27/1: Haenisch to the Oberkirchenrat, 13 Jan. 1919.

20. D.Z.A. Merseburg, Rep. 76, III Sekt. 1, Abt. XVII, 212/Beiheft 1: minutes of the meetings of 12–14 Dec.

21. *Zentralblatt für die gesamte Unterrichtsverwaltung in Preußen*, 1918, pp. 721–2.

22. E.K.U., Gen. II. 27/1: Hirsch to Oberkirchenrat, 9 Jan. 1919.

than Hoffmann and at the end of November 1918 he had threatened to resign.[23] In December Hoffmann was ill and he left the government on 3 January with the other Independent Social Democrats. This removed the radical influence from the Kultusministerium. Secondly, Haenisch was worried by the reaction of the churches and the effect it would have on separatist movements and on the forthcoming elections to the National Assembly.[24]

Further pressure against Hoffmann's policy came from the departmental officials of the Kultusministerium. They defended the churches' subsidies, condemned Wessel's appointment, and protested to the head of the Prussian government.[25] The senior official sent a copy of this protest to the Oberkirchenrat through Wilhelm Kahl—a striking example of the solidarity of the old officials in church and state against the new political authorities.[26] Four officials of the Kultusministerium even asked the Chairman of the Zentralrat (the central council of the workers' and soldiers' councils with authority over the provisional governments of the Reich and Prussia) for Hoffmann's dismissal, claiming that they had Haenisch's approval.[27] After Hoffmann's resignation, Haenisch accepted the validity of the officials' criticisms and promised to consult them in future.[28]

23. Thimme, *Revolution und Kirche*, pp. 36–7.

24. He was especially concerned about Catholic frontier provinces. See his letter to Hoffmann, 31 Dec. 1918, in E. Kolb, *Der Zentralrat der Deutschen Sozialistischen Republik* (Leiden, 1968), pp. 139–41.

25. D.Z.A. Potsdam, Reich Min. f. d. kirchl. Angelegenheiten, 22166: memorandum of 25 Nov. 1918. G.St.A., Rep. 90, 2380: Die geistliche Abteilung (Kultusministerium) to Prussian government, 21 Dec. 1918.

26. E.K.U., Gen. II, 27/1: Kahl to Voigts, 15 Dec. 1919, and note by Voigts, 28 Dec. W. Kahl (1849–1932), church lawyer and DVP politician, leader of the middle group (*Evangelische Vereinigung*) in the General Synod of the Old Prussian Union, member of the *Nationalversammlung* and its constitutional committee 1919, and of the Reichstag (1919–32). Kahl was active in educational questions and Chairman of the Reichstag committee on penal reform. He was also a notable exponent of a *Vernunftrepublikaner* attitude; see below, p. 60. Biographical details in *Religion in Geschichte und Gegenwart*, iii. 1088–9.

27. Nachlaß Becker, 81: memorandum about the meeting of 30 Dec. 1918. It is quite likely that they had Haenisch's approval since on 31 Dec. 1918 he wrote to Hoffmann saying that one of them must resign and he thought it should be Hoffmann; Kolb, *Der Zentralrat*, pp. 139–41.

28. G.St.A., Rep. 90, 2380: Haenisch to Prussian government, 25 Jan. 1919.

b. *The Weimar constitution*

The church leadership did not respond to Haenisch's request that it should reassure the parishes. On the contrary, since Haenisch had made it clear that the decisions over church-state relations would be taken by the new constituent assemblies of the Reich and Prussia, church leaders attempted to exploit the shock of parishioners at the initial measures of the government, so that the political parties should be made to feel the importance of the Protestant vote.[29]

The campaign was directed in the Old Prussian Union by a subcommittee of the Vertrauensrat. It published a news-sheet edited by Otto Dibelius.[30] The news-sheet explained that the Protestant church stood above political parties but only those parties that represented Protestant interests should be supported.[31] The decree on religious education was bitterly attacked and its suspension greeted as a triumph.[32] Extracts from Dieterich's programme for separation of church and state were reproduced as late as 20 January, despite Haenisch's assurances.[33] Special attention was given to the Protestant female vote. On 8 January the results of an inquiry into the political parties were published.[34] The religious programmes of the DNVP (right-wing conservative), DVP (national liberal) and the Centre party (Roman Catholic) were considered sound but the Centre party was rejected because it was Catholic. Dibelius argued that the local clergy should tell their congregations whom to support

29. Over 800 protests from Catholic and Protestant associations were sent to the Prussian government, G.St.A., Rep. 90, 2380.

30. *Mitteilungen aus der Arbeit der dem Evang. Oberkirchenrat und dem Generalsynodalvorstand beigeordneten Vertrauensmänner der Evangelischen Landeskirche.* Similar campaigns were conducted in other German churches especially by groups formed at the revolution, for instance the *Volkskirchenbund* in Hanover, which by December 1919 claimed 300,000 members (Hanover *Landeskirchenamt* newspaper archive).

O. Dibelius (1880–1967), 1915 Pastor in Berlin, 1921 member of the Oberkirchenrat, 1925 Generalsuperintendent of the *Kurmark*, 1933 forced to retire, 1945 Bishop of Berlin and President of the Oberkirchenrat. Autobiography, O. Dibelius, *In the Service of the Lord* (Engl. edn., London, 1964).

31. *Mitteilungen*, No. 1, 17 Dec. 1918.

32. Ibid., No. 3, 30 Dec. 1918.

33. Ibid., No. 5, 20 Jan. 1919.

34. Ibid., No. 4, 8 Jan. 1919.

and he recommended that they march together to vote after the church service on polling day. A Reich petition in support of Christian education was sent to the National Assembly at Weimar.[35] By the end of April 1919, almost 6,500,000 signatures had been collected.[36] There is little doubt that there was wide support among the electorate, including social democratic voters.[37]

The National Assembly met at Weimar on 6 February 1919. Although the parties favoured by the Protestant church had not been successful, the provisions of the Weimar constitution were favourable to the churches. This was because of the power of the Centre party within the government coalition[38] which made the SPD conciliatory. In addition the DDP (left-wing liberals) wanted agreement with the churches.[39] Protestant interests were represented on the constitutional committee by four members of the Vertrauensrat of the Old Prussian Union—Wilhelm Kahl (DVP), Reinhard Mumm and Gottfried Traub (DNVP), and Adolf von Harnack as a government expert on educational questions.[40]

The Protestant church presented the National Assembly with a list of demands for the new constitution.[41] These aimed to maintain the privileged position of the church while

35. *Mitteilungen*, No. 6, 1 Feb. 1919.

36. E.K.D., A 2/238: Deutscher evangelische Kirchenausschuß to Deutsche evangelische Kirchenkonferenz, 26 Apr. 1919.

37. *Mitteilungen*, No. 8, 12 Mar. 1919.

38. R. Morsey, *Die Deutsche Zentrumspartei 1917–1923* (Düsseldorf, 1966), pp. 208–20.

39. T. Heuss, *Friedrich Naumann* (2nd. edn., Stuttgart, 1949), pp. 477–83.

40. *Verhandlungen, Nationalversammlung*, vol. 336, pp. 76–8, 187–230, 515–37. R. Mumm (1873–1932), *Reichstag* deputy of the Christian Social party 1912–18, of the DNVP 1918–29, and of the Christian Social *Volksdienst* party 1929–32; formed the Protestant Reich committee of the DNVP, 1921. See his autobiography, R. Mumm, *Der christlich-soziale Gedanke* (Berlin, 1933), also *RGG* iv. 1190. G. Traub (1869–1956), 1912 suspended from being a *Pfarrer* because of his liberal theology, reinstated 1918; 1913–17 Prussian Landtag deputy for the *Fortschrittliche Volkspartei*, 1917–18 for the *Vaterlandspartei*, 1919 Reichstag deputy of the DNVP, 1920 Kultusminister of the Kapp regime, 1921–34 editor of the *München-Augsburger Abendzeitung* in the Hugenberg interest, 1914–39 also editor of *Eiserne Blätter*. See his autobiography, first two chapters published as G. Traub, *Erinnerungen* (Munich, 1949), the remainder in Bundesarchiv, Nachlaß Traub, 5.

41. Kirchenausschuß to Nationalversammlung, 13 Mar. 1919, in *Allgemeines Kirchenblatt für das evangelische Deutschland*, 1 Apr. 1919 (Stuttgart, 1919), pp. 154–7.

giving it independence from the state. The National Assembly was warned against offending the religious feelings of the nation expressed in the petition on religious education.

The Weimar constitution (11 August 1919) differed from previous Reich legislation in the extent of its provisions on church matters.[42] This met the desire of the church that radical *Länder* should be restrained by the Reich. Article 137 declared that 'there is no Staatskirche', a formula for separation of church and state which everyone could accept. Churches were given the right to administer their own affairs and to appoint their own officials, but they retained the privileged *Körperschaft* status. The counterpart to this generous settlement was that *Weltanschauung* organizations, i.e. agnostic groups, could acquire the same rights, but in practice few did.[43] The end of state subsidies was foreseen but compensation was too expensive and they remained. The educational provisions were less satisfactory for the churches. In an ambiguous clause (Article 146) a unified educational system was given slight preference over separate denominational and secular schools. Details were left to a Reich School Law which never came into existence because no majority could be found on the subject. The clauses about religious education, however, met the wishes of the church. Harnack, unexpectedly, spoke strongly in favour of keeping religious education denominational and closely connected with the churches.[44]

The Protestant church had every reason to be pleased with the Weimar constitution. The November fears of a hostile programme of separation were dispelled. Church privileges were confirmed while state control over the church was reduced. The SPD was justified in arguing that this had produced a situation in which the church was free of the state but the state was not free of the church.[45]

42. E. R. Huber, *Dokumente zur deutschen Verfassungsgeschichte* (Stuttgart, 1966), iii. 148–50, 155.

43. See the explanation of Article 137 (Article 134 in the draft of the constitution) by the reporter of the constitutional committee to the plenum of the National Assembly, *Verhandlungen, Nationalversammlung*, vol. 328, pp. 164–5, and speech of Kahl, ibid., pp. 1646–9.

44. Ibid., vol. 336, pp. 216–18.

45. Ibid., vol. 336, p. 188 (speech of Meerfeld), vol. 328, p. 1650 (speech of Quarck).

c. *The church constitution*

The Prussian Constituent Assembly met on 13 March 1919. As in the Reich, a coalition government of SPD, Centre, and DDP was formed. Relations with the church were complicated by a provisional regulation of the powers of the new Prussian government which set up three Ministers (dubbed the 'three kings') to exercise the former royal powers over the Protestant church.[46] This created a new state authority for church affairs beside the Kultusministerium.

The main problem facing the authorities was the procedure to be adopted for the new church constitution (which had become necessary as a result of the abdication of the monarchy). The state expected the church to make some concessions to democracy, otherwise the Prussian Constituent Assembly could refuse to ratify the church constitution. At the same time the state recognized limits to its competence to interfere in church matters, especially in view of the new constitution of the Reich. For its part, the church accepted the right of the state to confirm the new laws and, indeed, wanted the security and permanence given by this confirmation and the Oberkirchenrat also accepted the need for some reform. There had, however, been no revolution within the church and any solution would have to be acceptable to the old General Synod since, even if the synod were bypassed, the same people were likely to be powerful in any church assembly. This made radical reform impossible.

The first question was the type of assembly to grant the new constitution. The Oberkirchenrat and the Vertrauensrat[47] favoured a democratic body elected by direct, universal suffrage. This plan, however, aroused fierce opposition from conservative groups. All the provincial synods which met rejected it.[48] In view of the opposition the Oberkirchenrat agreed to a compromise. This was to elect the church constituent assembly in two stages through a 'filter' of parish representative bodies.

On 30 May 1919 the Oberkirchenrat asked for government

46. *Preußische Gesetzsammlung*, Jg. 1919, No. 17 (Berlin, 1919), p. 53.
47. See above, p. 13.
48. Rhineland, Westphalia, Brandenburg, Pomerania, Silesia; *Verhandlungen, Generalsynode*, 1920, ii. 127–33, 136–40.

approval.[49] Kultusminister Haenisch, who was receiving conflicting advice from his liberal State Secretary, Ernst Troeltsch, and his conservative department officials, refused to commit himself.[50] When the Oberkirchenrat decided to go ahead and put their proposals to the General Synod,[51] the DDP tabled a motion in the Prussian Constituent Assembly accusing the church of acting illegally and violating the democratic rights of the Prussian people.[52] Their purpose was to force on the church a democratically elected constituent assembly in order to give church liberals the best possible chance within the new organization. Their power lay in the fact that the church needed DDP support to get confirmation of the electoral law by the Constituent Assembly.[53] Following the DDP action, the three Ministers refused to allow the General Synod to be summoned.[54]

The Oberkirchenrat countered that this violated the Reich constitution, which had guaranteed the independence of the church.[55] In negotiations the church was able to get agreement in return for some small concessions.[56] It is not clear why the Ministers gave way, but several explanations are possible.[57] The Catholic Centre party opposed its coalition

49. D.Z.A. Merseburg, Rep. 76, III Sekt. 1, Abt. XVII, 214/1: Oberkirchenrat to Kultusministerium.
50. Ibid., Troeltsch draft, 6 June 1919; Stalmann reply, 16 July, and Troeltsch's marginal comment. On Troeltsch, see W. Köhler, *Ernst Troeltsch* (Tübingen, 1941). E.K.U., Gen. II. 27/3: Haenisch to Oberkirchenrat, 21 July 1919.
51. D.Z.A. Merseburg, Rep. 76, III Sekt. 1, Abt. XVII, 214/1: Oberkirchenrat to the three Ministers and Haenisch, 30 Oct. 1919.
52. *Sitzungsberichte der Verfassunggebenden Preußischen Landesversammlung* (Berlin, 1921), *Drucksachen*, vol. 4, p. 1611.
53. The seats in the Prussian Constituent Assembly were divided as follows: DNVP 48, DVP 23, Centre 94, DDP 65, SPD 145, USPD 24, others 3. *Statistisches Jahrbuch für den Freistaat Preußen* (Berlin, 1920), vol. 16, p. 424.
54. The text of their letter is printed in *Verhandlungen, Generalsynode*, 1920, ii. 113–14.
55. Ibid. 114–21.
56. D.Z.A. Merseburg, Rep. 76, III Sekt. 1, Abt. XVII, 214/1: protocols of the meetings of 27 Jan. and 21 Feb. 1920.
57. Rittberg argues that with the support of the Centre Party the church had a majority of deputies friendly to it in both the Reich and Prussia but this was true only if the DDP supported the church, which was not the case on this issue. E. von Rittberg, *Der Preußische Kirchenvertrag von 1931. Seine Entstehung und seine Bedeutung für das Verhältnis von Staat und Kirche in der Weimarer Republik* (Diss. Phil., Bonn, 1960), p. 53.

partners in the government on this issue.[58] It is also likely that the Ministers were unsure of their legal position; they faced strong opposition from department officials and they may have feared that the Reich would support the church against them, as had happened in a comparable situation elsewhere.[59] Perhaps they had only intended to bring maximum pressure to bear on the church without allowing the dispute to end in open conflict and legal proceedings.[60]

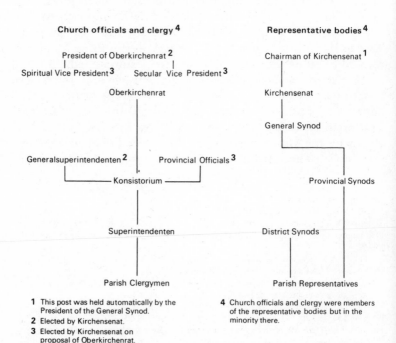

The Old Prussian Union Landeskirche
(Constitution of 29 September 1922)

Church officials and clergy [4]

President of Oberkirchenrat [2]
Spiritual Vice President [3]   Secular Vice President [3]

Oberkirchenrat

Generalsuperintendenten [2]   Provincial Officials [3]
└──────── Konsistorium ────────┘

Superintendenten

Parish Clergymen

Representative bodies [4]

Chairman of Kirchensenat [1]

Kirchensenat

General Synod

Provincial Synods

District Synods

Parish Representatives

1 This post was held automatically by the President of the General Synod.
2 Elected by Kirchensenat.
3 Elected by Kirchensenat on proposal of Oberkirchenrat.

4 Church officials and clergy were members of the representative bodies but in the minority there.

58. See the exchanges between Haenisch and the Centre deputy, Lauscher; *Preußische Landesversammlung*, vol. 6, pp. 7089–104, 7130–9, 7156–61.

59. Troeltsch fought a running battle with the officials; see D.Z.A. Merseburg, Rep. 76, III Sekt. 1, Abt. XVII, 214/1, and ibid., Rep. 77, Tit. 123, 157/1. Cf. E. Troeltsch, *Spektatorbriefe* (Tübingen, 1924), pp. 37, 89; and Kolb, *Die Arbeiterräte*, pp. 274–6.

60. The Prussian Cabinet discussed the attacks of the right-wing press on the three Ministers and the use made of the affair by the *Welf* (Hanover separatist) movement on 19 Dec. 1919; D.Z.A. Merseburg, Rep. 90a, Tit. III 2b, 6/168.

The elections to the Church Constituent Assembly were a victory for the right-wing parties.[61] By a small majority and against the advice of the Oberkirchenrat the assembly decided to return in future to a more indirect system of election.[62] It also resolved that a new committee should act as the executive body of the church when the General Synod was not in session. This committee, known as the *Kirchensenat,* was composed of synod deputies, members of the Oberkirchenrat, and the representatives of the General-superintendenten, with the synod deputies in the majority. Again despite the wishes of the Oberkirchenrat it was decided that its Presidency should be given to the President of the General Synod and not to the President of the Oberkirchenrat.[63] It is doubtful whether either of these victories over the Oberkirchenrat made much difference. Any election system would probably have given conservative groups a majority in the synod. Conversely, as a permanent and expert body the Oberkirchenrat retained important advantages in steering the Kirchensenat even though it did not chair the meetings.

There was general agreement that parts of the new constitution required state confirmation. The church was still a *Körperschaft des öffentlichen Rechts* with special privileges and the state therefore continued to exercise rights of supervision over it.[64] Despite the predominantly conservative character of the settlement, the church enjoyed, at least formally, increased legislative independence. The range of cases in which the state could object to church laws was restricted and church officials ceased to be state officials. A joint declaration was issued by the Oberkirchenrat and synod leaders to mark the introduction of the new constitution on 1 October 1924. It described the constitution as the first that the church had ever made for itself.[65] The constitution was well received by most church members though it was a disappointment to the liberals. Criticism also came from the

61. *Bericht über die Verhandlungen der außerordentlichen Kirchenversammlung zur Feststellung der Verfassung für die evangelische Landeskirche der älteren Provinzen Preußens* (Berlin, 1923), ii. 44–7.

62. Ibid. i. 1411, 1510–11.

63. Ibid. ii. 77–83.

64. State law of 8 Apr. 1924; G. J. Ebers, *Reichs- und preußisches Staatskirchenrecht* (Munich, 1932), pp. 639–48.

65. *Kirchliches Gesetz- und Verordnungsblatt,* 1924, pp. 255–7.

extreme anti-Republican Right: in the *Deutsche Zeitung*,
Maurenbrecher attacked the constitution for its half-hearted
parliamentary provisions. It was not a constitution of steel,
he said, but a broth, and the national, racialist ideology
would have to break through it.[66]

With the conclusion of the new constitution it was clear
that the church of the Old Prussian Union had survived the
attempts both from within and from outside to reform it. It
had retained its privileges and gained increased independence.
This was the result of many factors besides its own strength,
the most important being the division of the Social Democrats and the size of the problems they faced in the first
months of the Republic, and subsequently the strength of the
Centre Party and the guarantees inserted into the Reich
constitution through its influence. The church leadership was
also able to depend on the loyalty of the conservative
majority of its parishioners, the support of a group of
Protestant politicians, and the sympathy of the old officials
of the Kultusministerium. This enabled the Oberkirchenrat to
react strongly to state intervention and helped to ensure that
an already hard-pressed government would not risk a conflict
with the church.

There are good reasons for thinking that government
policy was, in any case, doomed to failure. There were two
possible courses. The first, most clearly expressed in
Dieterich's programme, was to weaken the church by a tough
policy of secularization and state control. It is improbable,
however, that this would have reduced the influence of the
church at least for a generation and it might well have proved
counter-productive by provoking a *Kulturkampf*. Republican
democracy could not carry out a successful programme of
persecution which, to be effective, would have had to be far
more drastic than Dieterich's. Hitler too did not feel strong
enough to embark on religious persecution within the
German Reich.[67]

The second possibility, favoured by Haenisch and
Troeltsch, was to put pressure on the church to adopt a
democratic constitution in the hope that this would give the

66. E.K.U., Gen. II, 27/Adhib. 1/1–2: *Deutsche Zeitung*, 17–18 Aug., Nos.
360, 362.
67. See below, pp. 148–56.

church a liberal majority. The weakness of this policy was that too few active church members were liberals. Troeltsch himself saw this clearly in 1919. In a memorandum for Haenisch, he wrote that even if the state succeeded in imposing the principle of direct elections, conservatives would win a big victory—'the liberals are too indifferent and too weak'.[68] The first effective use of the electoral system to challenge the traditional conservative majority in the church came from the pro-Nazi German Christians in 1932.[69]

The revolution settlement fell far short of Republican hopes. The new church constitution gave power to synods dominated by very large conservative majorities. The President of the new General Synod and therefore President of the new executive body of the church, the Kirchensenat, was Winckler, chairman of the DNVP in the Prussian Landtag. The conservatives, basically hostile to the Republic, recognized that a good settlement had been reached with the state. However, they regarded it as a victory over the Republican parties and were reluctant to give the Republic credit for its moderation. Even Dibelius's later reference to the revolution as 'the liberating storm' was too conciliatory for them.[70]

Nevertheless the fact that the church had been treated generously meant that there was between it and the Republic a possibility of gradual *rapprochement* which would not have existed if a harsh settlement had been imposed. This possibility might never have been followed up, however, but for the distinctive and influential position retained by the Oberkirchenrat. Ironically, this was because it was led until 1933 by men appointed to it by the state before the revolution[71] and as a result it remained more sympathetic

68. D.Z.A. Merseburg, Rep. 77, Tit. 123, 157/1: Troeltsch memorandum, 15 Aug. 1919.

69. See below, pp. 91–8.

70. O. Dibelius, *Das Jahrhundert der Kirche* (1st edn., Berlin, 1927), p. 75.

71. R. Moeller, President 1919–25, and H. Kapler, President 1925–33. Moeller's appointment as President took place before the new constitution came into effect and was confirmed by the Kultusministerium at his own request; E.K.U., Gen. II, 27/3: Haenisch to Oberkirchenrat, 21 July 1919, and the Oberkirchenrat reply, 30 Oct. 1919. Kapler was elected in January 1925 by a joint committee of the Oberkirchenrat and leaders of the old General Synod which had been empowered to act by the constituent assembly until the first Kirchensenat met in December 1925. E.K.U., Gen. III, 33/10: minutes of the meeting of 29 Jan. 1925.

towards the state than the synod majority. When Kapler was elected President of the Oberkirchenrat in 1925, Kultus-minister Becker (himself a former official of the Kultus-ministerium) expressed his confidence in Kapler as someone who had co-operated with the Kultusministerium for decades. Kapler, in reply, stressed the importance he attached to preserving good relations with the Prussian state.[72] During the period 1925-31 he demonstrated that this was more than a polite gesture and that in his view the welfare of the church would best be served by agreement with the Republic.

ii. The Other Protestant Landeskirchen

All Landeskirchen were faced with the same problem of reconstruction as the Old Prussian Union and most solved it in a similar fashion, giving more power to the synods but retaining an important place for senior officials and clergy in the church leadership. In most Landeskirchen, however, unlike the Old Prussian Union, the senior clergyman held the highest office in the church. There were some differences in the electoral systems adopted for the constituent assemblies, which are interesting as an indication of local feeling about democracy although of little practical importance.[73]

The Prussian *Land* treated all its Landeskirchen alike. This meant that the 'new' Prussian churches (Hanover-Lutheran, Schleswig-Holstein, and the Landeskirchen in the Prussian parts of Hessen) shared the experiences of the Old Prussian Union. The Old Prussian Union, however, bore the brunt of the opposition and, once agreement had been reached with it, no obstacles were put in the way of the 'new' Prussian churches; in any case, most of them opted for a system of direct election to their constituent assemblies. The Prussian law of April 1924, confirming the new church constitutions, was common to all Prussian Landeskirchen.[74]

Most of the other *Länder* gave the Landeskirchen little

72. E.K.U., Gen. II, 27/9: Becker to Kapler, 1 Apr. 1925 and Kapler's reply, 6 Apr.

73. F. Giese and J. Hosemann, *Die Verfassungen der Deutschen Evangelischen Landeskirchen* (Berlin, 1927) and *Das Wahlrecht der Deutschen Evangelischen Landeskirchen* (Berlin, 1929).

74. *Kirchliches Jahrbuch*, 48. Jg. (1921), 402; Ebers, *Reichs- und preußisches Staatskirchenrecht*, pp. 639–48.

cause for complaint.[75] In Baden, Württemberg, Hessen, Oldenburg, and Lippe, the revolutionary authorities made no attempt to interfere in the church and in Bavaria, Anhalt, and Mecklenburg, the Landeskirchen were soon granted independence. Most *Länder* retained rights of supervision over the church, but in Baden and the city states of Hamburg and Bremen (though not Lübeck) these were minimal. Württemberg was so well treated that it was afraid that the Reich constitution might restrict its privileges.[76]

It was common for the revolutionary authorities to take measures to reduce the influence of the church in education. In a notable case, the workers' and soldiers' council in Hamburg ordered the abolition of religious education. Most of these initial measures, however, did not long survive the meeting of the constituent assemblies of the *Länder* and the passing of the Reich constitution.

Important disputes occurred in Saxony and Brunswick, where radical governments survived beyond the constituent assemblies. In Brunswick the government attempted to impose a democratic constitution on the Landeskirche.[77] The dispute was referred first to the Reich Minister of the Interior and subsequently to the *Reichsgericht* (Reich Court). Both decided in favour of the Landeskirche, and this established a precedent which helped to prevent intervention elsewhere.[78] During the inflation of 1923 the governments of Brunswick and Saxony refused to pay church subsidies. The Saxon church leadership wrote to the Reich Chancellor describing how the clergy were forced to work in factories, mines, and offices to stay alive.[79] In both cases the courts

75. For details, see *Kirchliches Jahrbuch*, 46. Jg. (1919), 359-64; ibid., 47. Jg. (1920), 376–420; also a survey carried out by the Kirchenausschuß in E.K.U., Gen. II, 27/6.

76. Lk.A. Stuttgart, A 26/226: Konsistorium Stuttgart to Kirchenausschuß, 29 Dec. 1918. Cf. K. Weller, *Die Staatsumwälzung in Württemberg 1918–1920* (Stuttgart, 1930), pp. 145–8, 297.

77. E.K.U., Gen. II, 27/6: Kirchenausschuß survey.

78. D.Z.A. Merseburg, Rep. 76, III Sekt. 1, Abt. XVII, 214/1: Reich Minister of the Interior to Rat der Volksbeauftragten, Brunswick, 28 Oct. 1919 *Entscheidungen des Reichsgerichts in Zivilsachen*, vol. 103 (1921), pp. 91–4.

79. Bundesarchiv, R 431/2195: Saxon Landeskonsistorium to Chancellor Cuno, 5 Feb. 1923; cf. K-W. Dahm, *Pfarrer und Politik* (Cologne, 1965) pp. 140–2.

decided in favour of the churches.[80] These disputes were prolonged. Litigation over the payment of church subsidies in Brunswick lasted until December 1929. They also caused great bitterness.[81] However, they were confined to a few *Länder* and in every case the guarantees of the Reich constitution were eventually made effective by the courts. As a result, they did not prevent the church leadership as a whole, under Prussian guidance, seeking a stable relationship with the Republic.

iii. The Formation of the Kirchenbund

Shortly after the revolution several Protestant associations were formed independent of the Landeskirchen with the idea of holding a Kirchentag, a public conference representative of the whole of German Protestantism, following precedents from 1848 and 1871.[82] The Kirchenausschuß (the standing committee of the federal organization of the Landeskirchen) welcomed the suggestion because it wanted to strengthen the central organization of German Protestantism so that it could represent Protestant interests effectively to the Reich authorities and compete with the Roman Catholic church.[83]

The Kirchenausschuß and the free Protestant associations together summoned a preparatory conference which met in Cassel on 27-8 February 1919. The meeting decided unanimously in favour of a Kirchentag as a regular institution of German Protestantism. It was emphasized, however, that the independence of individual Landeskirchen would not be affected. The aim was not to establish a *Reichskirche* (Reich church) but only an organization to represent the common interests of the Landeskirchen. The first Kirchentag met in Dresden in September 1919. The Kirchenausschuß was given

80. *Entscheidungen des Reichsgerichts in Zivilsachen*, vol. 128 (1929), *Anhang*, pp. 16–46; ibid., vol. 113 (1926), pp. 349–403.

81. See *Kirchliches Jahrbuch*, 49. Jg. (1922), 399–404; ibid. 50. Jg. (1923), 384–7; ibid. 51. Jg. (1924), 427–32.

82. E.K.D., A 3/43: Arbeitsausschuß of the Konferenz Deutscher Evangelischer Arbeitsorganisationen to the Kirchenausschuß, 9 Jan. 1919; minutes of a meeting of the groups concerned at Elberfeld on 3 Jan. 1919.

83. Ibid.: Kirchenausschuß to the Arbeitsausschuß, 13 Jan. 1919; E.K.D., A 2/18: minutes of a meeting of the Kirchenausschuß and the Arbeitsausschuß 4 Feb. 1919. Protocol of the preparatory conference for a Kirchentag, Cassel, 27-8 Feb. 1919; a copy is in the Bundesarchiv, Nachlass Traub, 37.

fifteen new members and asked to prepare a detailed constitution.[84]

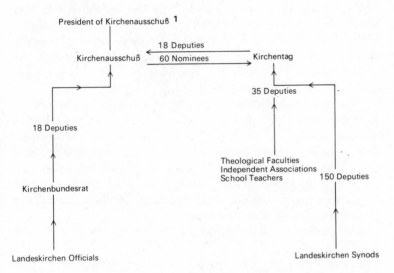

The Kirchenbund

President of Kirchenausschuß [1]

Kirchenausschuß — 18 Deputies / 60 Nominees → Kirchentag

35 Deputies

18 Deputies

Theological Faculties
Independent Associations
School Teachers   150 Deputies

Kirchenbundesrat

Landeskirchen Officials   Landeskirchen Synods

1 This post was held automatically by the President of the Berlin Oberkirchenrat

This foresaw a *Kirchenbund* which would represent the common interests of German Protestantism at home and abroad.[85] The Kirchenbund consisted of three main institutions—first, the Kirchentag which had 210 members with a majority (150) elected from the synods of the Landeskirchen. Beside the Kirchentag there was also a *Kirchenbundesrat* and the Kirchenausschuß. The Kirchenbundesrat was the successor of the old organization of church officials and had certain reserve powers to protect the Landeskirchen from too much central direction. The standing committee, the Kirchenausschuß, remained the most important body. It was the executive of the Kirchenbund and, as such, represented German Protestantism. It consisted of eighteen

84. *Verhandlungen des deutschen evangelischen Kirchentages*, 1919 (Berlin, 1920), pp. 26, 84–118, 153–237, 293–306, 345–7.
85. Ibid., 1921, pp. 30–45.

members appointed by the Kirchenbundesrat and eighteen elected by the Kirchentag. It had to meet at least every six months. The President of the Berlin Oberkirchenrat continued as of right to be President of the Kirchenausschuß.

The constitution was approved by the second Kirchentag which met in Stuttgart in 1921.[86] The individual Landeskirchen all decided to join and the Kirchenbund was formally inaugurated at a ceremony on Ascension Day 1922 at the *Schloßkirche* in Wittenberg. An administrative office, known as the *Kirchenbundesamt*, was set up in Berlin.[87]

The Kirchenbund was an important new departure. It provided a public platform—the Catholics already had a *Katholikentag*—and a more effective central organization than German Protestantism had previously possessed. Many matters were still settled at *Land* level by the local authorities but, in 1933, when the Reich became dominant, the Kirchenausschuß assumed responsibility for the policy of the Protestant church as a whole.

The power of the Berlin Oberkirchenrat remained great within the new federal organization and benefited from its increased prestige. In his capacity as President of the Kirchenausschuß, the President of the Berlin Oberkirchenrat was the foremost representative of German Protestantism. At the same time the power of the President of the Kirchenausschuß remained limited by the independence retained by the individual Landeskirchen. The importance of this limitation was seen when a minority of Landeskirchen repudiated the leadership of the Kirchenausschuß in 1933.

By 1924 the Protestant church in Germany was again secure. Only a few *Länder* persisted in an anti-clerical policy and they were restrained by the Reich. Most Landeskirchen had been treated generously and regarded the result as satisfactory. This reflected the failure of the revolution and the weakness of the Republican parties. But, as a result, a basis for co-operation between the church and the Republic had been created. There still remained strong emotional tensions dividing the two. The church found it difficult to

86. *Verhandlungen, Kirchentag*, 1921, p. 248.
87. Ibid., 1924, p. 15.

shed its loyalty to the old regime and the strongest Republican party, the SPD, often found it equally difficult to drop its hostility to the Protestant church.[88] Had the Republican parties been successful in imposing their original policy on the church, however, the church would have reacted with intransigent opposition. As it was, despite the tension between the two sides, progress was made towards a *rapprochement.*

88. See below, chapter 3.

2

PRUSSIAN CHURCH TREATY

In 1931 a Prussian church treaty was concluded, establishing a formal partnership between the Prussian *Land* and its Landeskirchen. It was preceded by a similar agreement in Bavaria and followed by another one in Baden.[1] Had the Weimar Republic survived longer, a Reich treaty (the equivalent of a Reich concordat) would probably have been concluded. The treaties gave the churches greater independence and a new status; in return the state obtained political guarantees to ensure that the leading officials of the church were loyal to the constitution of the Republic.

There were strong motives of self-interest behind the Protestant demand for a treaty. The main one was to keep abreast of the Roman Catholic church which concluded concordats with Bavaria in 1924, Prussia in 1929, and Baden in 1932–3.[2] Before the revolution the Protestant church had looked to the crown for protection. After 1918 it decided that it would have to defend itself and that it could not allow the Roman Catholic church to win special privileges without claiming equal rights for Protestants.

There were also objections to a treaty on ecclesiastical grounds. Some Protestants argued that their church was bound to be worsted if a concordat policy were successful. Because of its international power and the sovereign status of the Papacy, a concordat was like an international agreement, whereas a Protestant treaty was only an agreement between the state and one of its corporations. There was also a danger that by advancing counter-claims the Protestant church assisted the conclusion of concordats. If the Protestant

---

1. O. Friedrich, *Der evangelische Kirchenvertrag mit dem Freistaat Baden* (Lahr, 1933).
2. E. Deuerlein, *Das Reichskonkordat* (Düsseldorf, 1956), pp. 9–87, and D. Golombek, *Die politische Vorgeschichte des Preußenkonkordats (1929)* (Mainz, 1970).

church refused to negotiate a complementary treaty, it was
said, the state would be put in a difficult position. The
government might be unable to win enough support in the
Landtag for a concordat with the Roman Catholic church,
and even if it did, an agreement with only one church would
be seen to be a breach of the principle of parity.

The treaty also raised important political questions. In
return for the greater independence which the treaty would
give the church, the state demanded the right to make
political objections to the appointment of senior church
officials. This forced the problem of loyalty to the Republican
constitution on the church in a binding form. Some members
of the DNVP did not want the church to make a permanent
agreement with the Republic and were particularly bitter
about the 'political' clause. After 1929 this opposition
mounted, together with the general increase of radical
right-wing opposition to the Republic. This was embarrassing
to the church leadership, which had previously counted on
the DNVP for political support. The treaty was also
unwelcome to the SPD. It consented reluctantly to a
concordat with the Roman Catholic church because of the
importance of the Centre party to the Prussian government
coalition. It was openly hostile to a treaty with the
Protestant church which it considered an enemy of the
Republic.[3]

The senior officials and clergymen of the Prussian Landeskirchen, especially the Berlin Oberkirchenrat, decided that on
balance a treaty was desirable. They thought that its
advantages made the political concessions worthwhile.
Despite the opposition from both Republican and anti-
Republican parties, a treaty was negotiated and accepted by
the synods and the Prussian Landtag. It was the greatest
achievement of the church leadership during the Weimar
Republic and marked an important stage towards acceptance
of the Republic by the church.

The Kirchenausschuß first discussed a Protestant treaty in
1922 as a consequence of negotiations then in progress for a
Reich concordat.[4] Reinhard Mumm, a deputy from the

3. See O. Braun, *Von Weimar zu Hitler* (New York, 1940), p. 335.
4. E.K.D., A 2/20: minutes of Kirchenausschuß meeting, 26–7 May 1922.

Kirchentag and a DNVP politician, suggested to President Moeller that the Kirchenausschuß should demand a treaty of equal worth; he declared that he intended to make DNVP agreement to the concordat dependent on whether Protestant wishes had been satisfied.[5] President Moeller agreed that the Protestant church should receive a new settlement equivalent to the proposed concordat.[6] The legal subcommittee of the Kirchenausschuß considered the problem and decided in favour of a treaty because it would make the church independent of the Reichstag and Landtage.[7] The Landeskirchen were consulted and their leaders all agreed that a treaty was desirable, though doubts were expressed about whether a treaty could be the equal of a concordat.[8] On 18 December 1922 Moeller and Kapler met members of the Reich government who agreed to consider Protestant wishes for a treaty.[9]

Negotiations for a Reich concordat were delayed to allow a Bavarian concordat to be concluded first. The Bavarian concordat was signed on 29 March 1924 and ratified together with treaties with the two Protestant Landeskirchen of Bavaria by the Bavarian Landtag in January 1925.[10] The terms of these agreements provoked strong criticism from Protestant groups. The concordat was attacked for the extent of its concessions to the Roman Catholic church. The validity of canon law had been recognized without any restriction. The Catholic church acquired influence over some appointments to philosophical and history faculties in the universities as well as to theological faculties. Catholic schools, the great majority in Bavaria, were to be staffed only by teachers acceptable to the church. This clause applied not only to religious education, which was under the control of the church, but also to other subjects. The Catholic orders

5. E.K.D., B 3/236: Mumm to Kirchenausschuß, 19 Dec. 1921; Mumm to Moeller, 15 Mar. 1922.

6. Ibid.: Moeller to Mumm, 7 Feb. 1922.

7. Ibid.: memorandum of the legal subcommittee, 23 May 1922.

8. Ibid.: replies of the Landeskirchen to Kirchenausschuß circular, 15 June 1922.

9. Ibid.: note of Moeller about the meeting, cf. Bundesarchiv, R 431/2195: Moeller to Cuno, 5 July 1922; note of the State Secretary in the Reichskanzlei, 21 July 1922; and note of W., 22 Dec. 1922.

10. Deuerlein, *Das Reichskonkordat*, pp. 48–50.

were given every freedom, including the right to teach in state schools and to found private ones.

The *Evangelischer Bund*,[11] the *Christliche Welt*,[12] Gottfried Traub in a noted pamphlet, and many others[13] protested against these concessions. They also attacked the idea that the formal parity observed in the treaties with the Protestant churches gave them equality. It was noted that one of the school clauses of the concordat was only to apply to the Protestant churches should they ask for it: this was seen as proof that they did not really want it. Protestant critics pointed out that there was no Protestant equivalent of canon law or of the Catholic orders. Inequality was also alleged in the financial settlement to each church. Traub said that Protestants could stop the concordat by refusing to accept the corresponding Protestant treaties.[14]

The reaction to the Bavarian treaties changed the policy of the Protestant leadership. In 1924 a Reich concordat was again considered by the government, and the Ministry of the Interior asked President Kapler for the views of the Protestant church.[15] Kapler was deliberately dilatory[16] but after renewed requests from the Reich he asked the legal subcommittee of the Kirchenausschuß to consider the matter again. A leading Bavarian layman, von Pechmann,[17] strongly opposed a treaty and his views found the support of the Kirchenausschuß.[18]

---

11. E.K.D., B 3/236: *Evangelischer Bund* propaganda sheet. The *Evangelischer Bund* was an association independent of the Landeskirchen and quite distinct from the Kirchenbund. It was founded in 1886 primarily as an anti-Roman Catholic association. During the Weimar Republic it became a right-wing Protestant pressure group.

12. *Die Christliche Welt*, 1925, Nos. 1–6.

13. G. Traub, *Das bayerische Konkordat und was es für Volk und Staat bedeutet* (Munich, 1925). See also C. Mirbt, 'Das bayerische Konkordat vom 29. März 1924', *Neue kirchliche Zeitschrift*, XXXVI (1925), 371–411.

14. Traub, *Das bayerische Konkordat*, p. 15.

15. E.K.D., B 3/236: note of a visit by Ministerialrat Kaisenberg to Kapler, 25 Oct. 1924.

16. E.K.D., A 2/22: minutes of the meeting of the Kirchenausschuß, confidential protocol, 24–5 June 1925, speech of Kapler.

17. Freiherr Baron von Pechmann, President of the Bavarian Handelsbank, President of the Kirchentag, 1921–30.

18. E.K.D., A 2/22: minutes of Kirchenausschuß meeting, 24–5 Mar. 1925, confidential protocol, report of the legal subcommittee.

Negotiations for a Reich concordat were, however, then again postponed because the Prussian government insisted that Prussia must first have its own concordat, since Bavaria had been allowed a separate agreement. Attention therefore turned to Prussia.[19]

In December 1926, after retiring from the Berlin Ober-kirchenrat, President Moeller composed an important memorandum on the concordat problem.[20] He argued that while Protestants should oppose the conclusion of a concordat, if one nevertheless came about they would have to present their own demands. The Oberkirchenrat, under Kapler's leadership from 1925, followed Moeller's advice. It faced opposition from within the church both in the Old Prussian Union and the 'new' Prussian churches. All the provincial synods of the Old Prussian Union passed resolutions requesting the church leadership not to follow the example of Bavaria.[21]

This opposition was repeated at the General Synod which met in December 1925. Under the influence of the church leadership, however, a moderate resolution was passed.[22] The constitutional committee of the synod agreed that it was opposed to any concordat. It decided, however, that it should wait to see the content of the proposed concordat before publicly rejecting it. When it knew what was proposed, the committee would oppose anything contrary to Protestant interests, especially clauses concerning schools. At the same time, in return for harmless parts of the concordat the Protestant church would demand an agreement of equal worth.[23]

Ministerialdirektor Trendelenburg, the Kultusministerium official chiefly concerned with the negotiations with the churches, approached Kapler on 15 February 1926 about the

19. Rittberg, *Der preußische Kirchenvertrag*, contains a good account of the negotiations in Prussia; see also, E. Wende, *C. H. Becker* (Stuttgart, 1958), pp. 284–93, for an account from the government side. Becker was Kultusminister in Prussia in 1921 and again in 1925–30.

20. E.K.U., Gen. XII, 63/Beiheft (vertrauliches Material).

21. *Verhandlungen, Generalsynode*, 1925, i. 539–41.

22. Ibid., pp. 538–47.

23. E.K.U., Gen. XII, 63/Beiheft (vertrauliches Material): memorandum about the attitude of the General Synod to the question of a concordat.

concordat.[24] Kapler argued that it would bind the state by international law in a way that would be impossible in an agreement with the Protestant church. He also objected to the inclusion of any school clauses. Kapler later met Kultusminister Becker and sent him a memorandum explaining the attitude of the General Synod.[25] During the negotiations for the concordat with the Papal Nuntius, Pacelli, Becker supplied Kapler with confidential information about their progress.[26]

On 4 July 1927 Kapler told Becker that, if a concordat were inevitable, the Protestant church would present its own legal and financial demands.[27] When Becker said that the Prussian Finance Ministry believed that there could be no important new financial award to the Protestant church, Kapler replied that if Catholics were treated more generously than Protestants it would cause great bitterness. This would affect the behaviour of Protestant members of the Landtag whose support was necessary for the concordat. The next day, at a meeting attended by representatives of the Kirchensenat as well as the Oberkirchenrat and the Kultusministerium, the church leaders said they were prepared for provisional negotiations.[28]

These negotiations took place between March and May 1928.[29] At the last meeting, on 26 May, the 'political' clause was discussed. It was to cover senior church officials and the Generalsuperintendenten but not synod leaders. Trendelenburg said that the state had to insist on it in order to observe parity with the Catholic church, but in practice it would seldom be used against the Protestant church. He accepted that there should be a guarantee against objections of a party political kind (as against loyalty to the state) being raised under the clause. He also agreed that the church should be

24. Nachlaß Becker, 30: note of Trendelenburg, 16 Feb. 1926.
25. E.K.U., Gen. XII, 63/1: Kapler to Becker, 31 Mar. 1926.
26. Ibid.: Kapler to Becker, 31 Mar. 1926; ibid., 63/Beiheft (vertrauliches Material): memoranda on the progress of negotiations for a concordat from 18 Oct. 1926.
27. Ibid., 63/Beiheft (vertrauliches Material): note by Kapler, 9 July 1927.
28. Ibid.: note by Karnatz, 13 Oct. 1927; Nachlaß Becker, 34: minutes of the meeting.
29. E.K.U., Gen. XII, 63/Beiheft (vertrauliches Material).

allowed to examine any political objections raised by the state, but, he maintained, the state alone could judge whether the objections were sufficient for the candidate to be refused.

The negotiations with the Protestant church were broken off by the government in the summer of 1928. This change of policy was imposed on the Kultusministerium by the Social Democratic Minister President Otto Braun. Becker had intended to satisfy the demands of both churches simultaneously and hoped to have the support in the Landtag of all parties from the SPD to the DNVP. Braun declared, however, that the SPD would not support this policy and demanded that the negotiations should cease. Becker explained to a friend that the SPD was reluctant to agree to a concordat with the Catholic church despite the importance of the Centre party to the coalition; if the SPD were, in addition, asked to acquiesce in a treaty with the Protestant church, in which it saw 'the praetorian guard of the monarchy', it would revolt and both concordat and treaty would be rejected.[30]

This development had several important consequences. The Oberkirchenrat realized that it would have to persuade the government that the church was loyal to the Republic. At the same time, the prospect that a concordat with the Roman Catholic church would be concluded while the Protestant church was ignored made Protestants feel victims of injustice. This helped to unite them behind the demand for a treaty and made it easier for the church leadership to gain the support of the synods. Thirdly it became important for the church to win over some of the smaller, middle-class parties in the Landtag whose votes would be decisive for the concordat.[31]

At Trendelenburg's suggestion Kapler met State Secretary

30. Nachlaß Becker, 30: account of political developments 1928–9 by Becker.

31. The results of the Prussian Landtag elections of 20 May 1928 were: SPD 137, DNVP 82, Centre 71, DVP 40, KPD 56, DDP 21, *Wirtschaftspartei* 21, NSDAP 6, *Christliche Bauernpartei* 12, others 4; *Statistisches Jahrbuch für den Freistaat Preußen* (Berlin, 1929), vol. 25, pp. 321–5. The SPD and Centre were expected to support the concordat, giving it 208 votes; the DNVP, DVP, KPD, NSDAP, and some of the small parties were expected to vote against it—about 190 votes. The attitude of the DDP and the Wirtschaftspartei was therefore crucial.

Weismann, an official on Braun's staff, on 28 August.[32] He told him that he would like to meet Braun to discuss the concordat and the attitude of the Protestant church towards the present state. He said that he knew the Protestant church was criticized for not being Republican and for clinging to monarchism. Weismann told Kapler that a series of incidents, especially remarks of particular clergymen from the pulpit, seemed to justify this reproach.[33] Kapler replied that the Protestant church had had a different relationship with the crown from that of the Catholic church. The King of Prussia had been their *Summus Episcopus* and they had the Hohenzollern dynasty to thank that the Protestant church had prospered. He continued, according to Weismann's memorandum,

One should therefore be patient. It would be some time before everyone who held a position within the Protestant church had come to terms inwardly with the new situation. He must however emphasize that the Protestant church, as such, adhered to the state in its present form, as could be seen from many public and official declarations.[34] The reproach that it was anti-Republican was therefore unjustified. When individual clergymen went off the rails—which one could not prevent—they were always sharply reproved. He therefore asked that in future the government should treat the Protestant church with the confidence that it deserved.

Kapler added that the mere fact that a concordat was to be concluded had disturbed the Protestant population. He recognized that they would have to accept a concordat; he asked only that the rights of Protestants should not be impaired and that they should not be presented with a *fait accompli*.

Kapler met Braun on 9 October 1928. He wrote to Winckler (the President of the Kirchensenat) that it had been a very pleasant meeting but that the result was negative as far as a Protestant treaty was concerned. Braun declared that his opinion, shared by his party, was that a treaty could not be

---

32. E.K.U., Gen. XII, 63/Beiheft (vertrauliches Material): memorandum by Karnatz, 31 Aug. 1928. G.St.A., Rep. 90, 2383: memorandum of Weismann, 28 Aug. 1928.

33. Cf. G. Stresemann, *Vermächtnis* (Berlin, 1932), ii. 315–18.

34. Kapler gave Weismann a copy of the *Vaterländische Kundgebung* from the 1927 Kirchentag, see below, pp. 60–1.

concluded together with a concordat but must wait for later consideration. They had also discussed the general relationship of the Protestant churches to the state; Kapler thought that although this discussion would not influence the question of a treaty, it had been helpful in many respects in clarifying the situation.[35]

The whole Prussian church leadership now decided to support Kapler's initiative with a formal demand for a treaty.[36] On 23 October 1928 the Oberkirchenrat wrote to the Prussian government repeating its objections to a concordat but demanding a simultaneous treaty of equal worth and protesting against the break in negotiations.[37] It pointed out that Protestants outnumbered Catholics in Prussia by two to one. The other Prussian churches sent similar letters.[38] A full meeting of the Kirchensenat approved the action of the Oberkirchenrat and adopted a resolution making the same demands to be sent to the parishes.[39]

Otto Braun replied that no decision had yet been taken on the concordat; when it had, they would consider the consequences for the Protestant church and parity would, of course, be observed.[40] The Oberkirchenrat wrote again saying that Braun had not made it clear whether the government was prepared for a simultaneous treaty with the Protestant church.[41] To this they received no reply.

On 21 December 1928 Trendelenburg suggested to Karnatz that it might be possible to secure guarantees for the Protestant church while the concordat was being considered by the Landtag.[42] This could be achieved by persuading a majority of deputies to make their support for the concordat conditional on the Protestant church receiving a satisfactory

35. E.K.U., Pr. II, 61: Kapler to Winckler, 11 Oct. 1928.

36. E.K.U., Gen. XII, 63/Beiheft (vertrauliches Material).

37. G.St.A., Rep. 90, 2383/1: Oberkirchenrat to Prussian government, 23 Oct. 1928.

38. Ibid.: letters from the 'new' Prussian churches, Oct. 1928.

39. E.K.U., Gen. XII, 63/Beiheft (vertrauliches Material): minutes of the Kirchensenat meeting, 29 Oct. 1928.

40. E.K.U., Gen. XII, 63/3: Braun to Oberkirchenrat, 8 Nov. 1928.

41. E.K.U., Gen. II, 39/1: Oberkirchenrat to Prussian government, 23 Nov. 1928.

42. E.K.U., Gen. XII, 63/Beiheft (vertrauliches Material): note of Karnatz, 29 Dec. 1928.

equivalent. Kapler had already approached various politicians of the DNVP, DVP, and DDP explaining the demands of the Protestant church and sending them material on the attitude of the church to the Republic.[43] This lobbying had some effect. The DVP demanded that the Protestant church should be given equal treatment before any agreement with the Catholic church came into force.[44] The DNVP demanded a simultaneous treaty and refused a request from the Centre party that they should support the concordat in return for Centre party support for a subsequent treaty with the Protestant church.[45] Protestant members of the DDP put pressure on their party in the Landtag to prevent it agreeing to a concordat more readily than the DVP.[46] The Ober-kirchenrat also had intensive negotiations with the Wirt-schaftspartei.[47]

Despite this pressure, Braun insisted that the concordat should be concluded first. He did promise the opposition parties, however, that negotiations with the Protestant church would be resumed subsequently.[48] The concordat was signed on 14 June. The Kirchensenat immediately summoned an emergency meeting of the General Synod. The synod protested against the way the Protestant church had been treated and asked the Landtag to insist on a simultaneous Protestant treaty before ratifying the concordat. The Kirchensenat was empowered to conclude the treaty. The synod passed a resolution which declared that, 'the Protestant church is always ready to give the state what belongs to it . . . It demands, however, that the state should also give it what parity and justice require . . .'[49]

43. E.K.U., Pr. II, 61: Kapler to the President of the Rhine provincial synod, 20 Oct. 1928; to Pfarrer Graue (DDP), 23 Oct.; to Hallensleben (DVP), 27 Oct.; to Kriege (DVP), Boelitz (DVP), and Kahl (DVP), 2 Nov. 1928.

44. *Der Reichsbote*, 27 Nov. 1928.

45. E.K.U., Gen. XII, 63/Beiheft (vertrauliches Material): report of Koch, President of the Westphalian provincial synod and member of the Landtag, to Karnatz, 22 Feb. 1929, of a discussion between Brüning and Linneborn (Centre) and Keudell and Koch (DNVP), 7 Feb. 1929.

46. E.K.U., Pr. II, 61: confidential note of Kapler, 9 Feb. 1929, about information from Professor Hermelink, Marburg.

47. Ibid.: Kapler to a Generalsuperintendent in Hanover, 3 July 1929.

48. E.K.U., Gen. XII, 63/Beiheft (vertrauliches Material): report of the meeting, 7 June 1929.

49. *Verhandlungen, Generalsynode*, 1929, i. 23–5.

The Oberkirchenrat sent the General Synod resolution to the Prussian government on 26 June 1929 and demanded immediate negotiations for a treaty.[50] Becker replied agreeing to negotiations but only after the concordat had been passed and he did not specify whether the negotiations would be for a treaty or simply a further church law.[51] Becker had, however, privately recommended to Braun that he allow treaty negotiations.[52] This was, he said, in any case politically necessary as the support of the Wirtschaftspartei was essential to the concordat, and the party had made its support conditional on negotiations for a Protestant treaty being started immediately the concordat had been accepted.[53]

In the Landtag the DNVP and DVP voted against the concordat because the Protestant churches had not been given simultaneous treaties. These parties argued that promises of future negotiations were not an adequate guarantee. The DDP and the Wirtschaftspartei supported the concordat on condition that negotiations for a treaty began immediately. This was accepted by Braun on behalf of the government and passed by the Landtag with the SPD abstaining on 9 July 1929.[54]

Becker met the church leaders on 11 July 1929 to start preparatory discussions and, on 27 July 1929, the Oberkirchenrat sent Becker detailed proposals for a treaty.[55] Regular meetings were held from 16 August to 9 October.[56] They were then interrupted because of differences within the government, and because Braun did not consider it wise to give his opinion on the treaty proposals at a time when the national referendum over the Young Plan and Prussian

50. G.St.A., Rep. 90, 2383/1: Oberkirchenrat to Prussian government, 26 June 1929.

51. E.K.U., Gen. XII, 63/5: Becker to Oberkirchenrat, 28 June 1929.

52. G.St.A., Rep. 90, 2383/1: Becker to Braun, 20 June 1929.

53. Nachlaß Becker, 30: account of political developments 1928-9 by Becker.

54. *Verhandlungen, Landtag, 3. Wahlperiode*, vol. 6, pp. 7625-748, 7956-89, 8118-34.

55. E.K.U., Gen. II, 39/1: Oberkirchenrat to Kirchensenat, 11 July 1929; Oberkirchenrat to Becker, 27 July 1929.

56. Ibid. (Beiheft A): memorandum about the meetings.

municipal elections were being held.[57] The preparatory discussions were resumed in December.[58] After a further delay, during which Becker was replaced as Kultusminister by Grimme, who belonged to the Religious Socialist group within the SPD,[59] the Oberkirchenrat demanded formal negotiations and informed politicians of its demand.[60] The DNVP and Wirtschaftspartei asked questions in the Landtag[61] and Grimme then opened the formal negotiations on 8 February 1930.[62]

The main problem was the political clause. The church demanded that there should be provision for an arbitration court to settle disputes arising from the clause. Church representatives explained that this did not reflect mistrust of the existing government but the desire for a guarantee against any future regime.[63] This argument was probably quite genuine in the case of the Oberkirchenrat and its fears were shown to be justified in 1933 when the Nazi Kultusminister Rust used the political clause as a pretext for intervention in the church.[64] The main reason, however, for the demand for an arbitration court was that it would make the treaty less

57. E.K.U., Gen. II, 39/1 (Beiheft A): note of Karnatz, 30 Oct. 1929; ibid. 39/2: minutes of a meeting of the Oberkirchenrat and representatives of the 'new' Prussian churches, 30 Nov. 1929. See below, pp. 63–4.

58. Ibid.: memorandum about the discussions on 5, 7, 9, 17, and 19 Dec.

59. See Wende, *C. H. Becker*, pp. 294–301. Grimme was Kultusminister 1930–2. The Religious Socialists were a small group of Protestant theologians and laymen who belonged to the SPD and sought to reconcile German Protestantism and Socialism. See E. A. Suck, 'Der Religiöse Sozialismus in der Weimarer Republik' (unpublished Diss. Phil., Marburg, 1953).

60. E.K.U., Gen. II, 39/2: Oberkirchenrat to Becker, 25 Jan. 1930.

61. *Sammlung der Drucksachen des Preußischen Landtages, 3. Wahlperiode,* vol. 5, pp. 3263, 3361.

62. E.K.U., Gen. II, 39/1 (Beiheft A): minutes of the negotiations, 8 Feb. 1930.

63. Ibid. 39/5: minutes of the meeting of church and state representatives, 25 Feb. 1931, speeches of Kapler and von Berg.

64. See below, pp. 137, 143–4. At the time of the negotiation of the treaty the Oberkirchenrat probably imagined this threat coming from a KPD government rather than from the NSDAP which denied any anti-clerical leanings but the possibility of the NSDAP using the clause had been foreseen. R. Mumm wrote in the *Tägliche Rundschau*, 14 Apr. 1931, that a conflict would be more likely with a National Socialist Kultusminister than with the SPD, which showed reserve. The Frankfurt church leader, Kübel, suggested that the NSDAP would count race an adequate objection under the clause; J. Kübel, *Der Vertrag der evangelischen Landeskirchen mit dem Freistaat Preußen* (Berlin, 1931), p. 46. Cf. Braun, *Von Weimar zu Hitler*, p. 336.

offensive to Protestant opponents of the Republic since the
church would be able to appeal against government decisions
to an alternative tribunal. For the same reason the government was unwilling to grant the demand. It was a mark of
Kapler's skill that the treaty was nevertheless negotiated and
accepted by the General Synod.

In December 1929, Kapler told the Kirchensenat that if
they considered a political clause unacceptable in any form
they must say so.[65] Kapler pointed out that this would mean
the end of negotiations and would contradict the policy of
the 1929 General Synod, which had known that a political
clause was inevitable when it empowered the Kirchensenat to
start negotiations. One right-wing synod deputy, von Arnim-
Kröchlendorff, argued that a political clause should be
rejected, but he found no support.

At their first meeting in February Grimme told the church
representatives that the Landtag would not accept a treaty
without a political clause but he promised that it would
apply only to 'state political' objections, not party political
ones; it was a question of loyalty to the constitution.
Trendelenburg refused the church's request for an arbitration
court and said that after repeated statements from the church
confirming their loyalty to the state he could see no
difficulty for them in the clause. Kapler said he did not think
that the demand for a political clause raised any objections to
further negotiations.[66]

The General Synod, which met again in February–March
1930, expressed its confidence in the church negotiators and
renewed their commission.[67] Agreement was reached on
most points with the state by June 1930[68] and on 15
October Grimme sent the church leaders a draft treaty which
had been approved by the government.[69] The Kirchensenat
subcommittee decided to concentrate on achieving improve-
ments in the formulation of the political clause and to

65. E.K.U., Gen. II, 39/2: minutes of the Kirchensenat meeting, 13–14 Dec.
1929.
66. E.K.U., Gen. II, 39/1 (Beiheft A): minutes of the meeting of 8 Feb. 1930.
67. *Verhandlungen, Generalsynode*, 1930, i. 626–31.
68. E.K.U., Gen. II, 39/1 (Beiheft A): minutes of the meetings of February to
June 1930.
69. Ibid., 39/4: Grimme to Kirchensenat, 15 Oct. 1930.

demand some form of legal protection in the event of disputes arising from the clause.[70] The Prussian churches replied jointly to Grimme on 24 November welcoming the treaty in many respects but arguing that the political clause was unsatisfactory.[71]

After several further meetings and renewed political lobbying a majority of the Kirchensenat accepted a compromise. This represented a victory for Kapler over the President of the Kirchensenat Winckler, who, responding to right-wing political pressure, was prepared to allow the negotiations to fail rather than accept the political clause without provision for independent arbitration.[72]

The final formula provided that no one would be appointed a leading church official or Generalsuperintendent before the church had made sure that the government had no political objections to him. The clause applied only to 'state political' not party-political or church-party objections. If an objection were disputed, the government would give the facts on which it was based. Finally, if the facts were disputed a mixed commission could be set up to establish them.[73] In return for the last concession, the churches declared that they would consider only people of undoubted loyalty to the constitution for such appointments.[74] Both sides had the additional security of Article 12 which laid down that disagreements would be settled in a friendly manner. Kapler argued that the church would also be able to appeal to the *Staatsgerichtshof* (a special Reich Court) to protect its rights under the Reich constitution although the Kultusministerium disagreed.[75]

On 1 April 1931 the Kirchensenat agreed by 19 votes to 15 to Kapler's proposal to refer the treaty to the General Synod and to advise its acceptance. (Winckler proposed that

70. E.K.U., Gen. II, 39/4: minutes of the meeting, 29 Oct. 1930.

71. G.St.A., Rep. 90, 2383/1: Prussian churches' reply, 24 Nov. 1930.

72. For a detailed description of the negotiations, see J. R. C. Wright, 'The political attitudes of the German Protestant church leadership November 1918-July 1933' (D.Phil. thesis, Oxford, 1969), pp. 120-8.

73. E.K.U., Gen. II, 39/1 (Beiheft A): minutes of the meeting of 27 Mar.; ibid. 39/5: Trendelenburg to Oberkirchenrat, 31 Mar. 1931.

74. E.K.U., Pr. II, 61: Kapler to Trendelenburg, 31 Mar. 1931.

75. E.K.U., Gen. II, 39/5: minutes of the negotiations of 27 Mar. 1931. ibid., Gen. II, 39/6: Grimme to Oberkirchenrat, 4 May 1931.

the Kirchensenat should simply refer the treaty to the synod without giving an opinion.)[76] The General Synod met in April 1931 and approved the treaty by 166 to 47 votes.[77] Kapler argued that although the church had not obtained all its demands, on balance the treaty should be accepted.[78] The main opposition was to the political clause. Von Arnim-Kröchlendorff said millions of Protestants 'who could not forget that the colours Black-White-Red [the flag of the Empire] had waved over them' would be offended by the treaty.[79]

The treaty was signed on 11 May 1931 and passed by the Landtag on 13 June by 201 votes to 56. The SPD abstained, with the exception of Braun who voted for the treaty; the KPD and NSDAP voted against; the other parties, with the exception of a few individuals, voted in favour although the DNVP and DVP had reservations about the political clause.[80] The treaty was ratified on 29 June. In a speech at the ceremony, Braun said that it opened a new era in the history of the Protestant Prussian churches and in their relations with the state. The relations of church and state had been regulated 'in a spirit of trustful, peaceful co-operation to the benefit of both'.[81]

The treaty of 1931 gave the Prussian Landeskirchen many advantages.[82] Restrictions on church legislative freedom were reduced.[83] The state subsidy for the costs of church administration was increased by over 1,000,000 marks to an annual grant of 4,950,000 marks. Church property was guaranteed. It was laid down that appointments to the numerous parishes formerly in the patronage of the crown (there were over 2,000 in the Old Prussian Union)[84] would

---

76. E.K.U., Gen. II, 39/5: minutes of the meeting.
77. *Verhandlungen, Generalsynode,* 1931, i. 88.
78. Ibid. i. 31.
79. Ibid. i. 63–4.
80. *Verhandlungen, Landtag, 3. Wahlperiode,* vol. 15, pp. 21128–74, 21375–401, 21403, 21415–31.
81. *Amtlicher Preußischer Pressedienst,* 29 June 1931.
82. The text of the treaty is printed in, Ebers, *Reichs- und preußisches Staatskirchenrecht,* pp. 689–701.
83. Article 2. Cf. Kübel, *Der Vertrag der evangeiischen Landeskirchen,* p. 21.
84. See E.K.U., Pr. II, 61: Oberkirchenrat to Hindenburg, 21 Mar. 1931.

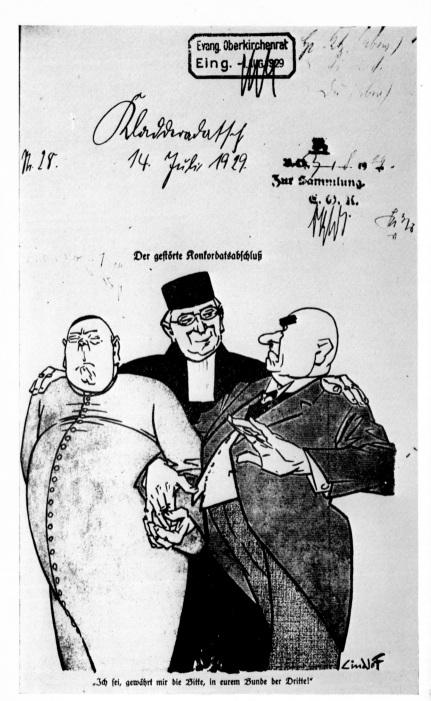

Der gestörte Konkordatsabschluß

„Ich sei, gewährt mir die Bitte, in eurem Bunde der Dritte!"

1. The Protestants demand a treaty (*Kladderadatsch*, 14 July 1929), see p. 47 fn. 87.

be made only after prior agreement had been reached between church and state. The new Prussian churches acquired rights in the appointment of theological professors similar to those previously enjoyed by the Old Prussian Union.[85]

More important than the individual clauses, the treaty gave the churches a new status. They became more than *Körperschaften des öffentlichen Rechts*; they were 'treaty-secured, autonomous, separation-churches'.[86] The difference was that none of the clauses of the treaty, unlike previous state laws concerning the church, could be altered unilaterally by legislation. The church was, in this respect, finally free of the Landtag. To gain this status, however, it had to concede the political guarantee contained in Article 7 which restricted its freedom of appointment. In 1924 the state had retained considerable powers over what the church did, but not whom it appointed; the treaty of 1931 did the reverse. The new system imposed a directly political criterion of loyalty to the Republic.

The significance of the treaty has to be weighed carefully. The main motive of the church had been to defend Protestant interests. The Protestant church wanted a share of the rights given the Roman Catholic church by the concordat.[87] It was not until it became clear that the state intended to conclude a concordat without a treaty that Protestant church leaders openly demanded a simultaneous treaty. The demand for a treaty became also a protest against government treatment of the church. The treaty was welcomed by Protestant leaders because it had increased the prestige and freedom of the church. In a letter of congratulation to Kapler, Dibelius wrote, 'even a few years ago it seemed unthinkable that the Protestant church could ever be

85. Rittberg, *Der preußische Kirchenvertrag*, pp. 174–205; *Verhandlungen, Generalsynode*, 1931, i. 67–70; ii. 144–5.
86. E.K.U., Gen. II, 39/5: minutes of the meeting of church and state representatives, 11 Feb. 1931; Trendelenburg quoted the phrase from an authority on church law.
87. Cf. the cartoon in the left-wing political satire magazine, *Kladderadatsch*, 14 July 1929; see Plate 1. It depicts Otto Braun arm-in-arm with a Roman Catholic clergyman. A Protestant pastor interrupts them saying, 'Pardon me, but I am the third partner in your union'.

an independent treaty partner of the state. . . . Now the prerequisite has been created for the Protestant to respect his own church.'[88] The political clause, on the other hand, was accepted by the majority only reluctantly as the price that had to be paid for these gains.

Nevertheless, the treaty did mark an advance in the relations of the Protestant church and the Republic. The mere conclusion of a treaty between the Prussian Landeskirchen and the Republic in 1931, when right-radical opposition to the Republic was already strong, was important. Those who rejected the treaty because of the political clause were those who belonged to the anti-Republican Right; they were seen to be in a minority (about one-quarter of the General Synod) and defeated. The acceptance of the treaty was a victory for Kapler and the moderate church leaders. It was also a victory for the Republic which had demonstrated that it was in a position to offer the church benefits and to demand its loyalty. The anger of extreme right-wing circles was understandable. In 1932 a perceptive observer, Professor Smend, wrote that the treaty established an official and legal *modus vivendi* between the church and the Republic but left open the question of whether the church would give democracy its moral support as well.[89]

88. Nachlaß Kapler: Dibelius to Kapler, 22 June 1931.
89. R. Smend, 'Protestantismus und Demokratie', reprinted in *Staatsrechtliche Abhandlungen und andere Aufsätze* (Berlin, 1955), pp. 287–308. See also Kübel, *Der Vertrag der evangelischen Landeskirchen*, p. 26.

3

DOMESTIC POLITICS DURING THE REPUBLIC

The progress towards a legal *modus vivendi* between the Protestant church and the Republic was accompanied by political *rapprochement*. The desire to obtain legal security for the church gave its leaders an incentive to be conciliatory. This was made easier for them because the Republic itself rapidly became more conservative than had seemed likely in January 1919. At the same time, Protestant leaders continued to feel strong resentment against aspects of the new regime and they never became emotionally committed to it.

Officially the church was 'neutral' in political matters, to avoid becoming identified with particular parties and alienating Protestants in others.[1] This did not prevent the church leadership from commenting on national problems which were considered above party politics. The idea of an exalted area of national life above party politics was itself, however, a feature of right-wing political attitudes. It was like the myth of the Kaiser as the impartial servant of the whole nation. Church leaders interpreted the national interest in their own terms. For instance, they did not regard the welfare of the church as a sectional interest and they were willing to act as a pressure group in its defence. Their natural political allies were the right-wing, conservative DNVP, the party most strongly opposed to the Republic in 1919. The situation was deftly summarized by the jingle, 'Die Kirche ist politisch neutral—aber sie wählt deutsch national' ('The church is politically neutral—but it votes German-National').[2]

Once the position of the church had been secured, however, its leaders became keen to take part in public life. They did not want to be permanently excluded by a

---

1. *Verhandlungen, Generalsynode*, 1920, i. 530–1.
2. K-W. Dahm, *Pfarrer und Politik* (Cologne, 1965), p. 104.

reputation for disloyalty. The benefit to the Roman Catholic church of having the Centre party as a normal member of Republican governments provided an incentive. The election of Field-Marshal von Hindenburg as President of the Republic in 1925 and government support for church work abroad also drew Protestant leaders closer to the new regime. They responded by proclaiming that the church was loyal to the state and by joining the celebrations of the anniversary of the Weimar constitution. Under Kapler, the Protestant leadership was aligned with those German conservatives who attempted to find a stable relationship with the Republic.[3] His ideas were close to those of Stresemann whom he knew and respected.[4]

The revolution of 1918 shocked the Protestant church. There was an irrational element in the Protestant reaction which never completely disappeared. As late as 1927 a comparatively cool observer, Dibelius, wrote that it had been caused by 'powers of darkness'.[5] The church leadership obeyed the Kaiser's request that they co-operate with the new rulers and took the oath of loyalty to the Republican constitution but their sense of loss was acute.[6] In his opening speech to the delegates of the first Kirchentag in 1919, President Moeller said:

The glory of the German *Kaiserreich*, the dream of our fathers, the pride of every German is gone and with it the exalted bearer of German power, the ruler and dynasty which we loved and honoured in our innermost being as the standard-bearer of German greatness.[7]

The next Kirchentag which met in 1921 was still predominantly hostile. Criticism was concentrated on the idea of

3. H. A. Turner, *Stresemann and the Politics of the Weimar Republic* (Princeton, 1963); M. Stürmer, *Koalition und Opposition in der Weimarer Republik 1924–1928* (Düsseldorf, 1967), pp. 249–54.

4. Kapler's son, Pfarrer A. Kapler, is no longer certain which party his father supported but believes it was mostly the DVP—'In any case this direction was relatively closest to my father's ideas'; letter from Pfarrer Kapler, 23 Aug. 1966.

5. O. Dibelius, *Nachspiel* (Berlin, 1928), p. 101.

6. The Kaiser's wish was reported in the *Staatsanzeiger*, 30 Nov. 1918; (E.K.U., Gen. II, 27/1). On the declarations of the Landeskirchen in 1918, see above p. 13, and Mehnert, *Evangelische Kirche und Politik*, p. 97. For an example of the oath, see Kapler's record in E.K.U., Personalia, Lit. K/16.

7. *Verhandlungen, Kirchentag*, 1919, p. 57.

a secular state. The spiritual vice-president of the Berlin Oberkirchenrat, Julius Kaftan, questioned the authority of an irreligious state since it did not recognize the authority of God.[8] In the closing speech to the Kirchentag, its President, von Pechmann, declared amid applause, '... the changes which have befallen public life in Germany in the last three years ... have not only struck at the very marrow of the German people but represent a serious danger for the Protestant church ...'[9]

To defend church interests, individual Protestants were encouraged to take part in politics. In 1918-19, the church leadership allowed an election campaign to be fought on its behalf by independent or ostensibly independent Protestant organizations. In Baden the Oberkirchenrat itself took part in election meetings.[10] In Prussia four Generalsuperintendenten were elected to the Landtag as DNVP deputies.[11]

The Protestant church also saw the preservation of German *Kultur* as its task. This was identified with a conservative, Christian philosophy. The Kirchenausschuß wanted legal restrictions on personal freedom maintained in support of its moral code. It supported censorship and licensing laws. It opposed penal reform and clashed with the more liberal views of one of its own members, Kahl, who was chairman of the relevant Reichstag committee. It opposed, in particular, change in the laws relating to sexual behaviour and divorce.[12] The decline in the birth rate was considered a national danger. One lay member of the Kirchenausschuß, Professor Titius, in a speech to the 1924 Kirchentag, attributed the decline partly to economic conditions and bad housing but also to a new code of sexual morality. For this, he blamed left-wing propaganda; 'radical socialism like radical

8. *Verhandlungen, Kirchentag,* 1921, p. 130. Cf. the correspondence of the brothers Julius and Theodor Kaftan, printed in W. Göbell, *Kirche, Recht und Theologie in vier Jahrzehnten,* ii. *1910–1926* (Munich, 1967).

9. *Verhandlungen, Kirchentag,* 1921, p. 252.

10. *Gesetzes und Verordnungsblatt für die Vereinigte Evangelisch-protestantische Kirche Badens,* 18 June 1919, No. 7; (E.K.D., A 2/427).

11. Mehnert, *Evangelische Kirche und Politik,* p. 239.

12. *Verhandlungen, Kirchentag,* 1924, pp. 17, 20–1; 1927, pp. 30–1, 71–3, 95–7; 1930, pp. 48, 109, 115, 140. E.K.D., A 2/20: minutes of the Kirchenausschuß meeting of 26–7 May 1922.

individualism have for decades attacked the existing marriage system'.[13]

It was easy for the Republic to become a symbol of the forces of modernism undermining the nation. The main enemy for conservative Protestants was socialism because of its doctrine of class war and its hostility to the church. By socialism they understood both the KPD and the SPD. The first officially opposed religion, and pastors were forbidden to join it. This was made explicit when a Pfarrer Eckert in Baden joined the KPD in October 1931 and was dismissed from the Landeskirche.[14] The Kirchenausschuß took the Communist threat particularly seriously because of the persecution of Christians in the Soviet Union.[15] In November 1930 it considered a report by a Kirchen-bundesamt official, Scholz, on the Communist atheist movement, *Ifa*, which claimed 3,000,000 members.[16] Scholz described how the *Ifa* programme condemned church treaties as 'cultural reaction', and attacked the 'school fascism' of the church and the 'slavery' of religious literature and art.[17]

The SPD was not as hostile to the church either in its programme or its policies but relations between the two remained cool. Although the great majority of SPD voters

13. *Verhandlungen, Kirchentag*, 1924, pp. 85–103. The 1927 Kirchentag issued an official declaration; ibid., 1927, pp. 358–9.

14. *Gesetzes und Verordnungsblatt für die Vereinigte Evangelisch-protestantische Landeskirche Badens*, 22 Feb. 1932, No. 2. The leader of the Religious Socialists, Pfarrer Piechowski, asked the Kirchenausschuß how Eckert's expulsion could be reconciled with the doctrine of political neutrality. He was told that the church could not allow this doctrine to be exploited to protect those who attached religion. Since this was the programme of the KPD, clergymen could not join it. E.K.D., A 2/28: minutes of the Kirchenausschuß meeting, 24–6 May 1932.

15. This was condemned by the 1930 Kirchentag in common with many other Western churches. J. Hosemann, *Der Deutsche Evangelische Kirchenbund* (2nd. edn., Berlin, 1932), pp. 152–3.

16. This was the *Interessengemeinschaft für Arbeiterkultur* and probably represented their total international membership. The German section of the *Internationale proletarischer Freidenker* had only about 100,000 members in 1930 although it was very active in Berlin; S. Bahne, 'Die Kommunistische Partei Deutschlands' in E. Matthias and R. Morsey, *Das Ende Der Parteien* (Düsseldorf, 1960), p. 666.

17. E.K.D., A 2/27: minutes of the Kirchenausschuß meeting of 27–8 Nov. 1930.

Von der Liebe

Liebe christliche Brüder und Schwestern! Es ist ein groß Geschrei und Lärmen erhoben worden in den christlichen Gauen teutscher Nation, weil ein klein fein Mägdlein, so ihr Herz einem Herzog ge-

Ingleichen: so man nicht zahlet und Seine Herzogliche Hoheit wird zwingen wollen, in die eigene Tasche zu greifen — wird's nicht letztlich Dero Hohe Herzogliche Familie entgelten müssen durch Verkürzung der Notdurft und Nahrung dieses Lebens, wird nicht des Herzogs liebe Frau vergeben müssen vom Nadelgeld, wird nicht Unfried und Hader getragen werden in die hohe durchlauchtigste Familie? Siehe: so zerstöret die Republik die Grundlagen des Familienlebens!

Miterben! Haltet an und seht
Empor zum großen Lohne!
Denn nur durch unsre Feinde geht
Der Weg zu jener Krone!
Ob tausend auch zur Rechten euch,
Zur Linken tausend sänken,
So sinkt doch nicht! Wird uns sein Reich,
Der Kraft zum Streit gab, schenken,
Wenn wir darin erliegen?
(Lied 426 des Evgl. Gesangbuches für die Provinz Brandenburg.)

Vater, kröne du mit Segen
Unsern König und sein Haus.
Führ ihn auf deinen Wegen
Herrlich deinen Ratschluß aus.
Deiner Kirche sei er Schutz,
Deinen Feinden biet er Trutz,
Sei du dem Gesalbten gnädig,
Segne, segne unsern König!
(Lied 507 des Evgl. Gesangbuches für die Provinz Brandenburg.)

Die Komtesse M., die eines deutschen Herzogs Herz ihr eigen nennen durfte.

schenket, vertrauend dem Staat sich genaht, ob er wohl Verständnis habe für die Glut eines liebenden Herzens und all ihrer Folgen. Denn es stehet schlecht um die christlichen Werke und die Westdeutschen Montanaktien notieren bekümmernden Stand. Und also hat man das klein fein Mägdlein eine Maitresse gescholten, und die Republik will nichts zahlen.

Lasset uns aber festhalten an den Grundlagen der öffentlichen Ordnung, wie solches uns geboten worden ist durch den Kirchensenat. („Ihr Knechte, seid untertan mit aller Furcht den Herren, nicht allein den gütigen und gelinden, sondern auch den wunderlichen." 1. Petr. 2, 18.) Die öffentlichen Grundlagen — jenes Mägdlein hat sie wohl gewahret. All ihr Liebeswerk vollzog sich in der Öffentlichkeit, ob sie gleich eines Herzogs genoß. Und gern sah man sie. Sie war in Wahrheit ein öffentliches Mädchen!

Siehe: die Grundlagen des öffentlichen Lebens will die Republik zerstören!

Die traute Landschaft, fern ab der Welt, darin sich der Herzog und die Komtesse zum erstenmal trafen.

Bedenket, liebe christliche Brüder und Schwestern, wenn jenes Mägdlein nicht abgefunden wird, wovon soll ihrer blühenden Kinder Schar Heim und Familie bereinst begründen und erhalten? Die Grundlagen des Familienlebens seien uns teuer und wert. Aber sie wollen nicht zahlen.

Siehe: so zerstöret die Republik die Grundlagen des Familienlebens.

O, wie betrübet uns der Mangel christlichen Sinns, wie wohl so herzlich wünschen wir, daß in den Amtsstuben des neuen Staates das Wort des Apostels stünde in flammenden Schrift: „Erweiset euch als die Armen, die doch viele reich machen!" (2. Kor. 6, 10.) Und: „Einen fröhlichen Geber hat Gott lieb!" (2. Kor. 9, 7.), und aber: „Erinnere sie, daß sie den Fürsten und der Obrigkeit untertan und gehorsam seien, zu allem guten Werk bereit seien." (Tit. 3, 1.)

*

Sonntagsfrühgebet
zu sprechen am 3. nach Trinitatis (20. Juni)

Ach bleib mit deinem Segen
Bei uns du reicher Herr!
Das fürstliche Vermögen
Bei uns reichlich vermehr!

2. Socialist satire on monarchism in the church (*Lachen Links*, 11 June 1926), see p. 53 fn. 23.

belonged to a church, if only nominally, this was not true of SPD deputies. In 1928 only twenty out of 152 Reichstag deputies belonged to a church. There was some local variation; in the state of Hessen over half the SPD deputies in the Landtag were members of a church but in Prussia the party was strongly agnostic.[18] Even the leader of the Religious Socialists, Pfarrer Piechowski, was reported as saying that it was almost impossible to be a member of the SPD in Berlin if one were religious.[19] The SPD press frequently criticized the church; it made fun of Christian festivals, attacked state subsidies for the churches and church social work, and opposed denominational schools.[20] Against this background, Protestant leaders assumed with some justification that the moderation of SPD policy towards the church was the result of pressure from the Centre party.

The referendum for the expropriation of the royal houses in 1926 led the Protestant leadership to take a public stand against the socialist parties. The referendum was demanded by the SPD and KPD after the Reichstag had rejected a motion for expropriation. Church leaders naturally opposed the plan but were divided about whether they should make their opposition public.[21] However, under strong pressure from the parishes, a majority of the Kirchenausschuß agreed to a resolution. It said that as well as the political and legal questions involved, the referendum affected the Christian conscience. 'The proposed expropriation of the royal houses without compensation means the removal of the rights of German fellow countrymen and contradicts clear and unambiguous principles of the Gospel.'[22] The church was sharply attacked by the socialist press for its attitude.[23]

18. H. Christ, *Der politische Protestantismus in der Weimarer Republik* (Diss. Phil., Bonn, 1967), p. 283.

19. E.K.D., A 2/478: *Evangelischer Pressedienst*, 15 Nov. 1929.

20. The press files of the Kirchenbund contain many examples, mainly from *Vörwarts*, see E.K.D., A 2/494–5.

21. E.K.D., A 2/425: von Pechmann to Kapler, 26 Mar. 1926. E.K.U., Gen. II, 32/Beiheft 1: Winckler to Kapler, 5 Apr. 1926 and Kapler's reply, 14 Apr.

22. E.K.D., A 2/24: minutes of the Kirchenausschuß meeting of 3–5 June 1926.

23. See, for instance, *Lachen Links*, 3. Jg. (1926), No. 24, a mock page from a Protestant Sunday paper satirizing the church's connections with monarchy (Plate 2).

In addition to their dislike of socialist influence within the Republic, conservative Protestants also objected to the power which the Roman Catholic church had gained in the new regime. The influence of the Centre party in Republican governments meant that the Roman Catholic church seemed to receive official favour, reversing the advantage enjoyed by Protestants in north Germany under the Empire. Protestants considered the policy of coalition with the SPD (which the Centre party adopted) an unprincipled attempt to win sectional gains by alliance with a party which was basically hostile to the church and politically undesirable.[24] Protestant leaders were indignant that the Roman Catholic church, whose demands were often more extreme than Protestant ones, was nevertheless relatively exempt from attack in the Republican press. Protestant leaders also believed that there was a systematic policy of excluding Protestants from government appointments, although they could not prove it.[25] Instead of gratitude for the concessions won by the Centre party for both churches, they resented their dependence on a Roman Catholic party and saw it as evidence of the basic indifference of the Republic towards Protestant interests.

Another threat to German *Kultur,* in Protestant eyes, was Jewish influence. In a lecture to the 1927 Kirchentag the theologian, Paul Althaus, criticized *völkisch* theories but maintained that there was a Jewish danger. He quoted with approval a statement of the Central Committee of the Inner Mission which said that 'evangelization is today opposed on all sides by a mentality under Jewish influence in business, the press, art, and literature'. Althaus said that the churches should not be afraid to speak out. It was not a question of racial or religious anti-Semitism, 'but only of the threat of a ... demoralized and demoralizing, urban intellectual class which is represented primarily by the Jewish race'.[26] The church leadership did not commit itself to a public state-

24. *Kirchliches Jahrbuch,* 59. Jg. (1932), 116.
25. E.K.D., A 2/28: minutes of the Kirchenausschuß meeting of 24–5 Nov. 1932; E.K.D., A 2/446: Kirchenausschuß to Landeskirchen, 10 Apr. 1933 and their replies.
26. *Verhandlungen, Kirchentag,* 1927, p. 216.

ment, but there is evidence that it agreed with Althaus's analysis.[27]

The Protestant leadership shared the objections to democracy common among German conservatives. They felt no attachment to a parliamentary system; their ideal was the authoritarian state of William I and Bismarck. Their dislike of German liberalism was increased by its reputation for anti-clericalism. During the Weimar Republic this reputation was no longer accurate, but there was still a difference between the educational policies of the liberal parties, the DDP and the DVP, and that of the majority of the church leadership. The DDP also made itself unpopular by trying to force a democratic constitution on the church through the Prussian Landtag. In addition, its reputation as a Jewish party may have counted against it.[28] The DVP had more support in the Protestant church because it was more conservative, and in some parts of the 'new' Prussian provinces, it was the main conservative party.[29] The DVP was also the natural party for the Vernunftrepublikaner[30] in the church leadership to choose, since it could be seen as a conservative and national party which was loyal both to the church and the Republic.

The failure of successive Republican governments to pass a Reich School Law in line with the wishes of the church leadership created a major obstacle to the development of good relations with the Republic. It also occasioned a sharp disagreement with the DVP. The Weimar constitution envisaged three types of school: denominational, inter-

27. See below, pp. 114–17. Cf. W. Jochmann, 'Die Ausbreitung des Anti-semitismus' in W. E. Mosse, *Deutsches Judentum in Krieg und Revolution 1916–1923* (Tübingen, 1971), pp. 409–510. For examples of anti-Semitism in the Protestant press, see I. Arndt, 'Die Judenfrage im Licht der evangelischen Sonntagsblätter von 1918–1933' (unpublished Diss. Phil., Tübingen, 1960).

28. Christ, *Der politische Protestantismus*, pp. 323–4.

29. This was partly to do with the size of farms—the medium and small farmers tended to vote DVP; owners of larger estates DNVP. It also reflected local dislike of the Prussian aristocratic tradition, associated with the DNVP. R. Heberle, *Landbevölkerung und Nationalsozialismus. Eine soziologische Unter-suchung der politischen Willensbildung in Schleswig-Holstein 1918–1932* (Stutt-gart, 1963), pp. 28, 117; W. Hartenstein, *Die Anfänge der Deutschen Volkspartei 1918–1920* (Düsseldorf, 1962), pp. 236–53.

30. Literally 'rational Republicans'—i.e. those who were prepared to work with the Republic although they felt no emotional loyalty to it.

denominational, and secular. Of these, it appeared to have a slight preference for the interdenominational *Gemein-schaftsschule*. Most Protestant leaders favoured a denominational school; only in Hessen, Baden, and Thuringia, where interdenominational schools had been long established, did church leaders support them.[31] The Kirchenausschuß pressed for a Reich School Law favourable to the denominational school.[32]

Several Republican governments attempted to pass a Reich School Law but none succeeded. Their failure seemed to bear out the criticism of conservative groups that in the Republic every party had its own *Kultur* programme but the state had none.[33] The type of educational system depended on political control in the *Länder*. Brunswick was a notorious example; every change of government was followed by a change in the schools.[34] Protestant hopes for a Reich School Law were almost realized by the coalition government formed in January 1927. The DNVP and the Centre party joined it partly with the aim of solving the school problem in favour of denominational education. The DVP, true to its national-liberal tradition, resisted this policy and supported the (interdenominational) Gemeinschaftsschule.[35] To find a compromise, the Kirchenausschuß became involved in negotiations with both the DNVP and the DVP.[36] A formula was

31. E.K.D., A 2/254: letters from the three Landeskirchen to the Kirchenausschuß, September 1927. The Hessen Landeskirche said that a change in their educational system would disturb the progress they had made towards reconciliation with the SPD and the teachers.

32. E.K.D., A 2/239: Moeller to Reich Minister of the Interior, 6 May 1921; ibid., A 2/253: Kirchenausschuß to same, 22 June 1925 and copies to politicians; ibid. A 2/254: Kapler to Reich Minister of the Interior, 27 Feb. 1926 and 18 July 1927. In 1927 all Protestant Reichstag members were informed of Protestant wishes and a social evening held for them, *Verhandlungen, Kirchentag,* 1927, p. 25.

33. Dibelius, *Nachspiel,* pp. 15–18. For a discussion of the effect of the Reich School Law question on the Catholic Centre party, see G. Grünthal, *Reichsschulgesetz und Zentrumspartei in der Weimarer Republik* (Düsseldorf, 1968).

34. See the account in the *Christlicher Volksdienst* (Berlin), 21 Jan. 1928, No. 3.

35. The formation and collapse of the coalition and the part played by the Reich School Law are discussed in, Stürmer, *Koalition und Opposition in der Weimarer Republik,* pp. 182–90, 230–5.

36. E.K.D., A 2/254: report by the Kirchenbundesamt official, Scholz, 16 Jan. 1928.

found but it was rejected by the DVP Reichstag party and the coalition government broke up. In the subsequent election campaign Kapler publicly denied DVP allegations that he had agreed with its policy.[37]

The political sympathies of the Protestant leadership, and of the church as a whole, drew it naturally to the right-wing, conservative, DNVP. In addition, the church could count on unconditional DNVP support until October 1928, when Hugenberg became chairman of the party and led it on an extreme anti-Republican course. It stressed Christianity in its programme; it supported the church in the Reichstag against radical *Länder*; it worked for censorship and licensing laws; a DNVP Minister, von Keudell, produced the Reich School Law project in 1927 which was favoured by the church leadership; the party voted against the Prussian concordat because there had not been a simultaneous treaty with the Protestant church and later, despite its objections to the political clause, it voted for the Protestant treaty.[38] The overwhelming majority of DNVP deputies were Protestants and they included several church leaders.[39] In 1922 a Protestant Reich Committee of the DNVP was formed.[40] It kept in close contact with the Kirchenbundesamt[41] and issued a confidential information sheet giving details of DNVP work for the church.[42]

37. E.K.D., A 2/255: Kapler to the Landeskirchen, 16 Mar. 1928, giving an account of the dispute.

38. The importance of this record was emphasized by Dr. Karnatz, a senior official of the Berlin Oberkirchenrat from 1919 to 1933, in an interview in Berlin on 20 Oct. 1965.

39. Christ, *Der politische Protestantismus*, pp. 281-2. R. Mumm and F. Behrens from the Kirchenausschuß were Reichstag deputies until 1930; Winckler, President of the Kirchensenat, was Chairman of the DNVP in the Prussian Landtag until 1928; four Prussian Generalsuperintendenten were DNVP deputies in the Prussian Constituent Assembly; Pastor Koch, President of the Westphalian provincial synod from 1927, was a DNVP deputy in the Prussian Landtag 1919-33 and 1930-2 in the Reichstag as well. In Württemberg, Wurm who was President of the Landeskirche from 1929, was a DNVP deputy in the local Constituent Assembly and first Landtag and in Hessen, Professor Diehl, President of the Landeskirche from 1923, was also a DNVP deputy in the local Landtag.

40. D.Z.A. Potsdam, *Evangelischer Reichsausschuß der DNVP*, 455: Mumm to Kähler, 20 Nov. 1922.

41. Ibid., 459: Hosemann to Mumm, 23 Oct. 1929; Mumm to Barthelheimer, 21 Oct. 1929; ibid. 455: invitation 28 Apr.? 1925.

42. The *Vertrauliche Mitteilungen des evangelischen Reichsausschusses der DNVP*.

If the DNVP had been stronger, the Protestant leadership might have been content to remain an unofficial partner of the party. Since, however, for most of the Republic the DNVP was a minority opposition group, it became important for church leaders to find a wider political base. This, in turn, made it necessary for them to come to terms with the Republic. The church leadership also disagreed with the more extreme anti-Republican groups within the DNVP on several issues.

The church leadership took no part in the Kapp *Putsch* (a right-wing attempt to overthrow the Republic in 1920).[43] It failed to comment on the murder of the Centre party politician, Erzberger, in 1921 but when this was followed by the assassination of Walther Rathenau, the Democratic Foreign Minister of the Republic in 1922, it joined in the general condemnation. Like other conservative groups it felt some sense of responsibility for the climate of opinion which led to the murder and it was anxious to clear its name. Chancellor Wirth's outspoken condemnation of 'the enemy on the right' and the legislation against anti-Republican groups which followed, may have acted as a further incentive.[44] Nevertheless, it was important that the church leadership spoke out clearly against political violence. It declared,

The Reich Minister for Foreign Affairs has fallen a victim to wicked assassination.

This atrocious outrage shames the German name. And while our unhappy nation, fighting for its like, needs inward peace and mutual understanding on the basis of respect for the law more than ever, we see passions inflamed to boiling point and our nation nearly at the brink of civil war ... The murder and what we have experienced since then illuminate in a glaring way the inner situation of our nation. We blame our enemies for thrusting our nation through their delusion into humiliation and crisis, from which the spirit of chaos comes ...

Above all, however, we call for self-examination ...[45]

43. Pfarrer Traub who agreed to be Kapp's Kultusminister held no position in the church leadership although he had been a member of the Vertrauensrat of the Old Prussian Union in 1918–19. J. Erger, *Der Kapp-Lüttwitz-Putsch* (Düsseldorf, 1967), p. 94.

44. On the background to the Rathenau assassination and its consequences, see A. Brecht, *Aus Nächster Nähe. Lebenserinnerungen 1884–1927* (Stuttgart, 1966), pp. 347–9, 382–94.

45. Hosemann, *Der Deutsche Evangelische Kirchenbund*, p. 161–2.

Although it condemned violence, the church leadership was very sympathetic to its lower-middle-class members who were driven to right-radical movements by economic despair. On several occasions it intervened with the Reich government on their behalf.[46] It believed, however, that the Versailles treaty and reparations were primarily responsible for economic distress, not the German government.[47] In general its public statements were aimed at foreign churches not the German authorities. In this it differed from the anti-Republican Right, which exploited national grievances as part of the campaign to overthrow the Republic. The church leadership regarded this movement of 'national opposition' as an understandable but wrong-headed reaction to an impossible situation imposed from outside.

Unlike the anti-Republican Right the church leadership also never completely lost its respect for the authority of the state. An attitude of continuous and general opposition did not come naturally to it. The election of Hindenburg as President in 1925 restored a personal symbol of authority towards which the Protestant church felt strong attachment. The Protestant leadership had treated Ebert, the first President of the Republic and a Social Democrat, with reserve.[48] In contrast, in 1925 Hindenburg enjoyed great popularity in the church. During the Presidential election campaign, the few Protestant liberals who had the courage to campaign for his main opponent, Marx (a Roman Catholic) aroused bitter local opposition.[49] To the pleasure of the Protestant leadership, Hindenburg held a reception for the churches. At the ceremony, Kapler said: 'The Reich President is a loyal Protestant Christian and it would be unnatural if I omitted to say here—intending no offence to anyone—with what pride the Protestant church counts the Reich President among its members.'[50]

46. Bundesarchiv, R 431/2195: Kirchenausschuß to the Reich Chancellor, 1 Aug. 1924; R 431/2196: ibid., 28 July 1932.

47. See below, Chapter 4.

48. Christ, *Der politische Protestantismus*, p. 368.

49. Rathje, *Die Welt des freien Protestantismus*, pp. 355–63; O. Baumgarten, *Mein Lebensgeschichte* (Tübingen, 1929), pp. 464–75; A von Zahn-Harnack, *Adolf von Harnack* (Berlin, 1936), pp. 527–9. An example of the opposition they aroused is C. Ringwald, *Offener Brief an Seine Exzellenz Dr. Adolf von Harnack (Berlin) von einem badischen Laien* (Freiburg, 1925).

50. E.K.D., A 2/477: copy of the speech, 12 June 1925.

By the time the next Kirchentag met in June 1927, the Republic seemed to have become a stable regime and the church was secure within it. The DVP was a regular member of Reich coalition governments and even the DNVP took office for a time in 1925 and again in 1927. By 1927 the Prussian church leadership was also beginning to consider the advantages of a treaty with the Prussian *Land*. It was therefore natural for it to want to improve its relations with the state. The Kirchenausschuß appointed one of its members, Wilhelm Kahl, to give a formal lecture to the Kirchentag on 'The church and the Fatherland'.[51] The choice of Kahl was significant. He was a leading DVP politician, a close colleague of Stresemann and the first to coin the term *Vernunftrepublikaner*.[52] He was himself approaching eighty and knew how to appeal to a conservative audience. His fondness for describing the struggle he had with his conscience before accepting the Republic led a colleague to comment that it was remarkable how often Kahl struggled with his conscience but always came out on top.[53] In his lecture, Kahl argued that Protestants should not allow their loyalty to the monarchy to prevent them coming to terms with the Republic. This would be in accord with Biblical and Lutheran principles. It would also enable Protestants to be influential in public life.[54]

The declaration, known as the *Vaterländische Kundgebung*, which the Kirchentag adopted was less specific than Kahl's speech. The original draft had mentioned the duty of Protestants to submit to the present state.[55] In the final version, the *present* state was not mentioned. The declaration affirmed that,

The church stands above parties. It serves all its members whatever their party . . . It has the task of applying the principles of God's Word. It allows and gives the state what belongs to the state. The state is, we

51. E.K.D., A 2/24: minutes of the Kirchenausschuß meeting of 3-5 June 1926.

52. Turner, *Stresemann and the politics of the Weimar Republic*, pp. 112, 254.

53. E. Schiffer, *Ein Leben für den Liberalismus* (Berlin, 1951), p. 212.

54. The lecture is in *Verhandlungen, Kirchentag*, 1927, pp. 234–50.

55. E.K.D., A/489: extract from the minutes of the Kirchenausschuß meeting, 14–15 June 1927.

believe, ordained by God with its own important tasks. True to the instructions of Scripture the church prays for nation, state and authority (*Obrigkeit*). Equally the church makes certain moral demands on the state. In particular, the church cannot renounce the right to apply independently and candidly eternal moral standards to legislation and administration and to represent Christian principles in all public life. The church makes three demands of its members: It wants each . . . to serve the whole and to be subject to the state for the sake of the Word of God. It wants each to be aware of his share of responsibility.[56]

The Kundgebung, which was accepted by an overwhelming majority of the Kirchentag,[57] was an important achievement. It made it possible for church leaders to claim that the church was a loyal body and it gave it a basis both for resisting the anti-Republican Right and for moving further towards the Republic. Although the Republic had not been mentioned, the church had accepted by the almost unanimous decision of its greatest representative body that it had a duty to obey the state and to take part in public life. The idea of counter-revolution had been rejected. The Kundgebung was given wide coverage in the national and church press.[58]

The question of loyalty to the Republic was also raised by requests from Reich and *Land* authorities that the church should hold special services as part of the Weimar constitution's anniversary celebrations. In 1924 the President of the Kirchenausschuß supported a request of this kind.[59] His action aroused considerable opposition from the right wing within the church.[60] Between 1925 and 1928 the church leadership simply passed on state requests to the parishes

56. *Verhandlungen, Kirchentag*, 1927, pp. 338–40.

57. Ibid.

58. E.K.D., A 2/25: minutes of the Kirchenausschuß meeting of 8–9 Dec. 1927. It was reported that there had been 913 notices in 288 daily newspapers, including the fifty-four most important ones.

59. E.K.D., A 2/480: Moeller to the leaders of the Landeskirchen, 17 July 1924.

60. Ibid.: summary of the replies of the Landeskirchen; letter from Landrat a. D. von Brockhusen to Moeller, 23 Aug. 1924, published in the *Neue Preußische Kreuzzeitung* and *Der Reichsbote*; E.K.U., Gen. IX, 54/1: minutes of a meeting of the joint committee of the Oberkirchenrat and General Synod executive of the Old Prussian Union, 16 Sept. 1924.

without comment.[61] During the same period, the church avoided the political controversy about use of the Republican flag by inventing a flag of its own.[62]

In 1929, the tenth anniversary of the constitution, the Kirchenausschuß decided to take a more active part and most Landeskirchen followed its instructions to hold some form of celebration.[63] At the same time, they avoided any political commitment to republicanism or democracy. The Kirchenausschuß had suggested simply that they should consider their attitude to the Fatherland and to the *Volksgemeinschaft* (community of the nation), expressed in the state, using the *Vaterländische Kundgebung* as a basis.[64] Nevertheless, it was important that the church publicly acknowledged the anniversary of the constitution. In Berlin, a service was held in the *Dreifaltigkeitskirche* where Hindenburg normally went; as well as him, it was attended by representatives of seven Reich Ministries and nine Prussian ones and other officials.[65] A report on the services elsewhere suggested that while some had been successful, others had been poorly attended by state officials. In Hanover the result was pathetic, as no state official appeared and a section of the regular congregation stayed away.

The church celebrations also received a mixed reception from the press. The extreme right-wing *Deutsche Zeitung* spoke of 'deep shame' at church policy and added that the tortuous language used by church leaders for the occasion was hardly in the vein of Martin Luther.[66] The less extreme *Reichsbote*, which was influential in conservative church circles, said it would have been better for the church to show reserve; it suggested that the church had been playing politics and that Minister President Braun would not be impressed.[67]

---

61. E.K.U., Gen. IX, 54/1: Oberkirchenrat to Landeskirchenamt Frankfurt, 31 Aug. 1927. During these years the requests came from the *Länder*, not the Reich.

62. *Verhandlungen, Kirchentag*, 1927, pp. 94, 333, and ibid. 1930, p. 121. E.K.D., A 3/91: minutes of the Kirchenbundesrat meeting of 11–12 June 1928.

63. E.K.D., A 2/480: minutes of the Kirchenausschuß meeting and collection of decrees of the Landeskirchen.

64. Ibid.: Kirchenausschuß to Landeskirchen, 17 June 1929, reported by *Evangelischer Pressedienst*, 11 July 1929, No. 27.

65. Ibid.: report on the celebrations throughout the Reich, 29 Aug. 1929.

66. *Deutsche Zeitung*, 31 July 1929, No. 177.

67. *Der Reichsbote*, 31 July 1929, No. 182.

The Religious Socialist leader, Piechowski, also accused the church of opportunism saying that the celebrations were a purely tactical manoeuvre to assist the conclusion of a treaty.[68] Some democratic newspapers welcomed the church celebrations, however,[69] and the SPD *Vorwärts*, reported that DNVP circles were bitter about them.[70] It was rare for *Vorwärts* to mention the Protestant church without attacking it.

Soon after the 1929 anniversary of the constitution, the church leadership was faced with a new test of its policy of *rapprochement* by the decision of the DNVP under Hugenberg to join with the NSDAP and groups like the *Stahlhelm* in a campaign against the Young Plan (the Allied plan for the final settlement of German reparations payments). The Plan was made the pretext for a general attack on the Republic by the new right-wing alliance. They proposed a law threatening any government which accepted the Plan with imprisonment for treason and a referendum was called to decide on it. The proposed law forced a division within conservative circles between the Vernunftrepublikaner and the anti-Republican Right.

The church leadership adopted a neutral position. Kapler refused to sign a circular, sent to him by Severing (the Reich Minister of the Interior), condemning the referendum. He explained that he did not want the Protestant church to be drawn into a bitter political battle.[71] In this he was more reserved than the Roman Catholic episcopacy which did sign the circular. In order that his silence should not be interpreted as approval, Kapler gave an interview to the Republican *Vossische Zeitung* in October 1929.[72] He said that the referendum was a political question which should be

---

68. *Zeitschrift für Religion und Sozialismus*, Heft 5 (Marburg, 1929).

69. The Berlin *Morgenpost*, 31 July 1929, No. 181, and the *Berliner Allgemeine Zeitung* (ibid.).

70. *Vorwärts*, 31 July 1929, No. 354. The Berlin Oberkirchenrat received about fifty protests against its measures from bodies like the *Nationaler Verband deutschen Offiziere*; E.K.U., Gen. IX, 54/2. In addition, Hugenberg wrote to the Kirchenausschuß suggesting that it should use the anniversary to protest against the refusal of the Prussian government to grant a treaty together with the concordat; E.K.D., A 2/480: Hugenberg to Kirchenausschuß, 20 June, 1 July 1929.

71. E.K.U., Gen. II, 32/Beiheft II: Kapler to Severing, 14 Oct. 1929.

72. *Vossische Zeitung*, 20 Oct. 1929, No. 496.

left to individuals but that he deplored the lack of moderation shown in the campaign. Kapler's attitude did not prevent individual clergymen supporting it.[73] Their action seemed to bear out the criticism made by an SPD deputy in the Prussian Landtag in March 1929, that although church authorities had made friendly gestures towards the Republic, there was no evidence that a large number of pastors had followed this lead.[74]

The policy of *rapprochement* with the Republic achieved its greatest success in 1931 with the conclusion of the Prussian church treaty. Its basic assumptions, however, were by then already threatened by the growth of the 'national opposition'. The policy of the church leadership had been based on enlightened self-interest. It believed that the Republic had come to stay and that it would be best for the church and for the nation if Protestants accepted it and were accepted by it. Given the conservative tradition of the church, this required skill and courage. The *Vaterländische Kundgebung*, the celebration of the tenth anniversary of the constitution, and the Prussian treaty of 1931 were considerable achievements. They could have formed the basis of a stable relationship with the Republic.

The policy remained one of *Vernunft*, of the head and not the heart, however. The objections of the Protestant leadership to many aspects of Republican life and institutions continued unchanged. This made it difficult to impress the doctrine of loyalty on church members, many of whom stood further to the Right than the leadership. Men like Kahl and Kapler were sincere, but their views did not have the straightforward appeal of the anti-Republican Right. The Vernunftrepublikaner were always in danger of seeming half-hearted and even hypocritical. The leadership did win large majorities for its policy in the Kirchentag of 1927 and in the General Synod of the Old Prussian Union (which accepted the treaty) in 1931. Impressionistic surveys of the Protestant press and Protestant literature designed to show

---

73. *Vossische Zeitung*, 24 Oct. 1929, No. 254; *Sonntagsblatt des arbeitenden Volkes*, 3 Nov. 1929, No. 44.
74. *Preußischer Landtag, Stenographische Berichte des Hauptausschusses 1928/29*, vol. 2, pp. 10–13, 21–6, 32–3.

that the church was consistently and overwhelmingly anti-Republican should be treated with caution.[75] The accusations of SPD spokesmen were also sometimes based on isolated instances used for political effect.[76] There is no doubt, however, that the policy of *rapprochement* with the Republic, cautiously advanced by the church leadership, failed to take root in the church as a whole, in the same way that Stresemann failed to attract the Protestant *Mittelstand*.[77] As the church leadership was aware, after 1929 many church members followed the national trend to the parties of the anti-Republican Right.

75. For instance, K-W. Dahm, *Pfarrer und Politik* (Cologne, 1965). An important critique of Dahm by Superintendent Cordes appeared in the *Hannoversches Pfarrerblatt*, 74. Jg. (1967), 78–99. On the basis of a study of the Hanover church newspapers of the Weimar Republic and a questionnaire to pastors who were active at the time, Cordes argues that the Hanover-Lutheran Landeskirche was not overwhelmingly anti-Republican. Until there have been a series of systematic local studies, it will be impossible to know the extent of the Vernunftrepublikaner element in the church.

76. An example was an attack on the political attitudes of Protestant clergy made by Minister President Braun in the Prussian Landtag in May 1930. It was, he said, based on a series of incidents, but he gave only one example. Under pressure from the Oberkirchenrat, he partially withdrew, saying that his remarks were not meant to be a complaint against the attitude of clergy or church bodies. E.K.U., Gen. VI, 16/3: Oberkirchenrat to Braun, 21 July 1930, and Braun's reply, 15 Sept. 1930. *Das Evangelische Deutschland* (18 May 1930, No. 20) commented that if attacks of this kind continued, they would be a greater threat to good relations between church and state than blunders by individual clergy.

77. Middle classes including peasants; see J. Noakes, *The Nazi Party in Lower Saxony 1921–1933* (Oxford, 1971), p. 108.

4

FOREIGN POLICY

The Protestant church thought of itself as a national church. During the nineteenth century German Protestants, on the whole, welcomed the achievement of national unity and the creation of a powerful Reich—although particularist sentiment lingered in some *Länder* like Hanover. Protestants felt they had a special claim to be seen as a national church in contrast to Roman Catholicism. This was vividly illustrated by the Court Preacher, Adolf Stoecker, who wrote in 1871, 'The holy, Protestant Empire of the German nation is brought to completion ... in this we can see God's hand from 1517 to 1871'.[1] During the First World War, the Protestant church was gripped by the patriotic fever of the time. It threw itself into the war effort, recruiting subscribers for the war loan and preaching at the front and at home in support of the national cause.[2]

Under the Weimar Republic, the church leadership continued to believe that it was its duty to promote German interests abroad. It protested against the 'injustices' of the Versailles settlement, maintained links with German Protestants in areas separated from the Reich by the peace treaty and identified itself with the aims of German foreign policy in meetings with foreign church leaders. This activity was deeply nationalist but it was not anti-Republican. The church leadership seems to have been careful to keep its foreign policy in line with the wishes of the German government of the time. As in domestic policy the church leadership also resisted extreme nationalist pressure, here against co-operation

1. W. Frank, *Hofprediger Adolf Stoecker* (2nd. edn., Hamburg, 1935), pp. 27-8.
2. The Kirchenausschuß sponsored its own official account of the *Kriegserlebnis* (war experience): M. Schian, *Die deutsche evangelische Kirche im Weltkriege* (Berlin, 1921, 1925). See also Mehnert, *Evangelische Kirche und Politik 1917-1919*, pp. 30-8; W. Pressel, *Die Kriegspredigt 1914-1918 in der evangelischen Kirche Deutschlands* (Göttingen, 1967).

with Christians abroad in the ecumenical movement. However, after 1929 it was gradually forced back into isolation by criticism from the anti-Republican Right and by despair at the economic crisis which was blamed on reparations. It is anyway difficult to see how the extensive revision of the Versailles treaty which the church leadership desired could have been achieved by negotiation.

The immediate post-war years were dominated by national grievances. The Kirchenausschuß and the first three Kirchentage issued declarations protesting against the 'hunger blockade', the retention of German prisoners of war by the Entente powers, the 'monstrous' claim to sit in judgement on the Kaiser and the German High Command, the expropriation of German foreign missions, the Versailles treaty—especially the war-guilt clause—the separation of Upper Silesia, and the use of negro troops by the French.[3] The attempts of the Allies to enforce reparation payments provoked further bitter protests.[4]

The existence of Protestant communities in areas separated from the Reich by the treaty of Versailles gave the church leadership an opportunity to serve national and Protestant interests simultaneously. The rights of German Protestants in Poland, Memel, and Danzig were protected by special laws and they were allowed to maintain a connection with the Old Prussian Union.[5] The least-favourable settlement from the German point of view was with Poland, where a rival pro-Polish Protestant church was formed.[6] The Kirchenbund received considerable financial assistance from the government for its work abroad as part of its programme of subsidizing German *Kultur*, especially in the territories it

3. *Verhandlungen, Kirchentag*, 1919, pp. 238, 308–12; ibid. 1921, pp. 24–6; ibid. 1924, p. 18.

4. *Allgemeines Kirchenblatt für das evangelische Deutschland*, 15 Mar. 1921, p. 230; 2 Jan. 1923, pp. 1–3; 15 Mar. 1923, pp. 131–2; 15 Dec. 1923, p. 244.

5. The rights of German Protestants in Upper Silesia were protected by the German-Polish treaty of 15 May 1922, in Memel by a treaty with the Lithuanian and Memel authorities, 31 July 1925, and in Danzig by a law of the Free City, 7 June 1921; G. J. Ebers, *Evangelisches Kirchenrecht in Preußen* (Munich, 1932), i. 148–76.

6. F. Siegmund-Schultze, *Ekklesia*, v, *Die evangelischen Kirchen in Polen* (Leipzig, 1938).

hoped to regain.[7] The government also assisted propaganda with foreign Christians on behalf of German Protestants in Poland which was conducted by Dibelius with the connivance of the Oberkirchenrat.[8] The church leadership showed no hesitation in acknowledging the political side of its work, indeed it was proud of it.[9]

The development of the international, Christian (in practice, non-Roman Catholic) ecumenical movement after 1918 created another opportunity for combined religious and political activity. The bitterness of the immediate post-war period prevented the German church attending the first meetings and Germany was represented only by private individuals. In 1920 the French and Belgians demanded official German acceptance of war guilt.[10] No action was taken as the German delegates were not official representatives but the church was, of course, totally unwilling to accept responsibility for the war. The church leadership did not, however, condemn the ecumenical movement. It was prepared to join as soon as the international situation and feeling within Germany allowed.[11] During 1921-2, when the German government tried to reach agreement with the Allies by a 'fulfilment' policy, the Kirchenausschuß decided it was time to take part[12] but the French occupation of the Ruhr immediately created a new obstacle.[13]

There were strong reasons against the church, excluding itself from the ecumenical movement. Unlike the League of

7. 450,000 marks p.a. until 1930 when the grant was reduced with the austerity programme. A. A., Kult. Pol. Abt. VI. A., 18/4, 4: summary of payments, 19 Jan. 1934. Cf. C. M. Kimmich, *The Free City. Danzig and German Foreign Policy, 1919-1934* (New Haven and London, 1968).

8. A.A., Kult. Pol. Abt. VI. A., 18/4, 1: Dibelius reports, 15 Feb. 1921, 2 Apr. 1925; ibid. 10/1, 1: Dibelius to Auswärtiges Amt, 21 Apr. 1921; cf. Dibelius to Kultusminister Rust, 28 Aug. 1933, photostat copy in *Hier spricht Dibelius* (Berlin, 1960), pp. 81-2.

9. D. Z. A. Potsdam, Präsidialkanzlei, 281/1: Kapler to Hindenburg, 19 May 1930.

10. N. Karlström, 'Movements for International Friendship and Life and Work, 1910-25' in *A History of the Ecumenical Movement, 1517-1948,* ed. R. Rouse and S. C. Neill (London, 1954), pp. 530-7.

11. E.K.D., A 2/18: minutes of the Kirchenausschuß meeting of 23-5 June 1920.

12. Ibid. A 2/20: minutes of 8-9 Sept. 1921 and 26-7 May 1922.

13. A.k.A., C. 1. 1/1: Moeller to Söderblom, 5 Feb. 1923, 12 Apr. 1923.

Nations, to which it was sometimes compared, it was the
brain-child not of Germany's former enemies but of the
Archbishop of neutral Sweden, the land of Gustavus
Adolphus, the champion of Protestant Germany in the Thirty
Years War. Archbishop Söderblom had much to recommend
him to German opinion. He had been a professor at Leipzig
before 1914[14] and one of his sons had been a German officer
in the war. He had also publicly criticized Allied treatment of
Germany since the war.[15] In these circumstances there was
every reason to suppose that Germany would be treated as a
full partner.

The improvement of the international atmosphere after
1924 provided the opportunity. In August 1925 a major
conference was held at Stockholm and despite the doubts of
some of its members, the Kirchenausschuß decided to
attend.[16] In this they had the support of the government.
President Kapler had contacted the departments concerned
to obtain a subsidy and to ensure that the delegation's
attitude on political questions would be in line with official
policy.[17] Kapler explained that if they did not attend, the
English and American churches would dominate the conference.

The usefulness of the ecumenical movement to the
national cause was demonstrated in the following year when,
at Kapler's request, the question of war guilt was considered.
After hard negotiations between German and French representatives a reply was sent, acceptable to both.[18] It declined
to treat political issues but asserted that a confession imposed
by force had no moral value and it suggested a general
inquiry into war guilt.

---

14. Nathan Söderblom (1866–1931), 1912 Professor of Religious History at
Leipzig University, 1914 Archbishop of Uppsala; see B. Sundkler, *Nathan
Söderblom* (London, 1968).
15. Bundesarchiv, R 431/2194: report on Söderblom.
16. E.K.D., A 2/22: minutes of the Kirchenausschuß meeting of 24–5 June
1925.
17. A.k.A., C. 1. 1/2: Kapler to Auswärtiges Amt, 10 Feb. 1925; Bundesarchiv, R 431/2194: Reichskanzlei note of July 1925, recording Kapler's visit to
explain the policy for Stockholm.
18. E.K.D., A 2/24: minutes of the Kirchenausschuß meeting of 8–9 Dec.
1926.

The decision was a victory for the Germans, particularly compared with the French attitude of the immediate post-war years. Most important, the victory was recognized within Germany. The church leadership was delighted. The correspondence over war guilt was published in full in a central position among the proceedings of the 1927 Kirchentag.[19] Kapler was warmly congratulated in the Kirchenausschuß and in the General Synod of the Old Prussian Union.[20] The way now seemed clear for the German church to give uninhibited support to the ecumenical movement.[21]

Under Kapler, the foreign policy adopted by the church leadership showed a clear similarity to that pursued by Stresemann (as Foreign Minister of the Republic) in the Locarno agreements and subsequently in the League of Nations. Both tried to win the maximum benefit for Germany by co-operation with the West.[22] In particular, Kapler's policy of persuading foreign churches of the need to revise the Versailles treaty was closely in line with Stresemann's general propaganda effort and was personally approved by him.[23]

This policy had both a negative and a positive side. The emphasis placed on the national advantages which had been derived from the ecumenical movement might feed nationalist appetites rather than further appeasement. On the other hand it had been shown over the question of war guilt that national grievances could be discussed with success in an international body. This was a first step away from isolation, which was the automatic inclination of many Germans after Versailles.

Kapler's policy remained unopposed until 1929, except by

19. *Verhandlungen, Kirchentag*, 1927, pp. 119–49.
20. E.K.D., A 2/24: minutes of the Kirchenausschuß meeting of 8–9 Dec. 1926, and *Verhandlungen, Generalsynode*, 1927, i. 11–12.
21. See the optimistic article in *Kirchliches Jahrbuch*, 54. Jg. (1927), 534–58.
22. On Stresemann's policy, see J. Jacobson, *Locarno Diplomacy. Germany and the West 1925–1929* (Princeton and London, 1972) and M-O. Maxelon, *Stresemann und Frankreich. Deutsche Politik der Ost-West Balance* (Düsseldorf, 1972).
23. E.K.D., A 2/545: Stresemann to Kapler, 23 June 1929.
24. E.K.D., A 2/25: minutes of the Kirchenausschuß meeting of 14–15 Mar. 1929.

a few extremists.[24] The tenth anniversary of the Versailles treaty, however, was a natural opportunity for the revival of nationalist sentiment. The aggressive tactics of the DNVP under Hugenberg's leadership and the Young Plan controversy also encouraged hostility to the ecumenical movement. At a meeting between representatives of the *Vaterländische Verbände* (right-wing 'Patriotic Associations') and General-superintendent Dibelius the church leadership was accused of a lack of enthusiasm for the national struggle, and co-operation in the ecumenical movement and the League were condemned.[25]

This type of criticism found increasing sympathy within the Kirchenausschuß. In June 1929 it issued a new declaration condemning the Versailles treaty,[26] and criticism of its part in the ecumenical movement grew as Germany's economic position deteriorated.[27] At the suggestion of the Prussian Kirchensenat and against Kapler's advice, the Kirchenausschuß issued a further declaration on war guilt in October 1931 which spoke of the crisis driving men to despair and violence; 'our people are near the limit of their moral and physical strength'.[28] This was followed by a declaration on the 'Present Crisis' in May 1932 which emphasized the damage done by the Versailles treaty and demanded 'deeds, not fruitless negotiations'.[29] In August 1932, as Chairman of the European section, Kapler painted a grim picture of the position in Germany to ecumenical leaders. He warned that as a result of the discrimination[30] still maintained against Germany the demand for withdrawal

25. An account of the meeting was given to the Prussian Oberkirchenrat by Dibelius; E.K.U., Gen. VI, 2/1: Bericht über die Tagung der vaterländischen Verbände am 24 Jan. 1929.

26. J. Hosemann, *Der Deutsche Evangelische Kirchenbund* (2nd edn., Berlin, 1932), pp. 171–2.

27. E.K.D., A 2/27: minutes of the Kirchenausschuß meetings of 12 Mar., 6 June 1931.

28. E.K.U., Gen. IX, 67/1: extract from the minutes of the Kirchensenat meeting of 9–10 Oct. 1931; E.K.D., A 2/28: minutes of the Kirchenausschuß meeting of 22–3 Oct. 1931; the text of the declaration is given in Hosemann, *Der Deutsche Evangelische Kirchenbund*, pp. 173–4.

29. E.K.D., A 2/28: minutes of the Kirchenausschuß meeting of 24–6 May 1932. It is printed in Hosemann, *Der Deutsche Evangelische Kirchenbund*, pp. 189–90.

30. This referred to reparations and disarmament.

from the ecumenical movement had been taken up by responsible people.[31]

By 1932 German participation in the ecumenical movement which had seemed well established in 1927 was again seriously threatened; the situation was comparable to 1923. The immediate cause was the economic crisis for which the Versailles settlement was held responsible; the demand for withdrawal from the movement was a natural, if irrational, response to despair. Even without the economic crisis however, it is unlikely that the process of appeasement begun in 1926 would have succeeded. In the period 1925–32, the German church raised the questions of war guilt, reparations, and disarmament in the ecumenical movement. Had these been satisfied earlier, other demands might have followed. The church leadership certainly regarded the Polish frontier and the prohibition against Austria joining the Reich as unjust,[32] although it did not protest against the Locarno settlement of the western frontier, nor did it raise the question of the Sudetenland.[33] The Polish frontier was, however, the crucial issue and it is difficult to see how any negotiated settlement acceptable to German opinion could have been reached on it.[34]

The foreign policy of the church leadership between 1918 and 1932 was in the spirit of Stresemann, not of the 'national opposition'. However, like Stresemann's policy, it was ambiguous. More important the church leadership did not face up to the fact that negotiated revision on the scale it wanted was extremely unlikely. There are therefore few grounds for

31. Nachlaß Kapler contains a copy of the speech.

32. The Kirchenausschuß protested against the separation of Upper Silesia; feelings about the exclusion of Austria were clear from the exchange of greetings between the German Kirchenbund and the Austrian Kirchentag of 1919; *Verhandlungen, Kirchentag*, 1919, pp. 71–2. In 1926 the Austrian Protestants joined the Kirchenbund and at the 1927 Kirchentag President von Pechmann commented that they belonged together by blood and history, divine providence, and justice; *Verhandlungen, Kirchentag*, 1927, p. 185.

33. Like most Germans, however, it did not show much enthusiasm for Locarno. Whem American church leaders sent the Kirchenausschuß a telegram of congratulations on the Locarno treaty and asked for it be be published, the Kirchenausschuß decided that there was no reason for publication and simply thanked the Americans for their message; E.K.D., A 2/22: minutes of the Kirchenausschuß meeting of 4–5 Nov. 1925.

34. Cf. Kimmich, *The Free City*, pp. 160–2.

thinking that it would have been appeased, even if the depression had not intervened and made it desperate. It is, however, possible that given continued economic recovery, in time national grievances would have come to seem less urgent.

5

THE 'NATIONAL OPPOSITION'

In its attempt to find a stable relationship with the Republic and in its co-operation with Republican governments over foreign policy, the Protestant leadership resisted the influence of the anti-Republican Right or 'national opposition' as it styled itself. Church leaders shared many of its political views but they thought that its inability to compromise with the Republic was short-sighted and against the national interest. They also disliked the violence and racialism of some groups within the 'national opposition' and during 1932 they became afraid that the most powerful group, the NSDAP, would seek to interfere in the church. On the other hand they were not as hostile to the 'national opposition' as they were to the socialist movement. Church leaders regarded the 'national opposition', as basically sound and blamed its 'faults' on the way Germany had been made to suffer by her former enemies.

Church leaders were also afraid that the church would be isolated if it rejected a mass movement of 'national people' and, in addition, they saw in it a powerful defence against Communism. As the 'national opposition' gathered strength and attracted the support of many church members—while the Republic seemed unable to meet the challenge of the economic crisis—church leaders became increasingly vulnerable to its propaganda. The NSDAP made concessions to the church and exploited its weaknesses. The result was that although church leaders were aware of some of the dangers of the movement, they did not condemn it.

i. The 'National Movement'

The proper attitude for the church to adopt towards the 'national movement' was the subject of a lecture to the Kirchentag in 1927, delivered by the theologian, Paul

Althaus[1] and his ideas subsequently formed the basis of the policy of the church leadership. Althaus saw the national movement as a reaction against modern urban civilization, which he described as 'rational organization instead of a growing organism'. The idea of rebirth through a return to national roots had stimulated a great, new secular movement, second only to socialism.[2] Its origins were to be found in the 'exalted, stirring, national experience of August 1914' and further back in the youth movements.

The church, Althaus argued, had a responsibility to this movement as both had a national mission. The church, however, asserted absolute claims whereas commitment to the *Volk* was secondary. Althaus explained that *Volkheit*, a term coined by Goethe, should be understood as 'the will of God over a people'; the converse idea that the *Volk* was divine in itself 'deified unholy *Volkstum*—it made something earthly and fallible unconditionally binding'. Althaus ridiculed the rediscovery of pagan, Germanic religion; he defended the Old Testament against the attacks of anti-Semitic circles and reaffirmed the Pauline doctrine of justification by faith (i.e. and not by racial pedigree). He recommended that the church co-operate in the task of national recovery but remain free of nationalist illusions. The *Vaterländische Kundgebung* issued by the Kirchentag accepted this view.[3]

In September 1927 General Ludendorff declared that he intended to leave the Protestant church. He said that he no longer believed in the Protestant faith and that he resented Protestant indifference towards his campaign against ultramontanism and free-masons.[4] Under the influence of his wife, Dr. Mathilde Ludendorff, the General turned to a pagan Germanic religion and their *Tannenbergbund* spread anti-

1. *Verhandlungen, Kirchentag*, 1927, pp. 204–24.
2. It is interesting to note that this lecture was delivered before the NSDAP became a mass movement.
3. *Verhandlungen, Kirchentag*, 1927, pp. 338–40.
4. E.K.D., A 2/493: copy of Ludendorff's letter declaring his exit from the church, 31 (sic) Sept. 1927; also Ludendorff to Pfarrer Langenfaß, Munich, 14 Oct. 1927.

Christian propaganda.[5] Although Ludendorff had become an eccentric figure in Germany, his action created a stir in Protestant circles.

In February 1928 President Kapler sent a circular to the Landeskirchen asking about their attitude to free-masons.[6] He also commented on the increasing concern of nationalist groups with questions of *Weltanschauung* and religion. The replies of the Landeskirchen to Kapler's circular did not show any very clear attitude.[7] The Kirchenausschuß discussed the matter in June 1928. Some members stressed the difficulty of making contact with nationalist groups until they had worked out a clearer position of their own; at the moment, they said, the church could expect little understanding for *its* Christianity from these movements.[8]

The differences between the political attitudes of the 'national opposition' and the church leadership were evident in a meeting with leaders of the *Vaterländische Verbände* held in Berlin on 24 January 1929.[9] The spokesman for the Verbände, himself a Pastor, thought that the church should give its full moral support to the national opposition. Generalsuperintendent Dibelius objected that the church could not become identified with nationalist, middle-class ideas since it also had a responsibility to the rest of the nation; 'the church must stand above parties and somehow come to a positive relationship with the new state'. Nevertheless, Dibelius conceded, the church approved of the spirit

5. D. J. Goodspeed, *Ludendorff* (London, 1966), pp. 235–6, 245–6; K. Witte, *Der Tannenbergbund,* in W. Künneth and H. Schreiner, *Die Nation vor Gott* (3rd edn., Berlin, 1934), pp. 416–63, and H. Buchheim, 'Die organisatorische Entwicklung der Ludendorff-Bewegung und ihr Verhältnis zum Nationalsozialismus' in *Gutachten des Instituts für Zeitgeschichte* (Munich, 1958), pp. 356–70. In 1933 the Tannenbergbund was prohibited both because it attacked the national socialist state and because it opposed Christianity and the 'Christian basis of the state'; E.K.D., A 2/491: Reich Ministry of the Interior to the Reichskirchenregierung, 14 Nov. 1933.

6. E.K.D., A 2/493; Kapler to the leaders of the Landeskirchen, 14 Feb. 1928.

7. Ibid.

8. Ibid.: extract from the minutes of the Kirchenausschuß meeting of 8–9 June 1928.

9. E.K.U., Gen. VI, 2/2: report of the meeting sent by Dibelius. The leaders of the *Vaterländische Verbände* included aristocrats like von der Goltz, von Arnim-Boitzenburg, von Arnim-Kröchlendorff (a member of the Kirchensenat of the Old Prussian Union), Vice-Admiral von Trotha, von Kleist-Schmenzin, and Prince August Wilhelm of Prussia.

of the national movement although not of incitement to hatred and revenge. In the discussion, Stahlhelm pastors complained about difficulties made for them by the church and demanded that the *Vaterländische Kundgebung*[10] be withdrawn. The church was accused of having found its way to the Republic 'peculiarly fast'. Dibelius remained firm and said that a Generalsuperintendent who did not agree with the Kundgebung should resign.

ii. The NSDAP

In the Reichstag elections of September 1930 the NSDAP won 18 per cent of the votes and 107 seats. The 'national opposition' had become a serious challenge to the Republic and the NSDAP the most important group within it. In December 1930 President Kapler sent a second circular to the Landeskirchen asking for information about groups, like the *Deutschkirche*,[11] which preached a 'German Christianity'.[12]

The Oberkirchenrat of the Old Prussian Union replied that a few members of the Deutschkirche belonged to the synods in five provinces.[13] They opposed collections for missions to the Jews, wanted to play down the Old Testament in religious education and to 'cleanse' religious language of Hebraisms. They also made eugenic suggestions, wanted to prohibit Jews holding positions in the church and to prevent clergy joining the free-masons. Unlike them, the Tannenbergbund (the Ludendorff movement) was hostile to Christianity as such. The racialist ideas of both groups had found wide support especially in rural districts and among young people. The National Socialist movement was connected with these groups in mood, though not in organization; it had not as yet formed a party within the church but it was expected to at the next elections.

The replies from the other Landeskirchen were less detailed.[14] Four—Bavaria, Schleswig-Holstein, Baden, and Anhalt—spoke well of the National Socialists and contrasted

10. See above, pp. 60–1.
11. A small *völkisch* group within the church. See H. Buchheim, *Glaubenskrise im Dritten Reich* (Stuttgart, 1953) pp. 45–8.
12. E.K.D., A 2/493: Kapler to the leaders of the Landeskirchen, 17 Dec. 1930.
13. Ibid.: Oberkirchenrat to Kirchenausschuß, 18 Apr. 1931.
14. Ibid.

them with groups like the Deutschkirche and the Tannen-bergbund. They said that the National Socialists were not critical of the church and helped to restrain the other movements.

The Kirchenbundesrat considered the Deutschkirche and allied movements in June 1931.[15] The result was a restate-ment of the policy outlined by Althaus to the Kirchentag of 1927. Bishop Mordhorst of Schleswig-Holstein, who intro-duced the discussion, said that the church should co-operate with the national movement. At the same time he criticized its theological shortcomings which centred on making a God of race; he quoted Rosenberg's *The Myth of the 20th Century* as an example. The Kirchenbundesrat accepted his analysis but rejected two of his proposals which would have committed the church clearly against the Deutschkirche. The Chairman, President Veit of Bavaria, concluded that the discussion had shown their sympathy for the *völkisch* movement—they rejected only those parts of its programme which were in conflict with religious faith.

This attitude was extremely vulnerable to Nazism since the party claimed to be a friend of the Christian churches. Hitler was responsible for this policy. It is reported that, on one occasion, in discussion with Hitler, Ludendorff criticized the Nazi party's programme for adopting 'positive Christianity'. Ludendorff said that the Christian churches would bitterly oppose a racialist movement. Hitler explained that the commitment to Christianity was necessary for electoral purposes: 'I need Bavarian Catholics as well as Prussian Protestants to build up a great political movement. The rest comes later.'[16]

In *Mein Kampf* Hitler was careful not to give direct offence to the churches. He said, 'The religious teaching and institutions of a nation must always be sacrosanct to the political leader . . .'. He criticized the nineteenth century Austrian pan-German movement for attacking the Catholic church. He admitted that the church in Austria had not been sufficiently nationalist, but said that this was a general

15. E.K.D., A 2/491: extract from the minutes of the Kirchenbundesrat meeting of 8–9 June 1931.

16. See the memoirs of Ludendorff's adjutant, W. Breucker, *Die Tragik Ludendorffs* (Oldenburg, 1953), p. 107.

weakness in German society and that the churches had shown by their contribution to the war effort that they could overcome it. In any case, it was not the task of a political movement to carry out a religious reformation and the two should not be confused. The attack on the Catholic church had cost the pan-Germans the support of countless of the best elements in the nation from the lower-middle class.[17] Elsewhere Hitler expressed 'deepest disgust' for the advocates of German paganism. He accused them of being anachronistic, failures and cowards—'völkisch comedians' who sidetracked the movement from its primary aim of combating the Jews.[18] He was equally forthright with those who opened denominational disputes by attacking 'ultramontanism'. This too simply served Jewish interests and split the National Socialist movement.[19]

There were some grounds for thinking that the views expressed by Hitler in *Mein Kampf* were genuine. The full text of point 24 of the party programme, adopted in 1920 and declared unalterable in 1926, read,

We demand liberty for all religious denominations in the state, so far as they are not a danger to it and do not militate against the morality and moral sense of the German race.

The Party, as such, stands for positive Christianity, but does not bind itself in the matter of creed to any particular confession. It combats the Jewish-materialist spirit *within* and *outside* us, and is convinced that our nation can achieve permanent health from within only on the principle:

THE COMMON INTEREST BEFORE SELF-INTEREST.[20]

When he was released from prison in 1925, Hitler dissociated himself from Ludendorff's attacks on the

17. A. Hitler, *Mein Kampf* (Munich, 1925), i. 112–22.
18. Ibid., pp. 381–3.
19. Ibid., (Munich, 1927), ii. 209–14. This is probably a reference to Ludendorff's speech at the trial after the Munich *Putsch*. It is interesting to note that Ludendorff's attacks on Catholicism threatened to produce the denominational division Hitler feared. The *Evangelischer Bund*, at a conference in Munich in 1924, warmly supported *völkisch* attacks on ultramontanism. This attitude was criticized by the Catholic press and the *Völkische Kurier* thereupon said that the *völkisch* movement would not be exploited by either denomination and that the movement was not bound by Ludendorff's statements. *Bundesarchiv*, R 431/2195: reports of the representative of the Reich government in Bavaria to the Reichskanzlei, 4, 5, 6, 9, and 12 Sept. 1924.
20. *Hitler's Official Programme and its Fundamental Ideas* (Eng. transl., London, 1938), p. 43.

Catholic church and again emphasized that religious disputes should be kept out of the party. He had a special motive for doing this since he had to persuade the Bavarian Minister President, a member of the BVP (the Bavarian equivalent of the Catholic Centre party), to lift the ban on the Nazis.[21] When the Thuringian Gauleiter, Artur Dinter, refused to obey Hitler's policy and continued to press his own brand of Aryan religion, which he called *Geistchristentum,* on the party, Hitler expelled him. Gregor Strasser (head of the party's political organization) asked all members to sign a form declaring their support for Hitler's religious policy and rejecting Dinter.[22]

Other aspects of the NSDAP were less reassuring. The most directly objectionable were the works of Alfred Rosenberg. In his commentary on the party programme, published in 1923, he made it clear that the purpose of point 24 was electoral and that its main emphasis was anti-Semitic. He added that it was deplorable that people should consider their primary loyalty a denominational one; only a *völkisch Weltanschauung* could overcome the differences.[23] *The Myth of the 20th Century,* first published in 1930, immediately aroused criticism from the churches. Rosenberg had, however, been careful to explain in the preface that the book contained only his personal views, not the programme of the NSDAP.[24] Unlike Dinter, he made no attempt to make his views official party policy. This enabled the NSDAP to dismiss criticism of the book by saying that it was no concern of the party.[25] Rosenberg was, however, an influential figure within the NSDAP and the editor of the *Völkischer Beobachter,* (the party newspaper).[26]

21. A. Bullock, *Hitler, a study in tyranny* (Revised edn., London, 1967), pp. 128-9.
22. A. Tyrell, *Führer Befiehl* (Düsseldorff, 1969), pp. 149, 202-5, 210-11. Also, A. Tyrell, 'Der Mann, der Hitlers Kreise störte' in *Publik* (16 Jan. 1970), 21.
23. A. Rosenberg, *Wesen, Grundsätze und Ziele der Nationalsozialistischen Deutschen Arbeiterpartei,* (Munich, 1923), pp. 41-3.
24. A. Rosenberg, *Der Mythus des 20. Jahrhunderts,* (1st edn., Munich, 1930), pp. 22-3.
25. e.g. *Völkischer Beobachter,* 17 Feb. 1931, No. 48.
26. On Rosenberg, see R. Cecil, *The Myth of the Master Race. Alfred Rosenberg and Nazi Ideology* (London, 1972).

The first official contact between the Protestant leadership and the NSDAP took place on 4 March 1931. With the approval of President Kapler, a Kirchenbundesamt official, Scholz, met Franz Stöhr, a member of the executive of the NSDAP Reichstag party.[27] Stöhr made it clear that the NSDAP regarded the parliamentary party simply as a means to reach its goal which he described as 'the creation of the real German Reich of German men'. Stöhr explained that the NSDAP was a secular, political movement but that it was led by Christians who intended to put Christian ethics into practice by legislation. Of the 107 NSDAP members of the Reichstag, two-thirds were Protestant and one-third Catholic; only one member did not belong to a church and that was because he had quarrelled with a clergyman, not because he was a freethinker. Stöhr emphasized that 'the party is far from hostile to the church'. In evidence he cited the case of Dinter whom Hitler had unhesitatingly dismissed from the party because he refused to give up his 'odious campaign against the church'.

In view of its goal of a united *Volkstum*, Stöhr continued, the party played down denominational differences. This did not prevent the leadership being 'Protestant in direction' (*protestantisch bestimmt*). Those leaders who belonged to the Catholic church were, in fact, inclined towards Prot-estantism. There was no danger that the movement would be captured by Catholics; it was a German movement and it rejected the claims of the Catholic episcopacy over German law and secular matters. In education the National Socialist ideal was a single school for both Catholics and Protestants with even religious education held in common. The party realized, however, that such a school was impracticable and it would therefore support the denominational school while resisting Catholic attempts at domination; 'The German state should be the master of the German school'. Free-thinkers and Jews would have their own schools and would not be allowed to teach in denominational schools.

Scholz then asked whether the NSDAP would be like the

27. E.K.D., A 2/490: confidential report of the conversation by Scholz.

English Labour party, both national and Christian,[28] but Stöhr rejected this comparison. The National Socialist party was governed by a 'spiritual idea'. It opposed the individual man of Liberalism, the collective man of Marxism, and the hierarchically controlled man of Catholicism. Their ideal was an independent German not living for himself but for the community.

Stöhr's remarks were an interesting mixture of truth and jargon calculated to win Protestant support. He was clearly at pains to allay fears that the NSDAP was under pagan or Catholic influence. The Kirchenbundesamt official, Scholz, was not convinced. In a note written a few days after the interview, he suggested that because of the importance of the NSDAP and the great confusion within it, a file of press cuttings should be kept to see whether the party in practice followed its principles.[29] After the elections of September 1930 a similar file had been started for the use of the Prussian Oberkirchenrat.[30] These show the kind of information about the NSDAP known to the Protestant leadership.[31]

They contain articles about the political violence and revolutionary aims of the NSDAP.[32] They also contain the official statement of the Nazi programme for the Jews—loss of civil liberties, legal restrictions on mixed marriages, and a 'positive' racial policy using eugenic and educational measures.[33]

Critical material directed particularly to a Protestant audience, was provided by the Religious Socialists and the

28. Scholz's comparison with the British Labour party seems bizarre but it reflected the envy felt by German churchmen for England's freedom from an anti-clerical, socialist movement and the corresponding hope for a Christian social party.

29. E.K.D., A 2/490: note by Scholz, 12 Mar. 1931.

30. E.K.U., Gen. VI, 27/1 (Beiheft).

31. In a few cases in the following section I have used material from files in the church archives apart from the two mentioned.

32. *Vossische Zeitung,* 11 Nov. 1932, No. 541; ibid. 26 Feb. 1931, No. 97; *Der Heimatdienst,* 2 Sept. 1930, No. 18. Cf. Hitler's decree forbidding party members to carry weapons, despite *Reichsbanner* 'attacks', because otherwise 'the system' would have a pretext to ban the party; *Völkischer Beobachter,* 18 Feb. 1931, No. 49.

33. *Völkischer Beobachter,* 28 Jan. 1931 (E.K.D., A 2/495).

Christian Social *Volksdienst*.[34] The Religious Socialists attacked the racial principle, demagogy, authoritarianism, and violence of the party.[35] The *Volksdienst* also attacked the racialism of the party, quoting Rosenberg's *The Myth of the 20th Century*, and pointing out that he was the official interpreter of the party programme and the editor of its main newspaper.[36] A Reichstag deputy wrote of the 'tasteless scorn' for religion shown by National Socialists like Göring and Goebbels.[37] Another article criticized Hitler's religious views: it admitted that there were passages in *Mein Kampf* which sounded friendly to the churches but argued that it was clear throughout the book that the Aryan race was Hitler's highest ideal; the rest was simply clever tactics.[38] The *Volksdienst* warned that the Nazis would carry the political battle into the church and that if they came to power they would re-establish a Staatskirche.[39]

The right-wing Protestant press was much more sympathetic to the NSDAP, although it too expressed some doubts. The most important Lutheran journal praised the Nazis' nationalism, courage, and integrity and their desire to build a 'Christian, German nation' but it also asked them about their educational programme and said that there was no such thing as an Aryan God, that to break with the Bible was to break with God and that Jesus had been a Jew. It added that though many Christians agreed that the influence of the Jews must be broken they were less in sympathy with the hatred of the Jews preached by the Nazis.[40] Even Pfarrer Traub (who had agreed to be Kultusminister to the Kapp regime) warned Protestants against the Nazi programme and asked

34. One of the small middle-class parties that continued to stand for co-operation with the Republic. See G. Opitz, *Der Christlich-soziale Volksdienst* (Düsseldorf, 1969).

35. *Sonntagsblatt des arbeitenden Volkes*, 30 Nov. 1930, No. 48.

36. *Tägliche Rundschau*, 23 Dec. 1930, No. 182; ibid., 29 Jan. 1931, No. 24; *Christlichsozialer Volksdienst*, 5 Sept. 1931, No. 36.

37. *Tägliche Rundschau*, 25 Oct. 1931.

38. Ibid. 28 May 1931, No. 121.

39. Ibid. 13 Nov. 1930, No. 149, and 4 Dec. 1931, No. 283.

40. *Allgemeine Evangelisch-Lutherische Kirchenzeitung*, 13 Mar. 1931, No. 11. This article is not in the files but it was quoted extensively in the *Völkischer Beobachter*, 1 May 1931, No. 121, which is there.

whether they would allow alcoholics and the mentally sick to be sterilized and incurable patients killed.[41]

The NSDAP defended itself energetically against its critics in both Christian churches.[42] The leader of the NSDAP in the Bavarian Landtag, Buttmann, explained that 'positive Christianity' meant rejection of both paganism and Jewish materialism in favour of a Christian attitude.[43] Professor Stark, a physicist and Nobel prize winner, wrote a short apologia for the NSDAP, primarily intended to counteract the criticism of Roman Catholic bishops, but also read by Protestants. He maintained that on the basis of the party programme, its official statements and its behaviour, the NSDAP was 'not an enemy but a friend of Christianity'.[44] Individual lapses were admitted and regretted but party officials argued that they could not be held responsible for everything party members did.[45] The accusation of violence was turned against the critics by emphasizing the *Totenliste* (death roll) as the party's proud record of sacrifice to the nation.[46] When Dibelius criticized the subjective legal norms of the party and insisted that 'murder is murder', *Der Angriff* rounded on him and said that it was easy for fine people like Dibelius to stand aloof—they risked nothing.[47]

41. *Eiserne Blätter*, 11 Sept. 1932, No. 37.

42. For an account of Roman Catholic press criticism of the NSDAP, see L. Volk, *Der Bayerische Episkopat und der Nationalsozialismus 1930–1934* (Mainz, 1965), pp. 40–2.

43. See *Völkischer Beobachter*, 1 May 1931, No. 121. On Buttmann, Volk, *Der Bayerische Episkopat*, p. 65.

44. J. Stark, *Nationalsozialismus und katholische Kirche* (Munich, 1931).

45. *Völkischer Beobachter*, 1 May 1931, No. 121. Examples of 'lapses' included parodies of hymns and prayers and the organization of a pagan festival. The church leadership also knew that the NSDAP employed disreputable clergymen. *Tägliche Rundschau*, 13 Aug. 1932, No. 51; *Der Freidenker*, 16 Feb. 1932 (E.K.D., A 2/491); *Tägliche Rundschau*, 31 Dec. 1931, No. 304; E.K.D., A 2/491: Hamburg *Kirchenrat* to Kirchenausschuß, 14 Apr. 1932; *Völkischer Beobachter*, 2/4 Apr. 1932, No. 94/5 and Kapler's marginal note (E.K.D., A 2/492); ibid. 20 July 1932, No. 202; *Tägliche Rundschau*, 12 June 1932, No. 161. *Ost Holsteinisches Tageblatt*, 19 Nov. 1932, No. 272; *Berichtigungsdienst des evangelischen Preßverbandes*, 22 and 29 Nov. 1932, Nos. 17, 18; cf. *Völkischer Beobachter*, 23 Feb. 1933, No. 54.

46. See, for instance, the dedication of *Mein Kampf*. An article in the main Lutheran journal illustrates the effectiveness of this propaganda. It said of the National Socialists, 'Even their enemies must admit that they stand up for their ideals with manly courage; they shun neither death nor wounds... One judge said: when Communists stand before the court they lie; when National Socialists, they confess'; AELKZ, 13 Mar. 1931, No. 11, quoted in *Völkischer Beobachter*, 1 May 1931, No. 121.

47. *Der Tag*, 4 Sept. 1932; *Der Angriff*, 14 Sept. 1932, No. 184. *Der Angriff* was a Nazi Berlin evening newspaper edited by Goebbels.

The Nazi press produced an aggressive political propaganda aimed at the Protestant vote. The *Völkischer Beobachter* published an enthusiastic account of a service in Magdeburg Cathedral, packed with S.A. and S.S. in uniform, where the clergyman described Hitler as a gift of God.[48] The Catholic Centre party was repeatedly attacked as an improper mixture of religion and politics and for its alliance with the SPD.[49] For the Prussian Landtag elections of April 1932, *Der Angriff* carried a full-page notice to 'Protestant Christianity' warning it of the plight of the church in Russia and Spain under Marxist rule, blaming the Centre party for not resisting the growth of atheist Marxism in Germany, and claiming that the National Socialists had been the first to stand up to the danger, suffering bloodshed, scorn, and persecution in the process.[50]

An apologia for the Nazi party from within the church was provided by Friedrich Wienecke, founder of the National Socialist *Pastorenbund* (Pastors' Union) and later one of the leaders of the *Deutsche Christen* ('German Christians'). In an article entitled 'Can a clergyman be a National Socialist?' he described how he had become one. He had been disillusioned, he said, with the 'materialism' of the DNVP (which he had previously supported).[51] When he read *Mein Kampf* (he knew Hitler's name since the Munich *Putsch* of 1923) he had been struck by how clearly Hitler rejected pagan *völkisch* ideas and also by Hitler's concept of race. Wienecke explained that he had been trained in liberal theology and this had led him to minimize the importance of racial differences. By reading Karl Barth, however, he was converted to the idea that man should not base himself on human enlightenment but on the reality given by God. This seemed to him parallel to the way Hitler talked of race as a 'thing of the Lord' and as the 'purpose of creation'. In another article, Wienecke criticized the middle class for

48. *Völkischer Beobachter*, 6/7 Nov. 1932.
49. Ibid. 19 Feb. 1932, No. 50 and *passim*.
50. *Der Angriff*, 19 Apr. 1932, No. 77.
51. *Die Reformation*, 22 Mar. 1931, No. 6. The issue over which Wienecke broke with the DNVP was its attitude to the Dawes plan. This plan, presented in 1924, established a schedule of reparations payments by Germany together with a loan to restore the German economy. The DNVP was split by the plan into those who opposed it on principle as a 'second Versailles' and those who supported it because of the material advantages it promised.

coming to terms with the 'religionless, Marxist state' (i.e. the Republic) and added that even the Prussian Protestant church was in danger of being fettered to the system by the church treaty. The cause of this degeneration was the influence of cosmopolitan, Jewish humanitarianism; 'It is a holy Christian duty to overcome this racially damaging spirit of humanitarianism', he concluded.[52] Wienecke admitted that the NSDAP suffered from many faults of immaturity and that there was a danger that it would make a god of race but, he argued, there was an important distinction between Hitler and Rosenberg and many members of the NSDAP rejected Rosenberg's views. Wienecke claimed that the experience of his Pastorenbund, working in close co-operation with the National Socialist Lehrerbund (Teachers' Union) under Hans Schemm showed that the National Socialist press appreciated their advice.[53]

An indication of how far the Nazi party lived up to its propaganda could be gained by an examination of its political record in church affairs. It voted against concordats and church treaties and against the Reich School Law proposal favoured by the church.[54] This was consistent with its attitude to clericalism and should have served as a warning to the Protestant church that this did not apply only to Catholic demands. In those Länder where the NSDAP entered governments before 1933, it had a patchy record. In Thuringia an NSDAP motion that the church should surrender part of its subsidy for unemployment relief was passed against the wishes of the church.[55] In the same state, the Minister for Education, Frick (later Reich Minister of the Interior), introduced strongly nationalist school prayers

52. Der Märkische Adler, 15 Aug. 1930.

53. Deutsches Pfarrerblatt, 20 Oct. 1931, No. 42. Hans Schemm was an NSDAP deputy in the Bavarian Landtag, 1918–32; he was also Gauleiter of the Bavarian Ostmark and later Kultusminister of Bavaria. He affected an interest in promoting good relations with the church. See G. Kahl-Furthmann, Hans Schemm spricht. Seine Reden und sein Werk (8th edn., Bayreuth, 1936) and G. Pridham, Hitler's Rise to Power. The Nazi Movement in Bavaria 1923–1933 (London, 1973), pp. 149–50.

54. E.K.D., A 2/479: letter to Kapler, 3 Nov. 1932.

55. Das evangelische Deutschland, 16 Nov. 1930, No. 46, and 14 Dec. 1930, No. 50.

despite protests from the Landeskirche.[56] In Oldenburg relations between the Protestant church and the Nazi government were bad. A Catholic was appointed to the Kultusministerium although two-thirds of the population were Protestant; the protest of the Landeskirche was rejected on the grounds that in the NSDAP what mattered was not a man's denomination but his national outlook.[57] When the Landeskirche invited a negro Pastor to speak to a church meeting, the Nazi Minister President described this as a provocation worthy of the death penalty. The Landeskirche initiated slander proceedings against him but the case was dropped.[58] In Brunswick, on the other hand, the NSDAP took measures calculated to please the church: free-thinkers in the teaching profession were dismissed and the 'Christian character' restored to education, though separate denominational schools were not set up.[59] In Anhalt, according to the *Völkischer Beobachter*, the NSDAP made it more difficult for people to resign membership of the church and again restricted the activity of free-thinkers among teachers.[60]

The files in the church archives show that the Protestant leadership did not lack information about the NSDAP. No Protestant leader and not many clergymen at any level became members of the party before 1933.[61] But the

56. E.K.D., C 3/143: Kapler to Reichardt, 12 Apr. 1932: Reichardt to Kapler, 23 Apr. 1932. The Landeskirche protested on the grounds that the prayers should be free of politics. They are printed in *Hitler's Official Programme and its Fundamental Ideas*, pp. 122–3.

57. *Nachrichten für Stadt und Land*, 20 Sept. 1932, No. 257, Beilage No. 1.

58. *Evangelischer Pressedienst*, 30 July 1932, No. 77; *Oldenburgische Generalpredigerverein*, 21 Sept. 1932; *Völkischer Beobachter*, 5 Nov. 1932, No. 310. E.K.D., A 2/479: letter to Kapler, 3 Nov. 1932.

59. *Völkischer Beobachter*, 21 July 1932, No. 203; ibid. 11 Aug. 1932, No. 224. The Bishop of Brunswick nevertheless thought that the educational plans of the NSDAP were 'thoroughly objectionable'; E.K.D., A 2/249: Bernewitz to Kirchenausschuß, 16 Apr. 1932.

60. *Völkischer Beobachter*, 19 July 1932, No. 201.

61. Pastor Hossenfelder, the leader of the *Deutsche Christen*, estimated that in 1932 there were only about fifty pastors in the whole Reich who were members of the NSDAP. (Interview, 16 Jan. 1968.) This is, however, probably an underestimate since there is a record of seventeen pastors belonging to the party in one Lower Saxon Gau; J. Noakes, *The Nazi Party in Lower Saxony 1921–1933* (Oxford, 1971), p. 208.

Protestant leadership failed to give a clear lead against the party on either religious or political grounds.

If the Nazi Party had officially identified itself with the philosophy of Rosenberg, church leaders would have been forced to condemn it, as they had the KPD because atheism was part of its programme. Hitler was too clever to do this. The result was that the Nazi party gave an impression of confusion in religious matters and Hitler appeared to be holding its radical elements in check. The confusion encouraged the political opponents of the NSDAP to point out the weaknesses in the party's propaganda and to warn the church of dangers which later materialized. The NSDAP replied that these warnings were signs of political prejudice and that the official position of the party on religion was impeccable.[62] This created sufficient doubt about the way the party would develop for churchmen, who were well disposed towards it, to be content with criticizing its 'faults' rather than condemning the movement as a whole.[63]

In general the Protestant leadership refrained from public statements and left the discussion to private individuals. There were several important private publications but no progress could be made because of the deliberate ambiguity of the NSDAP.[64] The views of the more critical members of the

62. For instance, when the President of the Reich Court attacked Nazism for replacing Christianity with a German faith, the NSDAP ridiculed him and said he must have confused them with another racialist group; *Das Evangelische Berlin*, 1 Jan. 1932, No. 1; *Frankfurter Volksblatt*, 6 Jan. 1932, No. 4. A marginal comment by the Kirchenbundesamt official, Scholz, shows that he accepted the Nazi statement.

63. Some Roman Catholic bishops took a stronger line. In the provinces of Paderborn and the Upper Rhine, Roman Catholics were forbidden to support the NSDAP, and in Bavaria Catholic priests were forbidden to take part in the Nazi movement. In addition, the errors of Nazism were condemned by Cardinal Bertram of Breslau and the Bishops of the province of Cologne. Bishop Schreiber of Berlin, however, indicated that Catholics could be members of the NSDAP and the bishops' conference at Fulda in 1931 decided not to condemn Nazism as hostile to Christianity. G. Lewy, *The Catholic Church and Nazi Germany* (London, 1964), pp. 8–15; cf. Volk, *Der bayerische Episkopat*, pp. 22–49 and W. J. Doetsch, *Württembergs Katholiken unterm Hakenkreuz* (Stuttgart, 1969).

64. See, for instance, L. Klotz, *Die Kirche und das dritte Reich* (Gotha, 1932); G. Wünsch, *Reich Gottes, Marxismus, Nationalsozialismus* (Tübingen, 1931); W. Künneth, Pf. Wilm, H. Schemm, *Was haben wir als evangelische Christen zum Rufe des Nationalsozialismus zu sagen?* (Dresden, 1931); H. Strathmann, *Nationalsozialistische Weltanschauung?* (Nuremberg, 1931); H. Sasse, 'Kirchliche Zeitlage' in *Kirchliches Jahrbuch*, 59. Jg. (1932), 65–74; von Kleist-Schmenzin, *Der Nationalsozialismus eine Gefahr* (Berlin, 1932).

church leadership were probably represented by a book produced under the auspices of the Inner Mission, which was widely distributed and may have had financial support from the Landeskirchen.[65] It argued forcefully that, despite the ambiguity of National Socialism, it was a religion of blood, irreconcilable with the Gospel. It emphasized statements of Rosenberg like, 'A sense of sin is the necessary accompanying phenomenon of physical bastardy'. It admitted that Hitler's philosophy was different but argued that the Nazi press showed that Rosenberg's views were more widely held in the party than Hitler's.

A much more friendly tone was struck by the *Christlich-Deutsche Bewegung* (Christian-German movement) for which one of the church leaders, Bishop Rendtorff of Mecklenburg-Schwerin was directly responsible. This movement originated with a group of Stahlhelm and DNVP supporters within the church, although Goebbels addressed one of its meetings.[66] The movement was later eclipsed by the more radical, exclusively Nazi, *Deutsche Christen*. Rendtorff praised Nazism because it sought to rouse the nation to its destiny and because, unlike most modern movements, it stood for 'positive Christianity'. At the same time, he argued that if the party took the phrase 'positive Christianity' seriously it would be subject to God and would not exploit Christianity for human ends.[67]

The church leadership also refused to condem the NSDAP on political grounds. Kapler dismissed evidence about the illegal, revolutionary aims of the party as inconclusive. Most Landeskirchen did issue decrees in 1931–2 intended to keep party warfare out of the church and some condemned

65. H. Schreiner, *Der Nationalsozialismus vor der Gottesfrage* (Berlin, 1931). In a critical review Wienecke asked who had paid for it to be sent to so many clergymen; *Deutsches Pfarrerblatt*, 20 Oct. 1931, No. 42. In reply to an inquiry from a German clergyman in Brazil, the Kirchenbundesamt recommended Schreiner's book. E.K.D., A 2/491: Kirchenbundesamt to Propst Francke, 11 Apr. 1931.

66. Buchheim, *Glaubenskrise im Dritten Reich*, pp. 60–2. F. Wienecke, *Die Glaubensbewegung 'Deutsche Christen'* (1st edn., Soldin, 1932), p. 10, and *Die Kampf- und Glaubensbewegung 'Deutsche Christen'* (Soldin, 1936), p. 5.

67. E.K.U., Gen. XII, 184: Rendtorff to Kapler, 29 Sept. 1932, enclosing the programme of the *Christlich-Deutsche Bewegung*; E.K.D., A 2/492: *Unser Werk*, Feb. 1932, vol. 2. Rendtorff joined the NSDAP in May 1933, but was soon disillusioned; see below, p. 133.

violence, but the church leadership deliberately avoided explicit condemnation of the NSDAP.[68]

The sympathy shown by the church leadership for the NSDAP had many causes. It reflected their common pre-judices—nationalist, anti-liberal, and anti-Semitic. This revealed the ambivalence of Vernunftrepublikaner conser-vatism, the extent to which their hearts remained with the opposition even as their heads led them to come to terms with the Republic. From 1932 there was a minority within the church leadership which favoured a more anti-Republican course. Church leaders also knew that there was strong support for the NSDAP among their parishioners.

The position was explained by an official of the Berlin Oberkirchenrat to two American visitors (representing the Federal Council of the Christian churches of America) who were anxious to know the attitude of the church to the Jewish question.[69] The official explained, as his personal view, that at the last Reichstag elections the National Socialists had won 13,000,000 votes; unlike the Communists and Socialists—who together had been equally successful and were hostile to the church—the National Socialists were overwhelmingly Protestant. This created special difficulties for church officials. He added that there was much that was welcome about the National Socialist movement and that the German nation should be protected from damaging Jewish influence, although legally and not violently. Where, however, the National Socialists idolized race, the church had to 'raise its warning voice'.

Like other conservative groups, church leaders tended to adopt a patronizing attitude to the NSDAP. While they recognized the crudeness of the Nazi movement, they attributed this to the social and educational background of the Nazi leaders. They believed in the basic integrity of the movement and they did not understand its revolutionary potential. An example of these attitudes is a report by church representatives of a meeting with a member of Hitler's staff in Munich in January 1932.[70] The meeting was authorized

68. This is examined in detail below, pp. 99–105.
69. E.K.D., C 3/170: account of the meeting, 11 July 1932.
70. E.K.U., Pr. II, 46/4: report dated 26 Jan. 1932.

by Kapler and kept secret. The Nazi representative is described as a loyal parishioner but otherwise unidentified.[71]

The church representatives criticized an article by Kube, the chairman of the NSDAP in the Prussian Landtag.[72] Kube had attacked the church leadership for its lack of support for the anti-Republican opposition; he also mentioned a financial scandal involving a subsidiary organization of the Inner Mission.[73] He proposed to make the church a single united Reichskirche and instructed party supporters to seize power through the parish elections. The church representatives protested that this kind of comment was no different to the left-wing press. They added that if the NSDAP organized a separate church party in the parish elections, this would contradict the principle of non-intervention in church affairs which Hitler had repeatedly proclaimed—instead the church would be reduced to an instrument of politics. The Nazi representative promised to raise the matter at the next policy meetings. He assured the church that he knew from repeated confidential conversations with Hitler that it could expect the best if Hitler came to power.

The church representatives noted in their report that one had to use a special vocabulary in negotiating with the National Socialists; one had to master an odd habit of saying something different to what was meant. One of the representatives, a Bavarian Protestant leader who claimed to know most members of Hitler's staff, thought they were very respectable and well-meaning but mostly just beginning to think about the problems. The report added more perceptively that the only thing that counted was Hitler's decision.

iii. The German Christians

Hitler decided to allow the organization of a pro-Nazi church party to contest the parish elections in the Old Prussian Union in November 1932. Apparently, the Nazi leadership calculated that because of their support among church

71. He may have been Hans Schemm, who had been involved in correspondence about a suggested meeting between Hitler and Kapler; E.K.D., A 2/491: Ihmels to Kapler, 2 and 31 Dec. 1931; Kapler to Ihmels, 28 Dec. 1931.

72. *Völkischer Beobachter*, 10/11 Jan. 1932.

73. See H. Brüning, *Memoiren 1918–1934* (Stuttgart, 1970), pp. 406–7.

members they could disregard the wishes of the church leadership. The church leadership was faced with a new, direct challenge.

This development seems to have come about as a result of pressure from both church members and Nazi party leaders. Previously, consistent with Hitler's principle of non-intervention, the church had been exempt from the Nazi system of specialized groups to penetrate professional associations like Schemm's Lehrerbund. Wienecke's Nazi Pastorenbund had worked with the Lehrerbund, but remained a private affair. In 1931 an increasing number of Protestants became dissatisfied with the existing church parties and felt the need to form a party sympathetic to the NSDAP. This was not a new idea—the existing church parties had loose connections with other political parties. In the elections to the Hessen-Nassau Landeskirchentag in 1931, the first Nazi-oriented church party won fifteen of the sixty seats. In November 1931 the first group to call themselves *Deutsche Christen* contested the parish elections in Altenberg in Thuringia.[74]

In 1932 the connection with the NSDAP became closer. A Nazi church party was organized at Reich level with the approval of the *Reichsleitung* (Reich leadership) of the NSDAP and Gauleiter were instructed to appoint *Kirchenfachberater* ('experts for church affairs') to co-operate with it. The initiative for this development seems to have come from Protestant Nazis and Kube (the leader of the NSDAP in the Prussian Landtag). Hitler appears to have remained doubtful about becoming involved in church affairs. He opposed the original name taken by the group, *Evangelische Nationalsozialisten* ('Protestant National Socialists') since it would commit the party too blatantly. Instead the title *Glaubensbewegung 'Deutsche Christen'* literally, 'Faith movement "German Christians" ', was adopted. Hossenfelder, the *Reichsleiter* ('Reich leader') of the new movement, gained the impression that Gregor Strasser, the head of the NSDAP political organization, was keener on the formation of a church party than Hitler. Strasser told Hossenfelder that, unlike Hitler, he did not believe that a political movement

74. K. Meier, *Die Deutschen Christen* (Göttingen, 1964), pp. 2–17.

could succeed without metaphysics, and when Hossenfelder asked him what Hitler thought of the new church party, Strasser shrugged as though Hitler's opinion was of no importance.[75] Lip-service continued to be paid to the principle of non-intervention in the church: ostensibly the German Christians remained independent of the NSDAP although they enjoyed the support of its organization.

The first signal for Nazi participation in the elections of the Old Prussian Union was given in January 1932 in the article by Kube in the *Völkischer Beobachter*, against which the church representatives had protested. In February 1932 the Berlin Oberkirchenrat received a copy of a circular from the NSDAP Gau Silesia which provided unmistakable evidence of the party's intentions.[76] It said that the NSDAP Reichsleitung had given permission for a Nazi church party to be formed to compete in the church elections which were of the greatest importance for the Third Reich. The programme was to be 'positive Christianity in the spirit of Martin Luther'. This meant rejection of the liberal spirit of Jewish-Marxist enlightenment with humanitarianism, pacifism, and Christian cosmopolitanism, emphasis on a warlike faith, and preservation of the race. The programme called for a new spirit in the church leadership which had failed in several respects—by concluding a church treaty with the black-red (i.e. Catholic-Socialist) coalition, by appointing people who were unreliable by *völkisch* criteria to many central positions, by restricting the attendance of the S.A. at church services, and by their reserve over the Young plan and other issues. The programme repeated Kube's demand for the creation of a single strong Reichskirche. Party members were to reject the accusation that the NSDAP was bringing politics into the church: they were to explain that they were acting not as a party but as Protestants, following a call of faith which came

75. Interview with Hossenfelder, 16 Jan. 1968. Gregor Strasser was a powerful figure within the party. In the autumn of 1932 he challenged Hitler's policy of refusing to enter a coalition government and resigned. He was murdered during the Röhm purge. See also H. Beyer, 'Volk, Staat und Kirche in der Übergangs-und Krisenzeit 1932–1934', in G. Kretschmar, B. Lohse, *Ecclesia und Res Publica* (Göttingen, 1961).

76. E.K.U., Gen. III, 51/1 (Beiheft): Westphalian Konsistorium to Oberkirchenrat, 26 Feb. 1932. In April it was published in the *Christliche Welt* (2 Apr.

from their 'national' movement; as loyal church members they had a right to demand that their movement should receive proper consideration in the life and administration of the church. Local party organizations were to appoint experts for church affairs; these were to report to the Gauleitung the names of any party members who were active church members or clergymen. Participation in church elections was obligatory for all party members; the local experts for church affairs would see that party members were properly registered. Agreements with other church parties on a joint list of candidates (making an election unnecessary) were only to be concluded if the National Socialists were given two-thirds of the seats.

At the beginning of June 1932 the programme of the Nazi church party, under its new name *Glaubensbewegung 'Deutsche Christen'*, was made public and Pastor Hossenfelder's appointment as leader was announced.[77] The programme was very similar to that of the Silesian circular but it was more detailed on the application of racialism. With reference to the charitable work of the Inner Mission it demanded protection of the race from the incapable and the inferior. The mission to the Jews was described as a serious danger because it might open the way to intermarriage, 'racial bastardy'; the mission was to cease as long as Jews had full civil rights and intermarriage with Jews was to be prohibited. It is interesting to note that the east Prussian German Christians under *Wehrkreispfarrer* (military chaplain), subsequently Reich Bishop, Ludwig Müller issued a separate programme which did not have the same racialist emphasis and was little different to the programme of the combined traditional church parties, who in some areas formed a common front against the German Christians.[78]

Following their instructions, the German Christians denied

77. J. Hossenfelder, *Die Richtlinien der Deutschen Christen* (Berlin, 1932); *Völkischer Beobachter*, 2 June 1932.

78. An east Prussian German Christian programme is printed in Buchheim, *Glaubenskrise im Dritten Reich*, p. 93. The programme of the traditional church parties, combined under the name 'Gospel and Nation', was printed in *Die Reformation*, 4 Sept. 1932. It was most closely representative of the church policy of the DNVP. It demanded freedom for the church from interference by the state or political parties; at the same time it was strongly nationalist, anti-Communist, and anti-Semitic.

that they were bringing politics into the church although they admitted that they had close contact with the NSDAP and used its propaganda.[79] They tried to select candidates who were members of the NSDAP although they were allowed to have people who simply voted for the party.[80] No German Christian could be a member of any other church party and German Christian candidates had to give a written undertaking promising to obey the party leadership.[81] The election campaign was fought with typical Nazi *élan*: one German Christian meeting in Berlin had to be dispersed by the police.[82]

The church leadership which normally observed neutrality in church elections tried to resist the German Christians by instructing the clergy and parishes to keep the elections free of political issues.[83] In June 1932 the Oberkirchenrat reminded electors and candidates that the elections were for a church office and asked them to show a non-party attitude.[84] Several suggestions were made to postpone the elections until the political atmosphere became less heated. In October 1932 the Oberkirchenrat issued a further statement, in the name of the Kirchensenat, refusing a postponement but repeating in strong terms that the purpose of the elections was non-political. Only candidates who could be guaranteed to promote the spiritual, moral, and social welfare of the parish on the basis of the Gospel should be elected. The statement was to be circulated to all clergy, read from the pulpit, and published in the local church press.[85] Although the German Christians were not named, it was clear that these statements were aimed primarily against them.[86]

79. E.K.U., Gen. III, 51/2: report of a German Christian meeting, 29 Sept. 1932; ibid. 51/1 (Beiheft): *Vossische Zeitung*, 25 Oct. 1932.

80. Ibid. 51/1 (Beiheft): *Merkblatt*, No. 1, for the church elections, Gau Cologne–Aachen; L.K.A. Hamburg, *Deutsche Christen, Rundbriefe 1932/33: Rundschreiben* No. 8, 31 July 1932.

81. Ibid., *Merkblatt*, No. 1.

82. Ibid. 51/2: *Deutschvölkische Freiheitsbewegung*, 30 Sept. 1932; copy of a parish council meeting of the Kaiser Wilhelm Gedächtniskirche, 28 Sept. 1932.

83. Ibid. 51/1 (Beiheft): Oberkirchenrat to Generalsuperintendenten (confidential), 24 May 1932.

84. Ibid.: decree, 18 June 1932.

85. Ibid. 51/2: Oberkirchenrat to Konsistorien, 14 Oct. 1932.

86. Ibid.: protest of German Christian *Ortsgruppe*, Wittenau, to Kapler, 28 Oct. 1932; ibid. 51/1 (Beiheft): *Vossische Zeitung*, 16 Sept. 1932; *Montagspost*, 24 Oct. 1932.

The church leadership did not, however, condemn the German Christian programme despite its pronounced racialism. It adopted the same attitude of critical sympathy to the German Christians as it had to the NSDAP. This ignored the special responsibility of the church in face of a movement which claimed to be a Protestant church party. The senior spiritual authority of the Oberkirchenrat, Vice-President Burghart, met Hossenfelder (Reich leader of the German Christians) in August and September 1932. Burghart objected to the declaration demanded of German Christian candidates binding them to obey the party leadership; members of parish bodies, he said, were bound only by their oath to the church constitution and their conscience. Hossenfelder gave way and an alternative declaration was substituted which was allowed by the Oberkirchenrat although it was ambiguous.[87] When Burghart, not in his official position but as an 'elder Christian', criticized parts of the German Christian programme, Hossenfelder replied that nothing more could be altered, whereupon Burghart said that further discussion was futile.[88] Burghart's failure to condemn the German Christians was repeated throughout the church leadership. One reason was no doubt the convention of neutrality during elections. The discussions of the provincial Superintendenten show, however, that although there were strong objections to the movement, there was also a general feeling that the German Christians contained 'healthy' elements and that the church should show, as one official put it, friendly receptiveness, not careworn defensiveness.[89]

In the elections the German Christians won about a third of the seats: in the western provinces they were least

87. E.K.U., Gen. III, 51/1 (Beiheft): Burghart to Hossenfelder, 6 Aug. 1932; reports on discussions between Burghart and Hossenfelder, 19 Aug. and 9 Sept. 1932. The second declaration explicitly accepted the terms of the church constitution though it also acknowledged loyalty to the leadership of the movement. Hossenfelder explained that this meant simply attending meetings of the movement and that there was no question of interfering with freedom of conscience.

88. Ibid.: letter 6 Aug. and report 19 Aug. 1932; also Burghart to Weinecke, 8 Aug. 1932.

89. Ibid.: minutes of a meeting of the Oberkirchenrat and Generalsuperinten-denten, 10 Mar. 1932, and minutes of the meetings of the provincial Superintendenten.

successful, winning only about a fifth, but in east and west Prussia and in Pomerania they won about half the seats.[90] The results are difficult to interpret.[91] The German Christians had not reached their goal; they had not conquered the church.[92] They had also done less well than might have been expected on the basis of the political elections in 1932.[93] This may indicate that the warnings of the church leadership against bringing politics into the church had some effect and that a significant number of Protestants who voted NSDAP in political elections did not want to see the party invade the church. Even the third of the seats won by the German Christians may give an exaggerated impression of their support among church members. The German Christians had the advantage of the NSDAP organization and the obligation laid on all party members to vote, regardless of whether they were regular church members. These tactics were likely to be especially effective in areas where church elections were not normally contested but settled by agreement between the parties.[94] Another factor in the German Christian gains was the special attitude taken by the east Prussian branch of the movement, where a moderate programme and agreements with other parties to share the seats produced one of their most successful results.[95] To summarize, the first German Christian attack had been contained but, as a report from the statistical office of the

90. See the analysis by Dibelius in *Der Tag*, 20 Nov. 1932, No. 279.

91. One of the main difficulties is to estimate the level of participation in the elections. The statistical office of the Kirchenbund reported that despite the excitement in Berlin, in some parishes only 75 per cent voted, in many not over 60 per cent, in some not 50 per cent. This probably represents a percentage of those registered to vote, not of all those entitled to register. What percentage registered to vote out of the total Protestant population is not reported, although there were reports of increases in registration because of the activity of the German Christians. E.K.U., Gen. III, 51/2: report of the statistical office, 23 Feb. 1933; *Evangelischer Preßverband für Deutschland* to Karnatz, 1 Nov. 1932.

92. This did not prevent them claiming success; L.K.A. Hamburg, *Deutsche Christen, Rundbriefe* 1932/33: *Rundschreiben* No. 14, 8 Dec. 1932; *Evangelium im dritten Reich*, 27 Nov. 1932.

93. See below p. 106.

94. See Dibelius in *Der Tag*, 20 Nov. 1932, No. 279, and report on a meeting of the Superintendenten in Silesia, 4/5 Nov. 1932 in E.K.U., Gen. III, 51/1 (Beiheft).

95. *Königsberger Anzeiger*, 14 Oct. 1932.

Kirchenbund pointed out, a church party had never before achieved such a high vote in so short a time.[96]

The Protestant leadership did not join the 'national opposition' before 1933 but neither did it condemn the movement. Church leaders resisted the attempt of the German Christians to make the church an instrument of the political ambitions of the NSDAP. They also supported warnings on religious grounds against some aspects of the movement especially its racialism. The church leadership failed, however, to direct its criticism publicly, officially, and unambiguously at the NSDAP. Church leaders hoped that if the movement were treated with understanding it would grow out of the faults they disliked in it. They were victims of their own prejudices and skilful propaganda. As a result, like other German conservative groups, the church leadership failed to appreciate the nature of Nazism before it became subject to Nazi rule.

96. E.K.U., Gen. III, 51/2: report of 23 Feb. 1933.

6

THE CRISIS OF THE REPUBLIC

The trend towards an authoritarian, right-wing government in Germany, which developed after the formation of Brüning's cabinet in March 1930 and became blatant with von Papen's illegal *coup* against Prussia on 20 July 1932, destroyed the basis of the policy pursued by the Protestant leadership from 1925 to 1931. The future of the Republic was jeopardized and it was uncertain what was to replace it. The rival ambitions of Hugenberg (the leader of the DNVP) and Hitler in the 'national opposition' appeared to make it impossible to form a stable government of the Right. Meanwhile the Communist vote increased. The political crisis developed against a background of severe economic depression, violence, and lawlessness. It seemed that Germany might sink into civil war.[1]

The church leadership responded by condemning violence and proclaiming the ideal of a civilized community. It tried to keep the church free of political strife and stressed the duty of the church to set an example to the rest of the nation. It failed, however, to condemn those who were responsible for violence by name, preferring general exhortations. On the political front, the Protestant leadership watched the subversion of parliamentary government without comment and probably without regret. It was anxious that the sections of the Reich constitution guaranteeing the privileges of the church should be upheld but it overlooked their dependence on the rule of law. It hoped to protect its rights by personal contact with individual Reich authorities.

---

1. W. Conze and H. Raupach, *Die Staats- und Wirtschaftskrise des Deutschen Reichs 1929/33* (Stuttgart, 1967), especially R. Vierhaus, 'Auswirkungen der Krise um 1930 in Deutschland. Beiträge zu einer historisch-psychologischen Analyse' and W. Conze, 'Die politischen Entscheidungen in Deutschland 1929–1933'.

The Kirchentag which met in June 1930 declared that the duty of the church in the existing crisis was 'to offer a torn and divided nation a discernible and living community in the strength of faith and love, stronger than all class and professional sectional interests, stronger than the conflict of power groups, stronger than economic compulsion'.[2] The internal threat to peace was taken up by individual Landeskirchen. In April 1931 the Hesse-Kassel Kirchentag warned against the increasing savagery of political life. Similar declarations were issued by the Thuringian Kirchentag and by Bishop Rendtorff of Mecklenburg-Schwerin.[3] Other church leaders followed in 1932 after Kapler had written to them supporting a request from the Reich Minister of the Interior, for church help in combating political violence.[4] In a New Year address the Bishop of Saxony referred to the terrible statistics of Germans murdering each other, and the Bishop of Brunswick asked how political parties could consider it an achievement to attack defenceless members of rival groups.[5] Kapler wrote to the Landeskirchen again in July 1932 after seventeen people had been murdered during fighting in Altona on Sunday 17 July, some of them during church services. Some Landeskirchen issued fresh appeals warning against civil war.[6]

These measures were sincere and salutary but their effect was blunted because church leaders avoided condemning particular groups. In October 1931 the Kirchenausschuß even decided against a general condemnation of violence, partly because a Nazi attack on Jews and Jewish shops had just taken place on the Kurfürstendamm (a main shopping street) in Berlin. The Kirchenausschuß was afraid that its statement

2. *Verhandlungen, Kirchentag,* 1930, pp. 312–13.
3. Copies of the declarations in E.K.D., A 2/478.
4. Ibid.: Groener to Kapler, 5 Dec. 1931; Kapler to the Landeskirchen, 31 Dec. 1931.
5. Ibid.: copies of the declarations.
6. Ibid.: Kapler to the Landeskirchen, 26 July 1932. The Old Prussian Union, Württemberg, Thuringia, Hesse-Kassel, Anhalt, and Bremen took action as a result; ibid. The pastors of Altona issued their own declaration, which anticipated principles later adopted by the Protestant opposition in the Third Reich. It is printed in K. D. Schmidt, *Die Bekenntnisse des Jahres 1933* (2nd edn., Göttingen, 1937), pp. 19–25; cf. the memoirs of one of its authors, H. Asmussen, *Zur jüngsten Kirchengeschichte* (Stuttgart, 1961), pp. 27–31.

would look like direct condemnation of the NSDAP.[7] The Berlin Oberkirchenrat also refused a request from Jewish circles that it should publicly condemn acts of desecration against Jewish cemeteries, on the grounds that there was no reason to believe that Protestants had been involved.[8] This evasion was consistent with the policy of political neutrality, but it was less forceful than the attitude previously adopted by the Kirchenausschuß on the occasion of the murder of Rathenau.[9]

Steps were taken to prevent exploitation of the church by political groups and to restrain clergy from party political activity but their effect was limited. The problem of 'Stahlhelm pastors' taking part in demonstrations against the Republic had embarrassed the Prussian church leadership since 1928. In 1929 the Oberkirchenrat issued a decree restricting the access of political groups to the church to purely religious occasions and recommending that, even then, they should attend the normal parish service.[10]

The increasing political bitterness of the years 1930-2 made the problem more serious. In January 1931 the Prussian Kultusministerium approached the Oberkirchenrat over complaints about Nazi pastors. The Kultusministerium official, Trendelenburg, mentioned government measures against civil servants joining the party and asked what the attitude of the church would be towards its pastors. Kapler said that the church would not consider mere membership of the NSDAP an offence but pastors who belonged to the party would have to obey the usual restrictions on political activity laid down by the church. When pressed by Trendelenburg as to whether the NSDAP was a violent, revolutionary organization, Kapler said that he did not think that it had been proved that it was; he did not consider remarks attributed to individual Nazis, or particular newspaper

7. E.K.D., A 2/478: Kapler to Graf Vitzthum, 18 Jan. 1932. cf. K. D. Bracher, *Die Auflösung der Weimarer Republik* (4th edn., Villingen, 1964), p. 376.

8. E.K.U., Gen. XII, 46/1: extract from the minutes of a meeting of the Oberkirchenrat and the Generalsuperintendenten, 26-7 Feb. 1931.

9. See above, p. 58.

10. E.K.U., Gen. VI, 16/2: extract from the minutes of a meeting of the Oberkirchenrat and the Generalsuperintendenten, 28 Sept. 1928; E.K.D., A 2/478: copy of the decree, 23 Apr. 1929.

articles, sufficient evidence. To underline his argument, Kapler added that the Prussian govenment would not accept all the remarks attributed to the SPD—such as threats to sabotage national defence, and a speech by Grzesinski, the Police President of Berlin (who had said he would like to see the enemies of the Republic hanged)—as responsible statements of that party.[11]

By the summer of 1931 the Landeskirchen of Thuringia, Württemberg, and Bavaria (right of the Rhine) had taken special precautions against party political exploitation of the church.[12] Following a request from the Kultusministerium, the Old Prussian Union issued a new decree in November 1931.[13] This laid down that church buildings, the pulpit, and church services (including those reserved for particular groups) were to be kept free of politics. The decree warned against the attendance of groups with their insignia at church services and said that parish councils must ensure that the church did not become involved in a political demonstration.

The decree was criticized by the Kultusministerium because it did not condemn the NSDAP as such.[14] It was also attacked by the Stahlhelm and the NSDAP who saw it as a threat to their propaganda.[15] It was in fact a weak measure. Uniformed groups were still allowed to attend church services provided that local parish councils decided they did not threaten the peace of the church.[16] The general

11. E.K.U., Gen. VI, 2/2: note by Kapler on a discussion with Trendelenburg, 30 Jan. 1931. On Grzesinski see P. A. Glees, 'Albert Grzesinski and the politics of Prussia 1926–1930' (B. Phil. thesis, Oxford, 1972).

12. On Thuringia, see Dahm, *Pfarrer und Politik*, pp. 81–7. Copies of the measurers taken in Württemberg and Bavaria are in E.K.D., A 2/478.

13. D.Z.A. Merseburg, Rep. 76, III Sekt. 1, Abt. XVII, 231/1: Kultusministerium to Oberkirchenrat, 19 June 1931; copy of the Oberkirchenrat decree of 21 Nov. 1931 in E.K.D., A 2/478.

14. Ibid.: Kultusministerium to Oberkirchenrat, 5 Jan. 1932.

15. *Der Stahlhelm*, 6 Dec. 1931, No. 49, and *Die Brennessel* (the Nazi satirical magazine) 16 Dec. 1931, No. 28 (see Plate 3). The cartoon depicts an indignant Martin Luther rejecting the Oberkirchenrat with its decree on church attendance and saying, 'Here I stand, I can no other. My Christianity was *Kampf!*'.

16. The spiritual vice-president of the Oberkirchenrat argued that the church leadership had to be cautious because technically the matter came within the autonomy granted to individual parishes by the constitution of the Old Prussian Union. Church leaders were, however, anyway anxious not to offend the 'national opposition'. E.K.U., Gen. VI, 16/4: minutes of a meeting of Burghart and the east Prussian Superintendenten, 22–3 Feb. 1932.

Oberkirchenrat wünscht keine S.A. in der Kirche

Luther: „*Hier stehe ich, ich kann nicht anders. Mein Christentum war Kampf!*"

3. Nazi satire on restrictions on the attendance of uniformed groups in church (*Die Brennessel*, 16 December 1931), see p. 102 fn. 15.

sympathy for the 'national opposition' meant that in most parishes the decree was likely to be interpreted generously in favour of anti-Republican groups. When the Stahlhelm asked for precise clarification, the Oberkirchenrat insisted only that party flags could not be erected within the church except at special services for the group concerned; otherwise, the Stahlhelm was told, it would have to make *ad hoc* arrangements with local parish authorities.[17]

Most Landeskirchen took comparable measures in 1931–2.[18] Detailed restrictions were imposed in Thuringia, Württemberg, Schleswig-Holstein, Oldenburg, Bavaria (right of the Rhine), and Lübeck. Other Landeskirchen simply recommended restraint by the clergy or condemned political violence in general. Some small Landeskirchen said that measures were unnecessary in their areas. Nowhere were clergy forbidden to join the NSDAP. Württemberg imposed the greatest restrictions and prohibited its clergy taking part in the campaign for the Reichstag election of November 1932.[19]

Some church leaders may have been prevented from taking firmer action by doubts about the legality of restricting political activity. In Thuringia the Landeskirche had to withdraw part of its decrees when Religious Socialists complained to the Reich Minister of the Interior that their constitutional rights had been infringed.[20] A more important motive, however, was fear of alienating the NSDAP. In a report to the Kirchenausschuß in November 1932, President Wurm of Württemberg said that the measures showed the desire of church leaders to preserve the neutrality of the church but also 'to bring to a mighty national movement, like National Socialism, even though it is objectionable in many respects, the greatest possible measure of understanding for

17. E.K.U., Gen. VI, 16/4: Der Stahlhelm—Bundesamt to Oberkirchenrat, 5 Apr. 1932; Oberkirchenrat reply, 22 Apr.

18. Copies are in E.K.D., A 2/478; see also, *Kirchliches Jahrbuch,* 59. Jg. (1932), 133–64.

19. E.K.D., A 2/479: text of a report by President Wurm of Württemberg to the Kirchenausschuß in November 1932. See G. Schäfer, *Die evangelische Landeskirche in Württemberg und der Nationalsozialismus.* Bd. 1 (Stuttgart, 1971), pp. 33–218.

20. Dahm, *Pfarrer und Politik,* pp. 81–7.

its motives. The mistake of the church towards socialism should not be repeated'.[21]

It is difficult to assess the contribution of the Protestant church to the anti-Republican Right. Political exploitation of the church caused concern to the Protestant leadership in most parts of Germany during 1930–2. Relatively few Protestant clergymen seem to have been involved, however. In 1931 the Prussian Kultusministerium reported thirty-two cases of anti-Republican activity; the church authorities took some action in fifteen of these; in one, the public prosecutor instituted legal proceedings which failed; in several cases the Oberkirchenrat reported that its investigation had shown that the accusations were tendentious. The Kultusministerium did not always agree with the decision of the Oberkirchenrat, but it recognized that the incidents involved only a small minority of the 9,000 Prussian Protestant clergy. The evidence in 1932 produced a similar conclusion.[22]

Nevertheless, a small group of dedicated pastors could be used to great effect. The most famous was 'Pastor' Münchmeyer, whose parish had been the anti-Semitic seaside resort of Borkum until he was expelled from the Hanover-Lutheran Landeskirche for immorality; thereafter he became one of the most successful Nazi orators in Lower Saxony.[23] In most Landeskirchen there were some pastors who were willing to campaign for the NSDAP. Wurm wrote that in Württemberg the Nazis had derived 'great benefit' from this type of support before the Landeskirche prohibited it.[24] Even where a Landeskirche imposed specific restrictions on its clergy, these could be evaded by bringing a pastor from another Landeskirche.[25]

21. E.K.D., A 2/28: minutes of the meeting of the Kirchenausschuß, 24–5 Nov. 1932.
22. D.Z.A. Merseburg, Rep. 76, III Sekt. 1, Abt. XVII, 231/2: draft by a Kultusministerium official for a statement to the Landtag, 19 Feb. 1932; ibid. 231/1: Oberkirchenrat to Kultusministerium, 19 Nov. 1931; Kultusministerium to Minister President Braun and Oberkirchenrat, 5 Jan. 1932.
23. Noakes, *The Nazi Party in Lower Saxony 1921–1933*, pp. 122–3; and E.K.U., Gen. XII, 46/1. For Bavaria see Pridham, *Hitler's Rise to Power*, p. 171.
24. E.K.D., A 2/479: Wurm to Kapler, 19 Oct. 1932.
25. Ibid.: *Evangelischer Presseverband für Bayern* to the Landeskirche authorities in Munich, 24 Nov. 1932, reporting that the DNVP and NSDAP had made use of this loophole.

Perhaps even more important was the degree of tolerance shown to the 'national opposition' by the church leadership. Religious Socialists alleged that the Landeskirchen connived at the political activity of anti-Republican groups but were hostile to the Social Democrats.[26] Even if these accusations were not wholly true of the practice of the church leadership, they accurately reflected its sympathies. Despite their general warnings, the attitude of the church leadership was deliberately permissive. This must have helped the NSDAP which drew much of its support from the Protestant *Mittelstand* and had a considerable following among church members.[27]

Some church leaders, however, continued to have strong reservations about the 'national opposition'. At the Reich Presidential election in 1932, Kapler and a number of others signed public declarations in support of Hindenburg.[28] They followed the small group of German conservatives who remained loyal to Hindenburg against the candidates of the 'national opposition'—Hitler and Duesterberg—although this meant voting with the Republican parties, the Centre and SPD. This was an unprecedented step for Kapler, since he had previously avoided public political commitment. He may have been persuaded that it was necessary because of Hindenburg's reluctance to stand again, and the value that the Reich President was known to attach to the support of individual leaders from all walks of German public life—especially those from conservative institutions.[29]

26. *Kirchliches Jahrbuch,* 59. Jg. (1932), 41-51. Suck, 'Der religiöse Sozialismus in der Weimarer Republik', pp. 152, 201-2. See also the criticism of the church leadership by a left-wing Professor of theology, Günther Dehn, who had a reputation as a pacifist and was driven from Halle University by a campaign of obstruction and intimidation organized by Nazi students. Dehn argues that the church leadership should have supported him but it remained silent. G. Dehn, *Die alte Zeit, Die vorigen Jahre* (Munich, 1962), pp. 247-85; cf. *Kirchliches Jahrbuch,* 59. Jg. (1932), 77-113, and E. Bizer, 'Der Fall Dehn' in W. Schneemelcher, *Festschrift für Günther Dehn* (Neukirchen, 1957), pp. 239-61.

27. Christ, *Der politische Protestantismus,* pp. 30-52.

28. The others included the spiritual vice-president of the Oberkirchenrat, Burghart; another member of the Oberkirchenrat, Domprediger Richter; the Generalsuperintendenten of Berlin and east Prussia; two members of the Konsistorium of the province of Brandenburg; the Bishop and President of the Landeskirche of Hessen-Nassau; the Bishop of Mecklenburg-Strelitz; Prälat Schoell and the President of the Württemberg Synod from the Württemberg Landeskirche. E.K.D., A 2/485: Kapler to Ministerialrat Doehle, 5 Apr. 1932.

29. On the background to the election, see A. Dorpalen, *Hindenburg and the Weimar Republic* (Princeton, 1964), pp. 268-71.

Kapler's action provoked criticism from church circles close to the 'national opposition'. Bishop Rendtorff of Mecklenburg-Schwerin complained that the signatures of the Prussian leadership would be considered as representative of opinion in the church as a whole. This was particularly regrettable since 'the Prussian Oberkirchenrat has so far shown and demanded the utmost reserve towards the German freedom movement'.[30] This marked the beginning of a challenge to Kapler's moderate conservative policy.

It is difficult to estimate the extent of support for Hitler among church members.[31] About 75 per cent of his vote in the second ballot probably came from Protestants. This represented only 35 per cent of Protestants entitled to vote; however, on the assumption that most of the SPD Protestant vote (which went to Hindenburg) came from nominal Protestants and not from those who went to church, the proportion of active Protestants who voted for Hitler may have been as high as 60 per cent, with 25 per cent voting for Hindenburg and 15 per cent (about the national average) abstaining. This suggests that the views of Kapler and the other church leaders who rejected the 'national opposition' were shared by only a minority of church members.

Kapler's public support for Hindenburg was the last Vernunftrepublikaner gesture of the Protestant leadership. The appointment of von Papen as Reich Chancellor, on 30 May 1932, confronted it with a new situation—the end of Republican democracy. The church leaders had to decide which parts of the Reich constitution they wished to see preserved and how they should respond to a regime which proclaimed the ideal of a 'Christian state' but had an uncertain political future.

The church leadership did not protest against the overthrow of the Prussian government on 20 July. It had reason

30. E.K.D., A 2/485: Oberkirchenrat Schwerin to Kirchenausschuß, 4 Mar. 1932. Copies were sent to all Landeskirchen.

31. The following figures are a rough calculation based on a comparison of the Presidential election results of 10 Apr. 1932 with the Reichstag elections of 31 July 1932 and the figures for the denominational division of the Reich at the census of 1925 and the estimated number of Protestant communicants at the same time. A. Milatz, *Wähler und Wahlen in der Weimarer Republik* (Bonn, 1965), pp. 137–44. *Kirchliches Jahrbuch*, 54. Jg. (1927), 144–5, 223.

to be pleased when the new *Reichskommissar* (Reich Commissioner), Bracht, promptly issued a decree restoring to the church some influence over religious education in schools. The Berlin Oberkirchenrat had worked for this since 1927 and had been involved in a bitter dispute with the last Prussian Kultusminister, Grimme, because, under pressure from the school-teachers' association, he repeatedly deferred a decision.[32]

In October 1932 von Papen promised in a speech in Munich that constitutional reform would be introduced during the next session of the Reichstag.[33] Kapler asked Professor Heckel (an authority on church law) to consider the consequences for the church. He reported that they should be concerned not only with the religious clauses of the constitution but also with proposals for political reform.[34] He said that the church 'would have to express its interest in the maintenance of stable, constitutional, government and the prevention of one-sided, "authoritarian" party rule'. Reform of the constitution should be introduced legally and not by 'dictatorial' methods. This was a reference to right-wing authors who were ready to justify reform by unconstitutional means.[35]

The legal subcommittee which had considered Heckel's report instead recommended an attitude of reserve. It argued that there was very little prospect of reform by constitutional methods (because of the opposition of the Reichstag), and that the threat of unconstitutional action would not be affected by any comment of the Kirchenausschuß. The

32. Details of the dispute are to be found in: D.Z.A. Merseburg, Rep. 76 VII neu, Sekt. 1 B Gen., Pt. I, 2/26 and E.K.U, Gen. XIV, 32/2–3. There is also a collection of press cuttings about it in E.K.U., Gen. XIV, 32/Beiheft, Pressestimmen.

33. The speech was reported in the *Vossische Zeitung*, 12 Oct. 1932; (E.KD., A 2/484).

34. E.K.D., A 2/484: copy of Hosemann to Marahrens, 18 Nov. 1932, with a statement of the main points of Heckel's report.

35. The best-known statement of their case was Carl Schmitt, *Legalität und Legitimität* (Munich and Leipzig, 1932). In his regular 'Sunday mirror' article for the DNVP newspaper, *Der Tag*, on 2 Oct. 1932, Dibelius argued that it might be necessary in the national interest for the highest authority of the Reich to break with the letter of the constitution. Dibelius argued that Luther had been prepared to sanction action of this kind, and that although the church could take no part in it, it could give those responsible a good conscience.

committee also felt that 'the danger of slipping into political
territory . . . must be avoided at all costs'. The report
expressed satisfaction with assurances given by the government.[36] The Kirchenausschuß simply took note of the subcommittee's report and asked Kapler to see that the interests
of the church were protected.[37]

The attitude of the Kirchenausschuß shows that the
church leadership was not prepared publicly to defend
parliamentary government or even the rule of law. It did not
acknowledge that the guarantees of the Reich constitution,
which it wished to see preserved, themselves depended on the
continuance of constitutional government. There is also no
evidence that it felt under an obligation because of its
previous declarations of loyalty to the constitution. It
sheltered behind the argument that political issues lay outside
its competence and that to comment on them would be
futile. The political confusion and atmosphere of crisis in
1932 made it natural for the church leadership to avoid
public controversy. At the same time, its attitude clearly
demonstrates the limits of the commitment felt by the
church leadership to the Republican constitution.[38]

Some church leaders were tempted to go further and to
support von Papen's authoritarian and avowedly 'Christian'
programme. At the Kirchenausschuß meeting on 24-5
November 1932, President Wurm of Württemberg referred to
the work of several theologians who argued that the liberal
state was coming to an end[39] while the phrase 'Christian

36. The Reich Minister of the Interior, von Gayl, had promised Kapler that
the religious guarantees of the constitution would not be affected; E.K.D. A
2/484; von Gayl to Kapler, 19 Nov. 1932.

37. E.K.D., A 2/28: minutes of the Kirchenausschuß meeting of 24-5 Nov.
1932.

38. There is one example, however, on the other side. Bishop Bernewitz of
Brunswick wrote to Kapler on 27 Jan. 1933 demanding a clear stand against 'the
small clique of politicians with vested interests' who were trying to gain power at
the expense of the constitution and who might thereby prepare the way for a
soviet dictatorship. E.K.D., A 2/484.

39. Wurm referred to F. Gogarten, A. de Quervain, W. Stapel, P. Althaus, and
H. Gerber. For the titles of their books see the bibliography, and for a general
discussion of the type of political theory to which they subscribed see K.
Sontheimer, *Antidemokratisches Denken in der Weimarer Republik*, (Munich,
1962).

state' had been revived by von Papen.[40] Although this caused him some uneasiness and there was no question of forcing people to be Christian again,

a state which makes it possible to be a Christian because it at least puts it [Christianity] in its programme should be welcome to us and we should gladly allow 'politics based on faith'[41] to be commended ... These are signs of a way of thought, which until recently was not considered possible any longer, a seeking after lost values, which it would be unjust to call reaction or restoration, even though one will bear in mind that it can border on this.[42]

The Kirchenausschuß treated Wurm's views with caution probably mainly because they were afraid that the so-called 'new course' in German politics rested on unsure foundations and might end in disaster.[43] Von Papen's government had already fallen after widespread fear that his plans would lead to civil war. As a result the church leadership avoided public political commitment until the formation of Hitler's coalition government and the quick assertion of its authority seemed to offer a solution to the national crisis.

40. The Centre party newspaper, *Germania*, 7 July 1932, No. 187, commented on the use of this phrase by the government and pointed out that it was meant to be a critique of Brüning's so-called 'alliance with godlessness'. See also, F. von Papen, *Memoirs* (Engl. edn., London, 1952), p. 160.

41. A phrase used by von Papen to contrast his 'conservative politics based on faith' with Nazi 'faith based on politics'; reported in *Vossische Zeitung*, 12 Oct. 1932, No. 490.

42. E.K.D., A 2/479: Wurm to Kapler, 19 Oct. 1932, and the text of his speech to the Kirchenausschuß, which he sent to Kapler on 15 Jan. 1933.

43. E.K.D., A 2/28: minutes of the Kirchenausschuß meeting, 24–5 Nov. 1932.

7

THE 'NATIONAL REVOLUTION'

Hitler's assumption of power came as a relief to the Protestant leadership after the uncertainty of 1932. However, the intentions of the NSDAP remained unclear. The contradictions within the party over religious policy were not resolved by the conquest of power; indeed they became more alarming. As a result, church leaders remained uncertain in their attitude towards the new government. They were filled with a mixture of hope and fear—hope that a 'Christian state' with strong leadership would be restored, fear that the Nazi revolution would not respect the independence of the church.

Neither the Nazi party nor the Protestant leadership preserved a united front towards the other. Within the Nazi party, Frick and Buttmann at the Reich Ministry of the Interior showed restraint in church matters but at the Prussian Kultusministerium Rust and Jäger adopted a policy of aggressive interference.[1] Hitler allowed both policies. His own attitude is uncertain.[2] In a private conversation in April 1933 he explained that the churches had to be destroyed but that an indirect approach would be more effective than open conflict.[3] At the same time he appointed a personal representative for the affairs of the Protestant church, Pfarrer Ludwig Müller, and encouraged Müller's attempt to take over the leadership of the church.

1. W. Conrad, *Der Kampf um die Kanzeln* (Berlin, 1957), pp. 12–31. Conrad was a senior official in the Reich Ministry of the Interior who had had responsibility for church affairs since 1922. In the Prussian Kultusministerium the chief official for Protestant affairs, Ministerialdirektor Trendelenburg, tried to restrain his Minister until he was dismissed at the end of June and replaced by Jäger. D.Z.A. Potsdam, Reich Min. f. d. kirchl. Angelegenheiten, 23463: memorandum by Trendelenburg, 22 June 1933; Conrad, op. cit., pp. 13–4.

2. See below, pp. 148–50.

3. H. Rauschning, *Hitler Speaks* (Engl. edn., London, 1939), pp. 55–65.

The Kirchenausschuß was split by the multiple challenge of Nazism. The majority of church leaders followed Kapler in a policy of co-operation with the government in its 'national' aims combined with defence of the church as an institution. A minority, however, felt that Kapler's concept of church independence was out of date and that the church should accept a closer relationship with the new state. The position was complicated by the activity of the 'German Christians' who considered themselves the representatives of the NSDAP within the church and who were themselves divided between moderate and extreme groups.

The tensions between church and state and within the church led to an open conflict in May–June 1933 over the appointment of the first Reich bishop, a post created by the church to give the central organization of German Protestantism greater authority. The conflict led to Kapler's resignation and ended in defeat for his policy. This defeat marks the beginning of the *Kirchenkampf*[4] and the end of an era in the history of the church leadership.

i. The New State

The Kirchenausschuß met on 2–3 March 1933 and approved a circular warning the Landeskirchen to serve the whole nation regardless of political change.[5] It also welcomed the government's intention to reform national *mores* and promised to co-operate; in return, it would ask the government to respect its interests. Several members of the Kirchenausschuß thought that the circular was lukewarm; the secular vice-president of the Oberkirchenrat, Hundt, declared himself a National Socialist and asked whether it would not be right for the church to express its 'gratitude, joy, and trust' in the change which had been 'given by God'.

Despite its undertaking to serve the whole nation, the Protestant leadership did not oppose any aspect of the political revolution carried out by the Nazis between March

---

4. Literally 'church struggle'—a term commonly used to describe the conflicts within the Protestant church and between the church and the state during the Third Reich.

5. E.K.D., A 2/28: minutes of the meeting.

and July 1933—except where the independence of the church was directly threatened. They ignored the destruction of trade unions and political parties and the purge of Catholic, Socialist, and Jewish civil servants. They did not try even to protect Protestant professors of theology with liberal or Socialist sympathies.[6] They also turned a blind eye to the violence which accompanied the revolution.[7] Even where Protestant leaders were unhappy about government reforms— for instance they were concerned that the Enabling Law could be used to nullify the religious guarantees of the Weimar constitution—they felt too weak to risk intervention.[8] They also accepted the destruction of *Länder* autonomy without protest.[9]

In a sermon at the special ceremony held in Potsdam on 21 March to mark the opening of the new Reichstag, Generalsuperintendent Dibelius defended the right of the government to take harsh measures to restore order but added a warning against arbitrary rule. He said,

If the state uses its office against those who undermine the foundations of public order, against those, especially, who seek with gibes and coarse language to destroy marriage, to make a laughing stock of religion, to besmirch the idea of laying down one's life for the fatherland—then let it use its office in God's name! But we would not be worthy to be called an Evangelical church did we not add with the same candor as Luther that public office must not be confused with private arbitrary power.[10]

6. Oberkirchenrat officials simply reported to the Generalsuperintendenten that they had heard from official sources that several professors would be dismissed on political grounds; E.K.U., Gen. III, 17/3: minutes of a meeting of the Oberkirchenrat and the Generalsuperintendenten, 11 Apr. 1933.

7. One case of a retired pastor who belonged to the Religious Socialists, being assaulted by the S.A. was reported to Kapler personally; he informed the police but he did not raise the matter in public; E.K.U., Gen. VI, 27/1: note of Kapler, 13 May 1933.

8. E.K.D., A 2/426: Hosemann (director of the Kirchenbundesamt) to Seetzen, 22 Mar. 1933, arguing that it would certainly be futile for the church to intervene and that it might jeopardize future co-operation with the government; Seetzen (acting for Kapler) agreed on 23 Mar. Kapler did write to Hindenburg about the rumours of a Reich concordat in connection with the Enabling Law. He asked Hindenburg to see that parity was observed; E.K.D., B 3/240: Kapler to Hindenburg, 23 Mar. 1933.

9. The Kirchenbundesamt just asked for information about the future organization of the German states to help the church in remodelling its own constitution; E.K.D., A 2/484: Hosemann to Pfundtner (Reich Ministry of the Interior), 12 Apr. 1933.

10. Dibelius, *In the Service of the Lord*, p. 138.

In confidential circulars to his clergy Dibelius warned that the church should preserve its neutrality and not become a political appendage of the new government.[11]

The Protestant leadership was encouraged by Hitler's speech of 23 March explaining the government programme to the new Reichstag. In order to win the votes of the Centre party for the Enabling Law Hitler gave certain assurances. He said,

The national government sees in both Christian denominations most important factors for the preservation of our *Volkstum* (nationality). It [the government] will respect the treaties concluded between them and the *Länder*. Their rights will not be infringed. It expects and hopes, however, that the work for the national and moral renewal of our people, which the government has made its task, will in turn be treated with equal esteem . . . The national government will give the Christian denominations the influence due to them in schools and education . . .[12]

However, the value of this declaration was almost at once thrown into doubt by the first Reich conference of the German Christians which met in Berlin from 3-5 April.[13] In a speech of welcome as leader of the NSDAP in the Prussian Landtag, Kube[14] declared that the NSDAP would ruthlessly use church subsidies and the Prussian church treaty to bring the revolution to the church. Kapler at once protested to the Prussian Kultusministerium declaring that Kube's remarks were irreconcilable with Hitler's declaration of 23 March—the first protest of the Protestant leadership against the Third Reich.[15]

In a report to the Kirchensenat of the Old Prussian Union, on 21 April, Kapler explained his view of the situation.[16] He

---

11. *Der Märkische Adler*, 2 Apr. 1933, No. 14 printed Dibelius's confidential circular of 8 Mar. 1933; cf. his further circular of 2 Apr.: E.K.U., Gen. II, 42/1. Dibelius was attacked by Kube and the German Christians for his reserve: ibid., Kapler to Kultusministerium, 5 Apr. 1933, and 'Fort mit Dibelius!' by Alfred Bierschwale, a German Christian leader, in *Neue Zeit*, 23 Apr. 1933, No. 113.

12. *Sitzungsberichte*, Reichstag, 23 Mar. 1933, in E.K.U., Gen. VI, 27/1.

13. J. Hossenfelder, *Volk und Kirche* (Berlin, 1933) contains the official record of the conference.

14. With the change of government he had been given the administrative position of *Oberpräsident* of Berlin and Brandenberg.

15. *Berliner Lokal-Anzeiger*, 4 Apr. 1933, No. 159; E.K.U., Gen. II, 42/1: Oberkirchenrat to Kultusministerium (represented by the Reich Kommissar, von Papen), 5 Apr. 1933.

16. E.K.U., Verhandlungen des Kirchensenats, 21 Apr. 1933.

applauded some aspects of the 'National Revolution'—the revival of national consciousness, the rejection of material-ism, and the emergence of a state leadership of great will-power which aimed to create a united nation rooted in Christianity. He described Hitler's guarantee of the freedom of the churches in return for their support of the government as the central fact. On the other hand, he was concerned about the independence of the church and its freedom to preach the Gospel because of 'the desire to draw all spheres of life including culture and the church into the power of a totalitarian state . . .'. The Berlin Oberkirchenrat had already issued an address, read from the pulpits on Easter Day 16 April, which illustrates Kapler's policy.[17] The address said that God had spoken to the nation by a great change and the church was ready to co-operate joyfully in the national revival. However, to do this the church needed to be free and it trusted the solemn guarantee of this freedom given by the government.

The Protestant church participated in the national celebra-tions to mark Hitler's birthday on 20 April. Prayers were offered for the Chancellor in the difficult work of restoring the Fatherland.[18] Such a gesture would have been un-thinkable during the Weimar Republic.[19] The churches flew the church flag and other church buildings were allowed to fly state flags which included the swastika.[20] Kapler sent Hitler a personal letter.[21]

The most extreme case of co-operation by the church in government policy was its decision to defend the measures

17. E.K.U., Gen. II, 42/1: Oberkirchenrat to Superintendenten, 11 Apr. 1933.

18. E.K.D., A 2/426: Kapler to the Landeskirchen, 10 Apr. 1933.

19. In 1932 the spiritual vice-president of the Oberkirchenrat, Burghart, had even refused a request that the church should pray for the Reich President H. Michael and D. Lohmann, *Der Reichspräsident ist Obrigkeit* (Hamburg, 1932), pp. 21-5.

20. E.K.D., A 2/426: Kapler to the Landeskirchen, 10 Apr. 1933; Ober-kirchenrat to the Old Prussian Konsistorien, 12 Apr. 1933; Kirchenausschuß to Landeskirchenamt, Darmstadt, 18 Apr. 1933. The swastika had been declared a Reich flag by decree of the Reichspräsident, 12 Mar. 1933. On 13 Apr. the Kirchenausschuß warned the Landeskirchen in a second decree only to fly flags if state buildings did; ibid.

21. Ibid.

taken against Jews.[22] In March and April 1933 the first
dismissals of Jewish civil servants, lawyers, and university
teachers took place and difficulties were placed in the way of
Jewish doctors. On 1 April an official boycott was organized
against all Jewish businesses throughout the Reich.[23] Individual Jewish Christians and representatives of the Jewish
community appealed to the church leadership for help. The
measures provoked hostile comment abroad and foreign
church leaders considered making a public protest.

A few German Protestants, including von Pechmann from
within the church leadership, demanded a church protest.
They were overruled by the majority however, and instead
Kapler defended government measures and used his influence
to prevent church circles abroad from condemning them. He
subscribed to the official view that foreign criticism was
'atrocity propaganda'[24] (a phrase which carried overtones
from the First World War). Kapler no doubt feared that
criticism by foreign churches would adversely affect Nazi
policy towards the church. Kapler tried to show the government that the church could be useful in defending official
policy, provided it was independent of the state and therefore commanded the confidence of foreign churches. At the
same time Kapler admitted to severe pangs of conscience and
asked government officials to show humanity and moderation.

Protestant leaders' defence of the government seems at
first to have been made on their own initiative. On 26 March
Generalsuperintendent Dibelius sharply criticized an
American bishop for joining American Jews to protest against
German actions and later he defended the government in a
broadcast to the United States.[25] On 27 March Kapler sent a
telegram to the President of the ecumenical council in New
York, asking him to prevent a public condemnation of

22. See A. Boyens, Kirchenkampf und Ökumene 1933–39 (Munich, 1969),
pp. 37–59.
23. K. D. Bracher, W. Sauer, G. Schulz, Die nationalsozialistische Machtergreifung (Cologne and Opladen, 1962), pp. 172–5, 277–81.
24. E.K.D., C 3/207: Kapler to the Landeskirchen, 1 Apr. 1933.
25. Der Tag, 26 Mar. 1933, No. 27. The text of the broadcast is printed in J.
S. Conway, The Nazi Persecution of the Churches 1933–45 (London, 1968), pp.
342–4.

Germany.[26] The government was informed of the action and Kapler received a message of thanks from Hitler.[27] To a request from the Reich representatives of the German Jews for 'a word soon' Kapler replied on 1 April simply that he was following developments with the greatest vigilance and that he hoped the boycott would end that day.[28]

Kapler's policy did not go unchallenged. Von Pechmann raised the matter at the next meeting of the Kirchen-ausschuß, held on 25–6 April.[29] He described the appeals from Jewish Christians he had received and the spiritual turmoil they revealed. He felt sure that the church owed its Jewish members protection; the Kirchenausschuß could not disperse without having said a word on their behalf. No other member of the Kirchenausschuß, however, supported a public statement. Several approved the reduction of the Jewish share in particular professions. President Kapler was one of these, though he added that he had had a heavy conscience about many of the measures taken and that he had raised the matter in his conversations with state representatives. During an interview with Hitler on the previous day he had asked that wherever possible harsh measures should not be enforced, though he had not felt it advisable to mention the Jewish question specifically at their first encounter. He had also tried to help a number of individual Jewish Christians—in some cases he had had no success, in some the outcome was still uncertain.[30] Despite Kapler's reservations the church continued to defend the government. On 7 June the Kirchenbundesamt sent a long memorandum

26. E.K.D., D 1/29 (formerly C. 1/22): copy of the telegram.

27. Ibid.: Reichskanzlei to Kapler, 8 Apr. 1933.

28. E.K.U., Gen. XII, 46/2: telegram to the Prussian Oberkirchenrat from the *Reichsvertretung der deutschen Juden* and Kapler's reply, 1 Apr. 1933.

29. E.K.D., A 2/28: minutes of the meeting. The text is published in Boyens, *Kirchenkampf und Ökumene*, pp. 295–9.

30. Requests for help from Jewish Christians appear in E.K.D., C 3/170 and E.K.U., Gen. XII, 46/2. The files do not contain details of how Kapler tried to help. Some petitioners seem to have received no reply; others were told that it was not possible to get exceptions to the law. The Vatican, in contrast, did intervene for Jewish Catholic civil servants. See G. Kent, 'Pope Pius XII and Germany' in *Am. Hist. Rev.*, 70 (1964), 61. The reaction of the German Roman Catholic episcopate, however, was very similar to that of the Protestant leadership. See Volk, *Der bayerische Episkopat*, pp. 76–82.

to foreign church leaders.[31] It argued that the Nazi revolution had saved Germany from Communism and it defended the government's anti-Semitic measures and its own silence. The memorandum cannot be taken without qualification as a statement of the view of the church leadership.[32] It served a tactical purpose—to underline to the government the importance of preserving church independence, which was gravely threatened by June 1933.[33] On the other hand, its defence of the government was in line with the views of the church leadership and its effect was to aid government propaganda.

ii. Revolution in the Church

By June 1933 the Protestant church was preoccupied with its own problems. The conflict between church and state and between the majority of the church leadership and the German Christians developed in three phases. Since the story is complicated, it may be helpful to have a brief outline in advance. The first phase lasted from the Reich Conference of the German Christians at the beginning of April until 25 April. During it, Kapler assumed special powers to carry out a reform of the central church constitution. This reform was undertaken partly in response to German Christian demands, but Kapler intended that it should be carried out by the church leadership. The threats made against the church leadership at the German Christian conference caused anxiety that the state would interfere. This anxiety was intensified when on 22 April the Minister President of Mecklenburg appointed a *Staatskommissar* (State Commissioner) over the Landeskirche of Mecklenburg-Schwerin. However, the incident proved to be the result of isolated local action taken without the support of the Reich authorities. The Staats-

31. The text is published in Boyens, *Kirchenkampf und Ökumene,* pp. 298–308.

32. It was in fact a private document which was simply used by the Kirchenbundesamt to give foreign church leaders a picture of the situation. E.K.D., D.1. 29: letter from Hosemann, 7 June 1933.

33. Copies were sent to the appropriate Ministries with a suitable accompanying letter. E.K.D., D.1. 30: President of the Kirchenausschuß to Auswärtiges Amt, Reichsministerium für Volksaufklärung und Propaganda and Reichsministerium des Innern, 21 June 1933.

kommissar was withdrawn after a few days and it looked as
though the affair had been a false alarm.

This impression was strengthened in the second phase
which lasted from the end of April until 23 May. It was
marked by greater confidence between the church leadership,
the state, and the German Christians. This was shown in the
co-operation of the church leadership with Ludwig Müller in
preparing the new church constitution. Müller had become
Hitler's personal representative for Protestant affairs; he was
also the chief representative of a 'moderate' group of German
Christians. During this second phase it seemed possible, even
likely, that the new church constitution would come about
by agreement between the church leadership and the German
Christian 'moderates' and that a conflict with the state would
be avoided.

This development was reversed during the third phase,
which lasted from 23 May until the end of June. A bitter
conflict arose over the appointment of the first Reich bishop,
the highest authority under the new constitution. The
majority of church leaders supported Friedrich von Bodelschwingh, the director of the Inner Mission's work for
epileptics at Bethel. The German Christians and a minority of
church leaders supported Müller. Ostensibly Hitler did not
interfere, though Müller enjoyed the advantage of his special
relationship with the Führer. The Prussian Kultusministerium, however, decided that the church leadership
was unreliable and in need of reform; at the end of June
Staatskommissare were appointed over all Prussian Landeskirchen. The conflict resulted in the disintegration of the
church leadership and victory for Müller.

Several reasons prompted Kapler to undertake a major
reform of the church organization. The weakening of the
authority of the *Länder* by the new government meant that
power was concentrated in the Reich. This made it desirable
that the church should have a central organization which
could speak and act for the Landeskirchen. The Kirchenbund
provided a basis but its authority was limited by the independence of the individual Landeskirchen. An immediate incentive was provided by the rumours of a Reich Concordat with

the Catholic church; it was felt that the Protestant church should have a central organization of sufficient standing to secure a parallel Reich treaty for the Protestant church.[34]

The conference of German Christians held between 3 and 5 April in Berlin gave new impetus to reform.[35] They repeated the demand for a Reichskirche and their threat to use the power of the NSDAP to force revolution on the church made it urgent. Hossenfelder declared that a Staatskommissar for the church was possible and the conference resolved that only church officials who were unconditional supporters of the national revolution need be obeyed.[36]

On 11 April Kapler explained the position to the General-superintendenten of the Old Prussian Union.[37] He referred to the danger of state interference exemplified by the threats of the German Christians. On the other hand, he had been reassured by conversations with government officials including Frick, the Reich Minister of the Interior. In addition, the German Christian leaders had since adopted a quieter tone: they had explained to Kapler that talk of revolution against the church leadership had been metaphorical—what they had meant was 'a spiritual encounter'. Kapler had also met Ludwig Müller, who told him that Hitler found the division of the Protestant church into twenty-eight Landeskirchen 'incomprehensible' and that he wanted a 'viable Protestant bloc' as a counterweight to the Catholics.[38]

The position in mid-April was that the church leadership considered a reform of the Kirchenbund necessary. Church leaders knew that the German Christians and Hitler wanted to see a single Reichskirche established and they feared that the state might be prepared to interfere to secure this. On the other hand, it did not seem that the threats made at the German Christian conference would be carried out at once. The church leadership therefore had the chance to introduce

34. E.K.D., C 3/207: Kapler to the leaders of the Landeskirchen, 1 Apr. 1933.
35. See above, p. 113.
36. *Tägliche Rundschau,* 5 Apr. 1933, No. 81.
37. E.K.U., Gen. III, 17/3: minutes of the meeting.
38. Müller was not formally appointed Hitler's representative for Protestant affairs until two weeks later.

reform under its own direction. This is what Kapler set out to
do. He may have had the parallel of 1918–19 in mind when
the Oberkirchenrat had taken a similar initiative and preserved the independence of the church.

There was one further factor in Kapler's calculations. The
desire for a major reform of the church constitution was not
confined to the German Christians or to church leaders
concerned about the possibility of a Reich Concordat. There
was a widespread desire among Protestants for a more united
church grouped around the different creeds. There was also
general hostility to 'parliamentism' in the church. It was felt
that the constitutions drawn up under the Republic had
made concessions to democracy which were now outdated.
In addition, the old parties seemed increasingly irrelevant;
they had grown up as a result of nineteenth-century theological disputes which now seemed less important than questions about the place of nation and race in theology. There
was also criticism of the leadership—that it was too old and
that lawyers had too much power. The time had come to
choose new men from the generation that had fought at the
front in the First World War and therefore belonged to the
modern world. There was enthusiasm for the general introduction of bishops, except in the Calvinist provinces. The
argument used was that the church needed spiritual leaders in
authority and not mere administrators, but it is difficult to
believe that the demand for bishops was not also inspired by
the *Führerprinzip* (the Führer model) prevalent in politics. In
the spring of 1933 there was a general feeling, especially
among young theologians, that a new era had dawned which
offered great opportunities after a long period of retreat.[39] If
the church were to reap the harvest it needed to be open to
new ideas and new men.

Many of those who wanted reform, including, for instance,
the eminent Lutheran theologian Emanuel Hirsch, joined the

39. The change in the religious climate is dramatically illustrated by statistics
for Berlin. In 1932 the Protestant Landeskirche suffered a net loss of nearly
45,000 members; in 1933 it had a net gain of over 52,000. Part of the 1933 figure
is due to Jewish 'converts' but there is no doubt that religion had again become
fashionable. F. Zipfel, *Kirchenkampf in Deutschland 1933–1945* (Berlin, 1965),
pp. 17–24.

German Christians.[40] Church members who feared that the German Christians would bring political pressure to bear, however, founded the rival Young Reformer movement to support the church leadership's plans for reorganization independent of the state.[41]

On 15 April the leader of the German Christians, Hossenfelder, wrote to Kapler asking him to summon German Christians to all representative bodies within the church of the Old Prussian Union.[42] On 19 April the *Tägliche Rundschau* reported a declaration by Bierschwale, a radical German Christian leader, in which he dismissed the idea that the old church leadership could introduce reform without the German Christians and demanded immediate elections.[43] On 21 April the *Tägliche Rundschau* reported under the headline '*Kirchenkommissar* for Prussia?' that Hossenfelder had been given a post in the Prussian Kultusministerium.[44] The paper speculated that this meant retrospective approval for the German Christian conference at the beginning of the month. It also suggested that Hossenfelder would advise the Ministry about the use of its powers over church appointments under the 1931 treaty. On 22 April the *Tägliche Rundschau* reported a rumour that if the Kirchensenat did not agree to the German Christian demand for representation 'the revolution of church people would take its course'.[45] On the same day Kapler heard that a Staatskommissar had been appointed over the Landeskirche in Mecklenburg.

At this point Kapler decided that it was necessary for him to take immediate action to keep the initiative.[46] On 23

40. Emanuel Hirsch, professor at Göttingen University 1921–45; *RGG* iii. 363–4. Hirsch's right-wing political views are clearly stated in his book, *Deutschlands Schicksal* (3rd edn., Göttingen, 1925). In May 1933 he joined the 'moderate' German Christians and became one of Müller's main advisers. See, E. Hirsch, *Das kirchliche Wollen der Deutschen Christen* (Berlin, 1933).

41. See *Denkschrift der Jungreformatorischen Bewegung über ihre Stellung zur Reichsbischofsfrage* (Göttingen, 1933); K. D. Schmidt, *Die Bekenntnisse des Jahres 1933* (2nd edn., Göttingen, 1937), pp. 145–6. See also, P. Neumann, *Die Jungreformatorische Bewegung* (Göttingen, 1971).

42. E.K.U., Gen. II, 42/1: Hossenfelder to Kapler, 15 Apr. 1933.

43. *Tägliche Rundschau*, 19 Apr. 1933, No. 91.

44. Ibid. 21 Apr., No. 93.

45. Ibid. 22 Apr., No. 94.

46. E.K.D., A 2/28: minutes of the Kirchenausschuß meeting, 25–6 April 1933; report of Kapler.

April he issued a notice to the press which said that reform of the church constitution with the goal of a federal German Protestant church was imperative and that Kapler, as President of the Kirchenausschuß, had summoned to help him Bishop Marahrens of Hanover to represent Lutheran interests and Pastor Hesse from Elberfeld to represent the Reformed (Calvinist) churches.[47]

Kapler's fear of losing control of events seems to have been exaggerated. The German Christians continued to demand and threaten until 25 April.[48] On the other hand the German Christians and the Reich authorities, including Hitler, disowned the Mecklenburg incident and the Staatskommissar with withdrawn when the church protested against it.[49] On 25 April, in a meeting which had been arranged before the Mecklenburg incident, Kapler warned Hitler against interfering in church affairs and Hitler reaffirmed the promises he had given to the churches in his Reichstag speech of 23 March.[50]

47. E.K.D., A 2/28; and *Vossische Zeitung*, 24 Apr. 1933, No. 194; *Tägliche Rundschau*, 25 Apr., No. 96. For Marahrens see E. Klügel, *Die lutherische Landeskirche Hannovers und ihr Bischof 1933–1945*, 2 vols. (Berlin and Hamburg, 1964–5). Pastor Hesse was a Calvinist theologian, who had been chosen by a meeting of the *Reformierter Bund* to represent their interests in the negotiations for a new church constitution; *Bielefelder Archiv des Kirchenkampfes im Dritten Reich*, Sammlung Hesse, 1. 21: Hesse to his family, 8 June 1933. Hesse later took a leading part in the *Bekennende Kirche*; he was interned in Dachau in 1943 and his son was executed there. *RGG* iii. 290.

48. In a statement printed in the *Tägliche Rundschau* on 23 Apr. Hossenfelder declared that the enemies of the Third Reich were sheltering behind the church and that any reform of the church in which the German Christians did not participate would be a dead letter. On 25 Apr. the *Tägliche Rundschau* reported that the German Christians were planning a march in Berlin with the slogan 'Peasants and workers conquer the churches'.

49. Bundesarchiv, Reichskanzlei, R 43 11/161, contains the protests, and notes by Lammers (22 and 25 Apr.) giving Hitler's instructions. Frick arranged a face-saving compromise whereby the Staatskommissar was withdrawn but the church admitted defects in its system of church dues; ibid.: letter from Frick, 29 Apr. The local bishop, Rendtorff, gave a full report on the incident to the Kirchenausschuß on 25 Apr. See, further, K. D. Schmidt, 'Eine folgenreiche Episode' in *Evangelische Theologie*, Jg. 22 (1967), 379–92.

50. See above, p. 113. The minutes of the Kirchenausschuß meeting of 25–6 Apr. 1933 do not contain details of Kapler's report on the interview. Notes made on the report during the Kirchenausschuß meeting by von Pechmann, however, survive in Lk. A., Nuremberg, Pechmann XXIII, 101/34. The *Deutsche Allgemeine Zeitung* (28 Apr., No. 197) also contains a report based on information from the Kirchenausschuß meeting. These both confirm the accuracy of the account given to me by Kapler's son, Pfarrer Kapler, from memory of what his father told him at the time (Interview, 13 Oct. 1965).

After the meeting, Hitler appointed Müller as his representative for Protestant affairs with special responsibility to advance the preparation of a Reichskirche.[51] Ludwig Müller, who was forty-nine when he became Hitler's representative, had served as a naval chaplain during and after the war.[52] In 1926 he became *Wehrkreispfarrer* (military chaplain) to the east Prussian army corps based on Königsberg. His office prevented him becoming a member of the Nazi party but his public statements brought him to the attention of the Prussian Ministry of the Interior which attempted to restrict his political activity without much effect.[53] In 1933 Müller claimed to have known Hitler for about six years; Hitler had stayed with the Müllers when visiting the army corps at Königsberg. Müller may have been influential in helping to convert his commanding officer, General von Blomberg, to Nazism and thus providing Hitler with a supporter in the army command of considerable importance in the conquest of power.[54] It was rumoured in Protestant circles that Müller was very close to Hitler in spiritual matters.[55] He was also considered to be a moderate: in 1932 he became leader of the east Prussian German Christians, who programme was significantly more conservative than Hossenfelder's programme for the Reich.[56] When Hitler appointed Müller as his representative in April 1933 church leaders expressed their

51. Bundesarchiv, Reichskanzlei, R 43 11/161: copy of Hitler's appointment of Müller, 25 Apr. 1933.

52. For biographical details of Müller see W. Ullmenried, *Die Reihe der deutschen Führer*, Heft 7 (Berlin, 1933). Also *Evangelischer Pressedienst*, 3 May 1933, No. 18. He died in Berlin in 1945.

53. Severing (Minister of the Interior) passed on material about Müller's activities from the Oberpräsident, Königsberg, to *Reichswehrminister* (Minister of War) Groener. In one reply Groener said investigation had shown that the allegations against Müller were false and that Müller had only opposed un-Christian and un-German activity (*Wesen*), especially *Kulturbolschewismus*. D.Z.A. Merseburg, Rep. 76, III Sekt. 1, Abt. XVII, 231/1: Severing to Prussian Kultusminister, 6 Aug. 1931; Groener to Severing, 15 Dec. 1930.

54. J. W. Wheeler-Bennett, *The Nemesis of Power* (2nd edn., London, 1967), p. 296; Bracher, *Die Auflösung der Weimarer Republik*, p. 712. He certainly acted as an intermediary between Hitler and Blomberg's Chief of Staff, Colonel von Reichenau. See Hitler to Reichenau, 4 Dec. 1932; the letter is printed in *Vierteljahrshefte für Zeitgeschichte*, 7. Jg. (1959), 429–37.

55. For example Pastor Hesse wrote to his family on 8 June 1933, 'Müller is Hitler's spiritual adviser (*Seelsorger*) and would appear to have been instrumental that Hitler is now reading Luther and drawing away from Rome'; Bielefelder Archiv, Sammlung Hesse, 1, 21.

56. See above, p. 94.

approval.[57] Müller at once declared his readiness to co-operate with them and explained that Hitler expected him to see that the battle for the future of the Protestant church was not fought like the political battle. 'Adolf Hitler does not want to start a religious war.'[58]

The Kirchenausschuß approved the goal of creating a Protestant church of the German nation in its meeting on 25-6 April 1933 and gave Kapler very wide powers.[59] During the next four weeks it seemed that a settlement would be reached by agreement. The committee of Kapler, Marahrens, and Hesse appointed to draw up the constitution of the new federal church declared their support for the new state,

A mighty national movement has gripped and raised up our German people. A comprehensive reshaping of the Reich is taking place in the awakened German nation. To this turn of history we say a thankful Yes. God has given it to us. To Him be the glory![60]

They were joined by Müller (in his capacity as Hitler's representative) and both sides soon reported satisfactory progress.[61]

If a settlement was to be reached, it was essential that Müller should win over or defeat Hossenfelder and the radical German Christians. On 6 May Hossenfelder gave Kapler a list of German Christian demands which showed little inclination to compromise.[62] It said that the German Christians did not want a state church but equally that they did not want a church which was a state within the state, that the new Protestant Reichskirche should be the church of Christian

57. An official information sheet of the Oberkirchenrat said that Hitler had appointed Müller in a form which deliberately avoided giving the impression of a Staatskommissar; a way had thus been found 'for confident and orderly co-operation between the church leadership and the Reich'; *Kirchliche Wegweisung*, No. I (Berlin, 15 May 1933), p. 7. According to one eyewitness, however, Kapler was initially shocked by the news of Müller's appointment since Hitler had not informed him of it at their meeting on the same day. G. Kretschmar, C. Nicolaisen, *Dokumente zur Kirchenpolitik des Dritten Reiches*, Bd. 1, *Das Jahr 1933* (Munich, 1971), p. 39.

58. *Kirchliche Wegweisung*, pp. 5-6; *Tägliche Rundschau*, 10 May 1933, No. 106.

59. E.K.D., A 2/28: minutes of the meeting.

60. *Kirchliche Wegweisung*, pp. 4-5.

61. Müller in *Tägliche Rundschau*, 10 May 1933, No. 106; Kapler to the Landeskirchen, 8 and 10 May in E.K.D., A 4/2.

62. *Kirchliche Wegweisung*, pp. 11-12.

Aryans and that the Reich bishop should be a German Christian. The whole Protestant population, excluding non-Aryans, should decide on the new constitution and the first bishop in elections to be held on 31 October. To prepare and supervise the elections Hossenfelder named a committee on which the German Christians would have had decisive influence. In contrast, the east Prussian German Christians (led by Müller) supported a joint declaration of east Prussian clergymen expressing their confidence in Kapler's committee.[63] In a press interview, reported on 10 May, Müller repeated that his relations with Kapler's committee were developing 'beyond all expectation . . . extraordinarily well, just as the Reich Chancellor had desired'.[64] A few days earlier the Prussian Kultusminister Rust, who had been suspected of favouring Hossenfelder, had publicly denied that he had any connection with the German Christians; Rust said that the dispute between the German Christians and the church leadership was an internal church matter in which he would not interfere.[65]

Hossenfelder appeared to accept Müller's policy and, in effect, to withdraw the demands of 6 May. On 13 May it was reported that Hossenfelder had instructed the German Christians to show full confidence in Kapler's committee.[66] At the same time Hossenfelder appointed Weichert, the most moderate of the German Christian leaders, to be their contact with Kapler's committee.[67]

Müller now attempted to consolidate his authority over the German Christian movement by imposing a new programme on it and formally taking over the leadership. With the help of Professors Fezer[68] and Hirsch, he drafted a programme

63. *Preußische Zeitung*, 4 May 1933, No. 103; *Mitteilungen der Glaubens-gemeinschaft Deutscher Christen, Königsberg*, 7 May 1933, in E.K.D., A 4/4.

64. *Tägliche Rundschau*, 10 May 1933, No. 106.

65. *Kreuzzeitung*, 7 May 1933, No. 125.

66. *Der Reichsbote*, 13 May 1933, No. 111.

67. K. Meier, *Die Deutschen Christen* (Göttingen, 1964), p. 21.

68. Fezer was a professor at Tübingen University and had been elected by the combined Protestant theological faculties of Germany as their representative for the work of church reform. Like Hirsch he believed that intellectuals should not stand aloof from the National Socialist movement. It was of considerable importance to Müller that he could count two respected theologians among his personal circle of advisers. E.K.D., A 4/1: Chairman of the *Fakultätentag* to Kapler, 30 Apr. 1933, and information from Pfarrer Fischer (Reutlingen) (Interview, 12 Dec. 1967).

which was published on 17 May. The programme was moderate, similar in tone to the east Prussian demands, though it made some concession to the racialism of the radical German Christians in its comments on missionary work overseas.[69] Müller explained to Kapler's committee that he attached great importance to the new programme which, he implied, would check the ambitions of the radical German Christians.[70]

On 17 May the *Tägliche Rundschau* gave details of the new moderate programme and reported that Müller had taken over the movement under the headline 'The march of the German Christians ended'.[71] In fact Hossenfelder did not surrender as easily as was, at first, believed. The exact sequence of events is uncertain. It seems that Müller submitted the new programme to Hitler who approved it and authorized him to take over the leadership of the German Christians.[72] According to Hossenfelder, Müller sent a member of his staff to tell the German Christian leaders that Hitler wanted him to have the leadership of the church and that therefore he wanted to take over the German Christians. Hossenfelder records that he and Weichert replied in writing that they were unable to give Müller the leadership.[73] In the week following the *Tägliche Rundschau* report, on the evening of 23–4 May, a meeting of German Christian leaders agreed to give Müller a special position as 'Protector' (*Schirmherr*) but it was unclear what this meant and whether the old programme had been replaced by Müller's new one.

The final meetings between Kapler's committee and Müller took place in a former monastery near Hanover, called Loccum, between 17 and 20 May. These meetings produced an outline of the future church constitution, known as the Loccum manifesto, and a private agreement on procedure for

69. H. Hermelink, *Kirche im Kampf* (Tübingen, 1950), pp. 37–9.

70. Lk. A. Hanover, Nachlaß Marahrens, *Die werdende evangelische Kirche deutscher Nation, Verhandlungen der 3 Bevollmächtigten*: minutes of the meeting of 17 May.

71. *Tägliche Rundschau*, 17 May 1933, No. 112.

72. This is according to Fezer's account given in a lecture in Tübingen on 7 June 1933; Lk. A. Stuttgart, Nachlaß Wurm, D 1/42: transcript of the lecture.

73. Hossenfelder to Dibelius, 7 July 1945. (Pastor Hossenfelder kindly gave me a copy of this important document which gives his account of events.)

introducing it.[74] A German Protestant church[75] was proposed with a Lutheran Reich bishop at its head supported by a 'spiritual ministry' to represent the non-Lutheran creeds. There was also to be a German National Synod which would take part in legislation and the appointment of church leaders and which was to consist of prominent church people, some elected and some appointed. The procedure suggested for introducing the constitution was first to hear the wishes of different church movements (in practice, primarily the German Christians and the Young Reformers); then there was to be a meeting of the representatives of the Landeskirchen who would authorize Kapler's committee to put the constitution into force and would also agree confidentially on the person to be bishop. Subsequently Kapler's committee would be received by Hitler and would tell him the name of the bishop. Afterwards the committee would issue a proclamation giving the main outline of the constitution and special services would be held throughout the Reich to celebrate. There would be no elections though objections could be registered in writing after the services. The choice of the first Reich bishop was crucial and it was natural that tension should build up around it. In their demands of 6 May the German Christians claimed the office for themselves.[76] In their first programme on 9 May the Young Reformers replied that the Reich bishop should be nominated at once by Kapler's committee.[77] The moderate course which the German Christians appeared to adopt during May raised hopes that a conflict could be avoided. On 18 May, however, it was made clear to the Young Reformers that Müller was the only candidate acceptable to the German Christians. The Young Reformers at once named an alternative candidate at a press conference held on 19 May. They said that the first bishop

74. The manifesto is printed in *Kirchliches Jahrbuch*, 60.-71. Jg. (1933-44), 15-16. A copy of the so-called *Modus procedendi* survives in Lk. A. Hanover, Nachlaß Marahrens, *Die werdende ev. e Kirche, Verhandlungen*.

75. The expression *Reichskirche* was not used for fear it would sound too much like *Staatskirche* and have adverse repercussions on links with the German Protestant communities in the separated territories.

76. See above, pp. 124-5.

77. *Denkschrift der Jungreformatorischen Bewegung über ihre Stellung zur Reichsbischofsfrage*, p. 3.

should be appointed by the church alone and that they were thinking of a man like Friedrich von Bodelschwingh.[78] At this point Müller may have feared that he was being out-manoeuvred: he had been persuaded by Kapler's committee to agree to a form of procedure which would minimize state influence; on the same day a rival candidate to himself had been proclaimed by a movement which stressed that the choice should be made by the church alone. Such a suspicion would explain Müller's sudden demand on 20 May that nothing further be done until there had been a meeting with Hitler.[79]

There is no evidence that Kapler's committee acted in collusion with the Young Reformers to frustrate Müller but they did not believe that Müller was a suitable candidate partly because of his close connection with Hitler.[80] They hoped that he could be persuaded to accept some lesser position, possibly the senior military chaplaincy (*Feldpropst*) or a special position for evangelism in the Reich bishop's 'spiritual ministry'. When these proposals were put to Müller on 25 May he neither accepted nor rejected them.[81] His behaviour strongly suggests, however, that he planned to become bishop. There can be little doubt that he had hoped that his commission from Hitler, the comparative moderation of his policies, and the control which he claimed to exercise over the German Christians would persuade church leaders to nominate him of their own accord. This solution, which would have avoided an open conflict would probably have been welcome to Hitler. When the church leadership did not choose Müller, his tactics changed and the *détente* which had been gathering momentum since 25 April ended abruptly.

The week following the Loccum meetings, starting on Monday 22 May, was of crucial importance.[82] First Müller

78. *Denkschrift*, pp. 3–4.

79. Lk. A. Hanover, Nachlaß Marahrens, *Die werdende ev. e Kirche, Verhand-lungen*: minutes of the meeting; E.K.D., A 4/24: memorandum by Kapler, 25 May 1933.

80. E.K.D., A 4/24: memorandum by Kapler, 25 May 1933.

81. Memorandum from Pastor Hesse (received by Marahrens 13 June 1933) in Lk. A. Hanover, Nachlaß Marahrens, *Die werdende ev. e Kirche, Verhandlungen*.

82. The following account is based on Kapler's memorandum of 25 May 1933 in E.K.D., A 4/24 and the official explanation issued on behalf of Kapler's committee to the Landeskirchen, 2 June 1933.

telephoned to say that the meeting with Hitler, planned for 22 May, had been postponed to 24 May and that the Chancellor did not want unrest to be created by the announcement of the person to be bishop. (Kapler's committee had consented not to do anything further about the person to be bishop until the meeting with Hitler had taken place.) On 24 May, after a meeting of the German Christians, a deputation, led by Hossenfelder, told Kapler that they had resolved that the bishop should be a German Christian, that he should have the confidence of the Chancellor, and that he should show within three of four weeks that he had the support of the majority of church people. Hossenfelder added that Müller had been elected unanimously as their candidate. Kapler treated this news as an ultimatum and replied that the churches were already united about the person to be bishop. In between, news had been received from Müller that for foreign policy reasons Hitler had cancelled all meetings that afternoon. Müller later telephoned Kapler and said that the German Christian deputation had not been authorized to mention his candidacy and that he would see that (contrary to their expressed intentions) nothing appeared in the press; Kapler replied that he doubted whether this would be possible.

Kapler suspected that the German Christians intended to create a *fait accompli* while the church leadership was waiting for the meeting with Hitler. A campaign for Müller, presenting him as the candidate of the Third Reich and suggesting that his election was a foregone conclusion, might quickly have created a situation which the church leadership would have been unable to reverse. Kapler therefore decided that he would again have to take extraordinary measures to retain the initiative. With the agreement of his committee, he issued a notice to the press which said that the churches were already united over the person to be bishop. News received during the afternoon of 24 May indicated that this would not be enough. It was reported that German Christians, returning from the meeting in Berlin, had announced that Müller had been elected bishop. Further inquiry revealed that the semi-official Conti bureau had told the press that Kapler's committee had agreed to elect Müller. Kapler's committee now felt forced to go further and to issue a name. With Bodel-schwingh's consent they therefore released a second notice to the press which appeared in the morning newspapers of 25 May and said that Bodelschwingh had been selected as the future Reich bishop.

It is possible that the German Christians were not respons-ible for the report that Müller had been elected, issued by the Conti Bureau.[83] Nevertheless, Kapler's fear that the church leadership might lose control of the situation was reasonable. The German Christians intended to secure Müller's election and Kapler's committee intended to prevent them. A dispute was therefore inevitable and there was a real danger that delay by the church leadership would allow the German Christians to create a public climate in favour of Müller.

Kapler's committee allowed Müller to address a meeting of the Landeskirchen held in Berlin on 26–7 May to discuss the choice of Reich bishop.[84] He used the opportunity to make an election speech for himself. He claimed that only the German Christians could win over the masses and he threatened that they would conquer the church in the same way as the Nazi party had conquered the state. He estimated that only a third of church members supported the leadership and indicated that he was ready for a conflict.

After the meeting had endorsed Kapler's choice of Bodel-schwingh by a majority, Müller repudiated its decision in a radio broadcast.[85] Müller was received by Hitler on 30 May and the press was informed that they were in full agree-ment.[86] At the beginning of June the German Christians circulated instructions issued by Ley, the leader of the Labour Front, saying that the Führer wanted the German

83. Professor Hirsch claimed later that the report had been caused by Kapler's own press notice saying that the churches were united over the person to be bishop; the Conti bureau, Hirsch argued, had assumed that Kapler's committee had chosen Müller. E. Hirsch, *Das kirchliche Wollen der Deutschen Christen* (Berlin, 1933), pp. 31–2.

84. E.K.D., A 4/24.

85. *Völkischer Beobachter*, 28–9 May 1933, Nos. 148–9.

86. *Vossische Zeitung*, 31 May 1933, No. 257; K-H. Götte, *Die Propaganda der Glaubensbewegung 'Deutsche Christen' und ihre Beurteilung in der deutschen Tagespresse* (Diss. Phil., Münster, 1957), p. 72. Cf. Hitler's subsequent assertions that he had not received either candidate out of loyalty to the principle of non-intervention. Kretschmar and Nicolaisen, *Dokumente zur Kirchenpolitik des Dritten Reiches*, pp. 91, 95.

Christians to oust the 'reactionaries' and that the NSDAP was to give them every support.[87]

Kapler was in a critical position, probably a hopeless one. Unlike 1918-19 the church leadership could not count on the support of the parishes where the German Christians had a strong following. It would be difficult to refuse the election now demanded by Hossenfelder[88] and, with the support of the Nazi party, the German Christians would almost certainly win.[89] If the church leadership had given Kapler its united support, however, his policy might still have had a chance. Hitler seems to have wanted to avoid direct interference in church affairs; he might, therefore, have preferred that Müller should accept a position under Bodelschwingh if the alternative had been conflict with a united church leadership.[90]

Kapler had assumed that he would receive united support from the church leadership but the meeting of the Landeskirchen on 26-7 May showed that he had miscalculated.[91] A

87. Lk. A. Hamburg, *Deutsche Christen Rundbriefe*: *Rundschreiben* No. 19, 7 June 1933.

88. D.Z.A. Potsdam, Reich Min f.d. kirchl. Angelegenheiten; 23463: copies of Hossenfelder to Kapler (two letters), 29 May 1933.

89. In the meeting of Landeskirchen representatives on 26 May, Kapler said that they would have to hold elections; Lk. A. Nuremberg, Rep. 101, XXXVI Meiser, 96: record of the meeting. In the new elections to the representative bodies of the Landeskirchen on 23 July (see below, pp. 140-1) the German Christians won an overwhelming majority. By this time, however, Bodelschwingh had withdrawn his candidacy and there was no real alternative to Müller around whom the opposition could gather.

90. There are indications that Bodelschwingh was not completely unacceptable to Hitler. One of Bodelschwingh's friends, Stratenwerth, reported from Berlin on 15 July 1933 that three conservative members of the new administration (Seldte, Schwerin von Krosigk and von Papen's political subordinate, von Tschirschky) agreed that Hitler had said, on 14 July, that he was quite indifferent as to who became Reich bishop. According to the same source, Hitler had told Schwerin von Krosigk ten days previously that he would be pleased if Müller were elected because Müller was the only representative of the Protestant church whom he knew, but that Bodelschwingh would also be acceptable and that he would not interfere in the matter. Hauptarchiv Bethel, Reichsbischof 1933, 2: Stratenwerth to Bodelschwingh, 15 July 1933. On the other hand, in an impromptu conversation on 28 June 1933, Hitler accused the church of departing from the agreed procedure and offending him by the election of Bodelschwingh. He added, 'The church must not be against our time and movement'. J. Glenthøj, 'Unterredung im Vestibül. Das Gespräch zwischen Pfarrer Backhaus und Hitler am 28. Juni 1933' in *Kirche in der Zeit*, 17.Jg. (1962), 389-94. Before the elections of 23 July Hitler came out openly on the side of the German Christians; see below, p. 140.

91. E.K.D., A 4/24: record of the meeting.

motion in favour of Müller was defeated by a majority of
only two churches (13 against, 11 in favour),[92] though following the usual practice of weighting the votes according to
the size of the Landeskirchen, there was a majority of 55 to
31 against Müller. When Bodelschwingh's candidacy was put
to the vote he received a majority of 11 churches to 8 (52
votes to 28), though in a second vote on the following day
(27 May) only Württemberg, Mecklenburg-Schwerin, and
Hamburg maintained their opposition to him. The disunity of
the church leadership had decisive consequences: Kapler decided to resign at the earliest opportunity;[93] the German
Christians were able to exploit the division and Bodelschwingh's position became untenable. The church leadership
as an effective body ceased to exist and the last hope of resisting Müller and the German Christians in the central church
organization disappeared.

Bodelschwingh's opponents acted for denominational as
well as political reasons. The Landeskirchen concerned were
almost exclusively Lutheran.[94] The Bavarian leadership, in
particular, was suspicious that the new German Protestant
church would be insufficiently Lutheran. When Bodelschwingh was nominated, it was suggested that he was the
candidate of the Old Prussian Union and (absurdly) that
Müller was more of a Lutheran.[95] The senior Lutheran
bishop, Marahrens, however, did not share these feelings. As a
member of Kapler's committee he had negotiated with Müller
and had come to suspect him. It was Marahrens who
persuaded Bodelschwingh to stand and remained his
staunchest supporter until Bodelschwingh was forced to
resign. The Lutheran leaders who opposed Bodelschwingh at
the same time rejected the policy of their own representative
on Kapler's committee.

92. E.K.D., A 4/24: These figures agree with two other records of the
meeting—one in E.K.D., A 3/93, and another in Nachlaß Marahrens. The Bavarian
record, however, reverses the order and gives 13 churches in favour, 11 against;
Lk. A. Nuremberg, Rep. 101, XXXVI Meiser, 96.

93. Lk. A. Hanover, Nachlaß Marahrens, *Die werdende ev. e Kirche, Verhandlungen*: memorandum from Pastor Hesse.

94. Of the eleven which voted for Müller only Waldeck was not Lutheran.

95. Lk. A. Nuremberg, Rep. 101, XXXVI Meiser, 96: notes on meetings in
Berlin, 23–5 May and ibid.: minutes of a meeting of Lutheran church leaders, 26
May: opening speech of Meiser. The Old Prussian Union contained both Lutheran
and Calvinist parishes, see above, p. 2.

The main motives of the Lutheran opposition were political. Two of their leaders, Bishops Meiser of Bavaria and Schöffel of Hamburg, were newcomers.[96] Both were elected in May 1933 in response to the 'national revolution' and were anxious to cultivate good relations with the new political authorities and the German Christians.[97] Another, Bishop Rendtorff of Mecklenburg-Schwerin had been sympathetic to the 'national opposition' before it gained power. He was now carried away by enthusiasm, hoping that it would prove a great opportunity for evangelization.[98] Bishop Wurm of Württemberg, though more cautious, was also anxious that the church should be accommodating towards the new state.[99]

These attitudes are not surprising. The whole church leadership had, after all, welcomed the 'national revolution' as did most of the Protestant population. There was also some reason to hope that the Third Reich would honour its promises. The Bavarian deputy, Buttmann, whose statements had reassured the churches before 1933, joined the Reich Ministry of the Interior in May;[100] the Bavarian Kultusminister, Schemm, coined the slogan 'Our religion is Christ;

---

96. They were also both Bavarians and old school friends; H. Kressel, *Simon Schöffel*, Heft 7 of *Veröffentlichungen des Historischen Vereins und Stadtarchivs Schweinefurt* (Schweinefurt, 1964), p. 37. J. Schieder, *D. Hans Meiser* (Munich, 1956).

97. 160 and 161 *Sitzung der Synode der Evangelisch-Lutherische Kirche im Hamburgischen Staate*, 16 Mar. 1933 and 29 May 1933, (cyclostyled copies in Lk. A. Hamburg); *Verhandlungen der Landessynode der Evangelisch-Lutherischen Kirche im Bayern r. des Rheins*, 1930–6, *Außerordentliche Tagung in Bayreuth 3–5 May 1933* (Bayreuth, n.d.).

98. See above, p. 89. Like the other Lutheran opponents of Bodelschwingh, Rendtorff later came into conflict with Müller and the German Christians; he resigned on 6 Jan. 1934. Meier, *Die Deutschen Christen*, p. 85.

99. See Wurm's remarks to the meeting of representatives of the Landeskirchen, 26 May 1933; Lk. A. Nuremberg, Rep. 101, XXXVI Meiser, 96: record of the meeting. Also Wurm's account of Bodelschwingh's election sent by him to the provincial authorities of the Württemberg Landeskirche; Lk. A. Stuttgart, D.1. 118: Wurm to the *Dekanatämter*, 30 May 1933. This is printed together with other associated documents in G. Schäfer, *Die evangelische Landeskirche in Württemberg und der Nationalsozialismus*. Bd. 2 (Stuttgart, 1972), pp. 106–9. Cf. T. Wurm, *Erinnerungen aus meinem Leben* (Stuttgart, 1953), pp. 84–8.

100. This was noted by Meiser in his speech to the Würzburg meeting of Lutheran leaders on 14 May 1933; Lk. A. Nuremberg, Rep. 101, XXXVI Meiser, 77: minutes of the meeting.

our politics, Germany'.[101] It was possible to argue that a
section of the Nazi party was friendly to the church and that
the church should encourage it.[102] Similarly, it was possible
to be optimistic about the German Christian movement
which in many parts of the Reich seemed less threatening
than the radical wing under Hossenfelder in Berlin.[103] The
opponents of Bodelschwingh succumbed to the illusion that
they could ride the tide of revolution by expressing confidence in the new regime and the 'moderate' German
Christians. More realistically, some of them were also afraid
of the consequences of refusing Müller.[104]

In view of the disunity of the church leadership, it would
have been natural for Bodelschwingh to decline the nomination. If he had, Müller might well have been elected; many
church leaders would have been relieved to have been thus
spared a conflict with the German Christians. Bodelschwingh,
however, accepted the nomination even on the basis of the
slender majority he had gained in the first vote (13 to 11
churches against Müller; 11 to 8 churches for Bodelschwingh); it was only then that, in a second vote, the opposition to him dwindled to three churches—several church leaders
withdrawing their opposition for the sake of unity.[105]

Bodelschwingh came from a Westphalian aristocratic
family; his father founded the great charitable organization
of Bethel and through its fame the family name had become
a household word in Germany, associated with social work
and particularly the care of epileptics.[106] When he learnt of
the division within the church leadership his first reaction
was to withdraw, but a small group of personal friends
(including Martin Niemöller who 'passionately' opposed the
idea of withdrawal) persuaded him to think it over. During
the night Bodelschwingh decided to accept. He wrote later:
'If the undertaking seemed hopeless, it was not a question at

101. K. Schwend, 'Die Bayerische Volkspartei' in E. Matthias and R. Morsey,
Das Ende der Parteien (Düsseldorf, 1960), p. 492.
102. Lk. A. Nuremberg, Rep. 101, XXXVI Meiser, 77: minutes of the
Würzburg meeting of Lutheran leaders, 14 May 1933, speech of Dekan Langenfaß.
103. Schöffel, for instance, told the meeting of Landeskirchen representatives
on 27 May 1933 that 'the German Christians in the country are 100 per cent
different from Berlin'; E.K.D., A 4/24: record of the meeting.
104. Lk. A. Nuremberg, Rep. 101, XXXVI Meiser, 96: meeting of
Lutheran leaders, 26 May 1933, and Meiser-Rendtorff conversation, 25 May.
105. E.K.D., A 4/24: record of the meeting.
106. See W. Brandt, *Friedrich von Bodelschwingh 1877–1946* (Bethel, 1967).

that time of success or failure but rather that a flag should be raised for the future under which a new troop could gather'.[107]

The German Christians were not prepared to accept Bodelschwingh's leadership. A national campaign was mounted with the help of the Nazi party machine. The pro-government press was instructed to support the German Christians and after 20 June the freedom of other papers was restricted by an order prohibiting discussion of Protestant affairs. Müller alone had access to the radio.[108] Bodelschwingh and Kapler's committee were refused an audience with Hitler.

Together with the Young Reformers, Bodelschwingh tried to rally support against the German Christians. A cyclostyled news-sheet was distributed which described the work of the new bishop.[109] It explained that the conflict with the German Christians was about whether the church would submit to the totalitarian claims of a movement which relied on the Nazi party; it was about whether the church would remain a church or become a cultural institute (*Kulturanstalt*) of the state.

Of the former members of Kapler's committee only Marahrens remained firmly and actively behind Bodelschwingh.[110] On 17 June he wrote to Hitler complaining

107. Hauptarchiv Bethel, Reichsbischof 1: memorandum by Bodelschwingh, entitled 'Thirty days at a turning point of German church history', composed in 1935. For a more detailed account of the Reich bishop crisis, see Wright, 'The political attitudes of the German Protestant church leadership', pp. 347–61.

108. Götte, *Die Propaganda der Glaubensbewegung 'Deutsche Christen'*, pp. 53–75.

109. *Kirchlicher Aufklärungsdienst*, 14 and 20 June 1933, in E.K.U., Gen. XII, 185/1. Also *Informationsdienst für das Kirchliche Reformwerk* in Lk. A. Hanover, Nachlaß Marahrens, *Die werdende ev. e Kirche, Verhandlungen*.

110. Kapler had reached the retiring age and was in poor health. He also felt out of touch with the world of the Third Reich and believed that the church needed new leadership. He had hoped to complete the transition to the new constitution before retiring but the disunity of the leadership and the opposition to his policy at the May meeting of the Landeskirchen led him to resign at once. E.K.U., *Präsidialia, Personalia Lit. K.*, No. 16: Kapler's letter of resignation to the Kirchensenat, 7 June 1933, and Kapler to Kultusminster Rust, 6 July 1933; E.K.D., A 2/28: minutes of the Kirchenausschuß meeting, 23 June 1933, Kapler's speech of resignation.

Pastor Hesse, the Calvinist representative on the committee was unenthusiastic about the idea of a Reich bishop and pessimistic about the outcome of a conflict with the German Christians. E.K.D., A 3/93: memorandum of Hesse on his attitude to the Reich bishop question; Lk. A. Hanover, Nachlaß Marahrens, *Die werdende ev. e Kirche. Verhandlungen*: memorandum by Hesse on the events which led to the nomination of Bodelschwingh; E.K.D., A 4/24: record of the meeting of Landeskirchen representatives, 27 May 1933, speech of Hesse.

about the triple position of Müller as the Chancellor's representative, a leader of the German Christians, and an opposition candidate for the bishopric, and about the support Müller received from the Nazi party and even from state sources.[111] Marahrens explained that this had aroused fear for the independence of the church which would prevent good relations with the state. In private letters Marahrens wrote that this was the point at which to make a stand; the decisive battle would be fought at the next Kirchenausschuß meeting.[112]

The Kirchenausschuß met in Eisenach on 23–4 June. On 22 June there was a private meeting of the Lutheran Landeskirchen, where Marahrens tried to win over the opposition to a united front behind Bodelschwingh.[113] He argued that the German Christians had purely political motives, that the church must stand firm and that it would win. He was unsuccessful; most of the Lutheran leaders upheld their opposition to Bodelschwingh and demanded that he should submit to an election.[114]

A personal appeal for support by Bodelschwingh to the Kirchenausschuß on 23 June was equally unavailing.[115] The meeting was interrupted when it was learnt that Professor Fezer and another German Christian were available to negotiate on Müller's behalf. In a meeting which lasted until 3 a.m. on 24 June, the German Christians indicated that if Bodelschwingh agreed to accept the terms of a future constitution which might require him to seek election, they would abstain from coercion and the Nazi party machine would be withdrawn. On 24 June a committee of the Kirchenausschuß agreed to make the offer. Before the next meeting with the

111. Printed in Klügel, *Die lutherische Landeskirche Hannovers*, ii. 14–6.

112. Marahrens to v. Issendorf, 22 June 1933 in ibid., 16–7; Marahrens to Heckel, 20 June 1933, in Lk. A. Hanover, Nachlaß Marahrens, *Die werdende ev. e Kirche, Verhandlungen*.

113. Lk. A. Nuremberg, Rep. 101, XXXVI Meiser, 254/1: record of the meeting from Meiser's diary. (I am grateful to Dr. H. Baier of the Landeskirchliches Archiv, Nuremberg, for providing me with transcripts of extracts from the diary.) The Landeskirchen of Bavaria, Schleswig-Holstein and Thuringia—in addition to Hamburg, Mecklenburg-Schwerin and Württemberg which had voted consistently against Bodelschwingh—raised objections to his nomination.

114. Record of the meeting in Meiser's diary and an account by Wurm, 30 June 1933, in Lk. A. Stuttgart, D.1. 119.

115. E.K.D., A 2/28: minutes of the Kirchenausschuß meeting, 23–4 June. These form the basis of the following narrative.

German Christians in the afternoon, however, news arrived that the Prussian Kultusminister had appointed a Staatskommissar over the Prussian Landeskirchen.[116] The German Christians now asked that Bodelschwingh should resign. He could remain a candidate for the bishopric but was to renounce any authority as bishop designate. Bodelschwingh's position was hopeless. The threat of state intervention, far from uniting the church leadership, increased the opposition to him. On the evening of 23 June, on hearing from German Christian circles in Berlin that if Bodelschwingh did not resign the state would intervene, the Lutheran leaders decided to demand his resignation and to refuse obedience if they were outvoted.[117] At 7 p.m. on 24 June, Bodelschwingh announced to the Kirchenausschuß that the appointment of the Staatskommissar had made it impossible for him to carry out the task he had been given and he therefore gave back his commission.[118]

iii. The Revolution Victorious

The June meeting of the Kirchenausschuß destroyed the last hope that the church leadership would offer concerted resistance to the German Christians. In the following week the Prussian Landeskirchen were subjected to the ruthless rule of Staatskommissar Jäger, a professional lawyer.[119] He

116. O. Söhngen, 'Wie es anfing. Die Einsetzung des Staatskommissars und die Usurpierung des Evangelischen Oberkirchenrates in Berlin im Juni 1933' in H. Kruska, *Gestalten und Wege der Kirche im Osten* (Ulm, 1958), pp. 176–89. See appendix, below pp. 143–4.

117. Lk. A. Nuremberg, Rep. 101, XXXVI Meiser, 254/1: record in Meiser's diary of a telephone message from Meiser's German Christian contact (Pfarrer Klein) in Berlin, 23 June 10 p.m., and meeting of Lutheran leaders subsequently.

118. E.K.D., A 2/28: minutes of the Kirchenausschuß meeting, 23–4 June. Although Bodelschwingh did not renounce his right to be a candidate for the Reich bishopric, in fact this became a dead letter and on 7 July he wrote to Marahrens saying that he should no longer be considered a candidate; Hauptarchiv Bethel, Reichsbischof 2. There is no doubt from his correspondence that Bodelschwingh would not have resigned, if he had had the united support of the church leadership: Hauptarchiv Bethel, Ki 37: Bodelschwingh to Rade, 11 July 1933. This was confirmed to me by G. Stratenwerth, Bodelschwingh's closest adviser at the time (Interview, 15 Sept. 1966).

119. An excellent selection of documents on the Staatskommissar episode is printed in Kretschmar and Nicolaisen, *Dokumente zur Kirchenpolitik des Dritten Reiches*, pp. 67–94. August Jäger seems to have been universally disliked; see Conrad, *Der Kampf um die Kanzeln*, p. 14. He later achieved notoriety as deputy *Reichsstatthalter* (Governor) in the Warthegau (a German administrative district in occupied Poland). In 1948 he was condemned to death by a Polish court for war crimes.

dismissed members of the Oberkirchenrat, appointed his own officials, dissolved elected church bodies, and ordered his subordinates to appoint new members without elections. Opposition was declared treasonable.[120] The church leaders protested to Hindenburg, Hitler, and Frick and opened legal proceedings in the appropriate Reich Court.[121] The General-superintendenten of the Old Prussian Union also protested, asking the parishes to observe the following Sunday as a day of prayer and repentance.[122] Hossenfelder (whom Jäger had appointed provisional spiritual vice-president of the Ober-kirchenrat) retaliated by threatening supporters of the Generalsuperintendenten with disciplinary measures and ordering a day of thanksgiving on the same Sunday.

The leaders of the Lutheran Landeskirchen who had opposed Bodelschwingh were shocked by the action of the Prussian Kultusministerium particularly as one of their number, the Bishop of Schleswig-Holstein, came under the Staatskommissar. The appointment of Hossenfelder also alarmed them since they had assumed that Müller would prevent the radical German Christians from gaining power.[123] In a meeting with Müller on 27 June they demanded Hossenfelder's removal.[124] Bishop Meiser warned that a mood of Kulturkampf was growing. Müller denied that

120. Kirchliches Gesetz-u. Verordnungsblatt, 27 June 1933, No. 9. In a meeting with his subordinate officials on 26 June Jäger said he did not want a 'blood bath' and that 'it should not look like persecution'; in areas like Westphalia, however, where there was strong support for Bodelschwingh, Jäger instructed his subordinates to make use of 'revolutionary justice' and to 'stamp out' the opposition. D.Z.A. Merseburg, Rep. 76, III Sekt. 1, Abt. II, Ldes. Sachen 49/1 (Beiheft H). See H. Baier, J. R. C. Wright, 'Ein neues Dokument zum Staatseingriff in Preußen 1933' in Zeitschrift für Kirchengeschichte, (forthcoming).

121. D.Z.A. Potsdam, Präsidialkanzlei, 281/3; Bundesarchiv, Reichskanzlei, R 43 11/161. D.Z.A. Potsdam, Reich Min. f.d. kirchl. Angelegenheiten, 23463: copy of the action brought by the Oberkirchenrat, 26 June 1933.

122. Hermelink, Kirche im Kampf, p. 42. O. Söhngen, 'Die Reaktion der "amtlichen" Kirche auf die Einsetzung eines Staatskommissars durch den national-sozialistischen Staat' in Arbeiten zur Geschichte des Kirchenkampfes (Göttingen, 1971), xxvi. 35–78. O. Söhngen, 'Der 2. Juli 1933, der "Sonntag der Kirche"' in Evangelisch-lutherische Kirchenzeitung. Festausgabe zum 60. Geburtstag von Präsident D. Heinz Brunotte, 11. Juni 1956, Nr. 12, pp. 239–42.

123. Lk. A. Nuremberg, Rep. 101, XXXVI Meiser, 96: records of a meeting between south German church leaders and German Christian representatives, 26 June 1933, and of a meeting of Lutheran leaders, 26 June 1933.

124. Ibid.: record of the meeting (held in the Reich Ministry of the Interior).

he had known in advance of the Prussian Kultusminister's appointment of a Staatskommissar; he had told Jäger that the present situation was intolerable. Jäger (who made a brief appearance at the meeting) gave an assurance that the Staatskommissar would remain limited to Prussia and would soon be withdrawn, and Müller promised that Hossenfelder would be given a different job. The Lutheran leaders then acquiesced in Müller's plan to reassert his authority by taking over the Kirchenbund.[125] On the evening of 28 June the Kirchenbundesamt was occupied by the S.A. and on the same day Jäger relieved Hossenfelder of his duties in Prussia and asked him to assist Müller instead.[126] The Lutheran leaders had once again allowed themselves to be exploited by Müller.

The progress to power of the German Christians was interrupted by the intervention of Reich President Hindenburg.[127] On 30 January he wrote to Hitler suggesting that negotiations should be held. The Reich Ministry of the Interior also intervened, proposing that the Staatskommissar (whose appointment they considered illegal) be removed and that new elections be held. Hitler accepted this solution.[128] Frick (Reich Minister of the Interior) who was authorized by Hitler to settle the matter, asked church leaders to co-operate with Müller in completing the new constitution.[129] Meanwhile they were to set aside the question of the legality of Müller's actions (in taking over the Kirchenbund) and, in return, once agreement had been reached on the constitution, he would help to solve the problem of the Prussian Staatskommissar. These terms weighted the negotiations heavily in

125. This was still technically independent, since, as a Reich organization, it did not come under the Prussian Staatskommissar.

126. D.Z.A. Potsdam, Präsidialkanzlei, 281/3: copies of protests from the acting President of the Kirchenausschuß to Frick, 29 June 1933, and from the successors to Kapler's committee, 30 June 1933 *Tägliche Rundschau*, 30 June 1933, No. 150, giving Jäger's decree transferring Hossenfelder, and Müller's decrees.

127. O. Söhngen, 'Hindenburgs Eingreifen in den Kirchenkampf 1933' in *Arbeiten zur Geschichte des Kirchenkampfes* (Göttingen, 1965), xv. 30–44.

128. Conrad, *Der Kampf um die Kanzeln*, pp. 16–17 and A. Jäger, *Kirche im Volk* (Berlin, 1937), p. 36.

129. Bundesarchiv, Reichskanzlei, R 43 11/161: note of Lammers, 30 June 1933; Lk. A. Nuremberg, Rep. 101, XXXVI Meiser, 96: letter from Frick, 4 July 1933. Klügel, *Die lutherische Landeskirche Hannovers*, i. 60–2.

Müller's favour; there was to be no withdrawal of the Staatskommissar until agreement had been reached between the church leaders and Müller. On 8 July Müller declared that unless the constitution were ready within a few days, the government would be forced to impose one.[130]

The constitution which Müller proposed was an authoritarian version of the draft previously agreed by Kapler's committee; it gave the Reich bishop, acting with his advisers, the right to decree laws without the agreement of the National Synod.[131] Although former opponents of Bodelschwingh, like Meiser and Schöffel, now joined Marahrens in criticizing the concentration of power on the office of Reich bishop, the church leadership decided it had no alternative but to accept Müller's terms.[132] The constitution was approved by the Landeskirchen and confirmed by a Reich Law of 14 July which ordered new elections to be held on 23 July. In return for the settlement the Staatskommissar and most of his subordinates were withdrawn.[133]

This gave the church leadership only temporary respite for, in the elections, the German Christians won an overwhelming victory, with the help of the Nazi party machine.[134] The previous evening Hitler broadcast in favour of the German Christians.[135] The church leadership observed the neutrality which was customary; its failure to unite behind Bodelschwingh had shown in any case its inability to give a lead against the German Christians. Only in Westphalia were the German Christians defeated by the Young Reformers who campaigned for a free and unpolitical church. In many areas united lists were agreed between the parties, giving German Christians about 70 per cent of the seats; where contests took

130. E.K.D., A 4/87: minutes of the meeting.

131. Text in *Kirchliches Jahrbuch,* 60.–71. Jg. (1933–44), 17–20. See also H. Kater, *Die Deutsche Evangelische Kirche in den Jahren 1933 und 1934* (Göttingen, 1970) pp. 93–129.

132. E.K.D., A 4/87: minutes of the meetings of 8 and 10 July; E.K.D., A 3/93: minutes of a Kirchenbundesrat meeting, 11 July 1933.

133. *Kirchliches Jahrbuch,* 60.–71. Jg. (1933–44), 20–1.

134. G. van Norden, *Kirche in der Krise* (Düsseldorf, 1963), pp. 81–92. Kretschmar and Nicolaisen, *Dokumente zur Kirchenpolitik des Dritten Reiches,* pp. 110–22.

135. *Kirchliches Jahrbuch,* 60.–71. Jg. (1933–44), 21–2.

place the German Christians won on average about 75 per cent.[136] These results concealed, however, a distinction between moderate and radical German Christians which later became important.

The elections had immediate consequences for the church leadership, particularly in the Old Prussian Union and in the new central organization. On 4 August the Kirchensenat of the Old Prussian Union elected Müller President of the Oberkirchenrat with the title *Landesbischof*.[137] This was in voluntary anticipation of the General Synod which met on 5 September and confirmed Müller's election. Ten bishoprics were created within the Old Prussian Union to replace the system of Generalsuperintendenten; Hossenfelder became Bishop of Brandenburg and resumed the office of spiritual vice-president of the Oberkirchenrat.[138] The new National Synod met in Wittenberg on 27 September and Müller was unanimously elected Reich bishop. 'The church struggle is over; the struggle for the soul of the nation has begun', he declared.[139]

In fact the 'church struggle' was just beginning. The story of the Kirchenkampf starts with the reaction against German Christian rule. The victory of the German Christians also marks the final disruption of the church leadership of the Weimar Republic. It may be that Hitler would not have tolerated an independent church. As it was, church leaders did not present him with a united front. Their illusions were particularly evident in the attitude of the Lutheran minority which was ready to give Müller and the 'moderate' German Christians the leadership of the central church organization. This attitude was, however, only an extreme form of the general welcome given by the church leadership as a whole to the Third Reich. Their false optimism was encouraged by the tactics of the Nazis and the deception (perhaps also self-deception) of Ludwig Müller. The government and the

136. van Norden, *Kirche in der Krise*, pp. 83–8.
137. Ibid., pp. 92–3.
138. Ibid., pp. 96–9.
139. Ibid., p. 99, and *Kirchliches Jahrbuch,* 60.–71. Jg. (1933–44), 27.

German Christians insisted that they believed in the independence of the church; even Staatskommissar Jäger was careful to reject the idea of a Staatskirche.[140] Müller astutely dissociated himself from Hossenfelder just as Hitler had earlier dissociated the NSDAP from Dinter. These tactics were enough to undermine men who were only too willing to be won over and feared the cost of resistance.

The Weimar church leadership also left a more positive legacy. Kapler's attempt to defend church independence by the election of Bodelschwingh brought to the fore men of a younger generation. Although they did not succeed to the leadership of the official church, they were later active in the *Bekennende Kirche*.[141] The most important was Martin Niemöller, who had worked with Bodelschwingh in Berlin during his period as Reich bishop designate. Niemöller had then anticipated the need for a clear break. On 21 June before the final meeting of the Kirchenausschuß, he wrote to Bodelschwingh urging him to be firm. He argued that either those who preached an alien Gospel or those who stood for the Reformation creed would be forced to secede. If the Kirchenausschuß rejected Bodelschwingh, he should become the leader of those who would be excluded from the church. 'Then', Niemoller predicted, 'the last word will not be spoken in Eisenach.'[142]

140. See the official explanation of the Kultusministerium for the appointment of the Staatskommissar printed in *Tägliche Rundschau*, 28 June 1933.

141. The Protestant opposition to the German Christians; for the importance of the Reich bishop conflict in the development of the Protestant opposition, see J. Schmidt, 'Studien zur Vorgeschichte des Pfarrernotbundes' in *Zeitschrift für Kirchengeschichte*, 79 (1968), 43–67.

142. Hauptarchiv Bethel, Reichsbischof 1: Niemöller to Bodelschwingh, 21 June 1933. Bodelschwingh seems at first to have considered the idea of remaining the unofficial leader of a 'free church'; Brandt, *Friedrich v. Bodelschwingh*, p. 138. It was, however, Niemöller himself who emerged as the leader of an uncompromising church opposition. For Niemöller's career see J. Schmidt, *Martin Niemöller im Kirchenkampf* (Hamburg, 1971).

APPENDIX

THE APPOINTMENT
OF THE STAATSKOMMISSAR[1]

The pretext for the appointment of the Staatskommissar was that the Kirchensenat had broken Article 7 of the treaty of 1931 by appointing a successor to Kapler, without first asking the Kultusministerium whether it had any political objections. In fact the Kirchensenat only appointed a provisional President because of uncertainty about how the new central church constitution would affect the post. It had been agreed at the time of the 1931 treaty that provisional appointments would not come under the 'political' clause. In any case, according to Article 12 of the treaty, the Prussian *Land* should first have tried to find a friendly solution to the dispute, before resorting to the appointment of a Staatskommissar.

The Kultusministerium officials seem to have believed that the Kirchensenat deliberately made a provisional appointment in order to evade the political clause and also that the natural successor to Kapler, the secular vice-president, Hundt, had been passed over because he was a National Socialist. These considerations may have influenced some members of the Kirchensenat. Hundt himself, however, maintained that it had acted both loyally and legally, and when he was offered the leadership of the Oberkirchenrat by Jäger, he declined (to Jäger's fury). According to his account, Hundt was bypassed by the Kirchensenat for a number of reasons. These included

1. This account is based on the following sources: E.K.D., Nachlaß Hundt, F2/2: chronological memorandum, 1932–3; Die Ereignisse von 24. Juni 1933 (dated 25–8 June 1933); account of his meeting with Jäger on 23 June; text of Rust's broadcast, 29 June; memorandum of a telephone conversation between Professor Heckel and Karnatz, 19 Dec. 1929. E.K.U., Verhandlungen des Kirchensenats, 2: minutes of the meeting of 8–9 June; E.K.U., Gen. III, 48/2: minutes of 21 June 1933. D.Z.A. Potsdam, Präsidialkanzlei, 281, 3/1: *Amtliche Preußische Pressedienst*, 27 June 1933, containing Göring's letter to Rust. D.Z.A. Merseburg, Rep. 76, III Sekt. 1, Abt. II, Ldes. Sachen 49/1 (Beiheft H): record of Jäger's conversation with Hundt, 23 June 1933, and minutes of a meeting of Jäger with his subordinate officials, 26 June 1933.

his disagreement with Kapler's policy in the question of the Reich bishop, but there was also a general feeling that the Old Prussian Union should have a clergyman as leader and not another lawyer. The new provisional President, General-superintendent Stoltenhoff, had been selected partly because he was thought to be on good terms with the German Christians and the National Socialists.

Internal Prussian considerations were, however, only part of the reason for the intervention of the Prussian Kultus-minister, Rust (supported by Göring, the Prussian Minister of the Interior). In a broadcast on 29 June Rust made it clear that he thought the Reich should have been asked for its approval of the person chosen to be Reich bishop. When this did not happen, Rust said, it became his job to prevent the growth of an 'opposition centre' and when Kapler resigned without telling him, he saw his opportunity to intervene. In his letter of support for Rust, Göring laid the whole emphasis on the Reich bishop problem.

There is no evidence to support the suspicion that Hitler directly encouraged the appointment of the Staats-kommissar.[2] The surviving documents suggest rather that Rust, Jäger, and Göring were responsible and that Hitler and Müller did not know about it in advance.[3]

2. See, for instance, K. Scholder, 'Die evangelische Kirche in der Sicht der nationalsozialistischen Führung bis zum Kriegsausbruch' in *Vierteljahrshefte für Zeitgeschichte,* 16. Jg. (1968), 19.

3. Hossenfelder was also consulted; letter from Pastor Hossenfelder, 7 Sept. 1972.

CONCLUSION

We may now suggest answers to the questions asked in the Preface: could the Protestant leadership have come to accept the Republic? How close was the sympathy between it and the Nazi movement?

Despite their close association with the German Empire, Protestant leaders did not adopt a consistently anti-Republican position after 1918. In the years of relative stability from 1925 they moved towards pragmatic acceptance of the Republic. Yet in 1933 they welcomed the Third Reich.

The simplest explanation for this ambivalent course is that they were primarily concerned to protect the interests of the church whatever the regime in power and they believed this could best be done by agreement and not opposition. There is no doubt that this was an important consideration but it leaves much unexplained.

Church leaders' policy was closely related to their interpretation of German history. Their ideal was the authoritarian, 'Christian' state which was presumed to have existed at some time before 1848.[1] By the end of the nineteenth century, however, it seemed clear that this ideal was Utopian and that the general trend lay towards an independent church in a secular, liberal state, which came about suddenly in November 1918. Despite their strong resentment against the revolution church leaders decided to come to terms with the new situation. This was facilitated by the Republic's quick retreat from its hopeless attempt to reform the church and the generous settlement it allowed. The Vernunftrepublikaner policy was particularly associated with President Kapler and its main achievement was the Prussian church treaty of 1931.

This policy distinguished church leaders from the overtly anti-Republican position of the intransigent Right. Their commitment to the Republic, however, was only a limited

---

1. Cf. R. M. Bigler, *The Politics of German Protestantism. The rise of the Protestant church elite in Prussia, 1815–1848* (Berkeley and London, 1972).

one. In practice they adopted a permissive attitude towards the activities of the 'national opposition' and they failed to recognize that the church's security depended on the survival of democratic institutions. It is not clear how far even this limited commitment was shared by church members. President Kapler won impressive majorities for his policy at the General Synod of the Old Prussian Union in 1931 and, albeit in a rather amorphous resolution, at the Kirchentag of 1927. However, church members may have voted for it more out of an appreciation of its advantages to the church than because they approved of its political implications.

The essential assumption of the Vernunftrepublikaner was that the Republic would last. The swift rise of the NSDAP from 1930, apparently reversing the whole development of German history since 1848, destroyed this assumption. Through the NSDAP the ideal of an authoritarian state became the programme of a mass movement and it seemed possible that the Hohenzollern dynasty would be restored.[2] As Reich Chancellor, Hitler announced that he attached the greatest importance to the two Christian churches and demanded their co-operation. Church leaders responded by welcoming the Third Reich as a gift of God.

The new regime did not conform, however, in all respects to the Protestant ideal. Protestant leaders were aware that its racialist ideology contained dangers and that it might try to exploit the church for political purposes in a way which would have been objectionable even under the monarchy. Why did they suppress their doubts?

The first reason was fear. They dared not criticize for fear that this would provoke the very state intervention they wished to avoid. This fear was particularly strong because of the general popularity of the new government among church members and the threat of revolution from within the church led by the German Christians. Unlike 1918–19, church leaders could not count on their members in a conflict. The result was that they tried to build up credit with the regime by public declarations of support and proofs of loyalty.

2. Dibelius confirmed that there seemed a real possibility that Hitler would restore the monarchy when Hindenburg died (Interview, 23 Oct. 1965); cf. Bracher, *Die Auflösung der Weimarer Republik*, pp. 715–16.

Secondly, Protestant leaders did not believe that it was their duty to criticize the Third Reich. They interpreted the Nazi victory as a natural reaction not only to the abuses of Republican democracy which had nearly ended in civil war, but also to over a decade of foreign oppression. Germany had not been a free agent since 1918. They did not feel, therefore, that Germany was to blame for the 'excesses' of the 'national revolution'. Particularly important in this respect was the widely accepted connection between reparations, economic instability, and political extremism.

This mixture of fear and the desire to justify made it impossible for the church leaders to unite even in defence of their own independence. In 1933 their surrender seemed complete.

EPILOGUE

THE THIRD REICH

i. Nazi Policy

The Third Reich is commonly supposed to have been a time of persecution of the churches and of Kirchenkampf. Neither of these descriptions adequately conveys what happened. The Christian churches were not persecuted in the way that German Communists, Jews, or Jehovah's Witnesses were. While the Nazi leadership was united in seeing their independence as a threat, it was divided as to how it should treat them. Where the Roman Catholic church was concerned, the general policy was nevertheless consistent: to undermine the church by indirect methods. This was in line with views expressed by Hitler in a conversation in April 1933 when he explained that he did not intend to repeat Bismarck's mistake and start an open conflict with the church; instead, he would accelerate the trend away from religious belief by making the church appear ridiculous and contemptible.[1]

The case of the Protestant church was more complicated. Here, in addition to the policy of indirect attack, an alternative scheme for making the church a pro-Nazi organization seems to have attracted Hitler for a time. This had been the programme of Hossenfelder's German Christian movement since 1932 but their patron within the party then seems to have been Gregor Strasser and not Hitler.[2] Hitler's interest in the idea coincides with the appearance of Ludwig Müller as a candidate for the office of Protestant Reich bishop. Probably Müller was responsible for arousing Hitler's interest and at the

---

1. H. Rauschning, *Hitler Speaks* (Engl. edn., London, 1939), pp. 55-65. Cf. T. Schieder, *Hermann Rauschning's "Gespräche mit Hitler" als Geschichtsquelle, Rheinisch-Westfälische Akademie der Wissenschaften, Vorträge G 178* (Opladen, 1972).
   2. See above, pp. 92-3.

same time won Hitler's support for his ambition to lead the new Reichskirche.[3]

Hitler's real views about Müller are uncertain. In the conversation of April 1933, Hitler dismissed the idea of a combination of German racialism and Christianity as 'all the same old Jewish swindle'. Later he said, 'Let it run its course. But it won't last. Why a uniform religion, a German Church independent of Rome? Don't you see that that's all obsolete? German Christians, German Church, Christians freed from Rome—old stuff!' Hermann Rauschning, who recorded the conversation, and who happened to know Ludwig Müller, noted that Hitler did not share Müller's views.[4] However, this is in conflict with a quotation from his wartime conversations (7 June 1942), 'He was honest enough to admit that he, too, had been hard at it trying to create order in church affairs. He had tried, namely, to clarify the confused conditions of the Protestant Church by the appointment of a Reich bishop.' (He went on to say that he was glad after all that he had failed.)[5] Two interpretations are possible. It may be that Hitler genuinely supported Müller and that the opposite views he expressed in April 1933 were intended to satisfy Nazi extremists (the audience included Streicher).[6] Or perhaps he had not made up his mind and was prepared at that stage to encourage both those who planned to undermine the church and those who aimed to make it a Nazi organization.[7] In either case, it was probably important that despite his contempt for Christianity, Hitler believed that some substi-

3. See K. Scholder, 'Die Kapitulation der evangelischen Kirche vor dem nationalsozialistischen Staat' in *Zeitschrift für Kirchengeschichte*, 81 (1970), 195, and H. Schmid, *Apokalyptisches Wetterleuchten* (Munich, 1947), p. 62.

4. Rauschning, *Hitler Speaks*, pp. 59, 61.

5. H. Picker, *Hitlers Tischgespräche im Führerhauptquartier 1941–1942* (2nd edn., Stuttgart, 1965), p. 395. The importance of this quotation was pointed out by K. Scholder, 'Die evangelische Kirche in der Sicht der nationalsozialistischen Führung', in *Vierteljahrshefte für Zietgeschichte*, 16. Jg. (1968), 16. A similar remark by Hitler is recorded in Rosenberg's diary for 19 Jan. 1940; H-G. Seraphim, *Das politische Tagebuch Alfred Rosenbergs 1934/5 und 1939/40* (Munich, 1964), p. 117.

6. Speer noted the inconsistency of Hitler's remarks on church affairs and attributed it to Hitler adapting his comments to his audience. A. Speer, *Inside the Third Reich* (Engl. edn., London, 1970), p. 95.

7. This was the conclusion of Hitler's Minister of Finance; L. Graf Schwerin von Krosigk, *Es geschah in Deutschland* (3rd edn., Stuttgart, 1952), p. 259.

tute would have to be found for it and that the new religion was still incomplete.[8]

Whatever Hitler's motives, there was no unity in Nazi policy. On 25 January 1934 Hitler renewed his support for Müller despite the opposition which his policies as Reich bishop had aroused and despite the suspicion of the Vatican that the German government was developing a special relationship with the Protestant church.[9] Yet the previous day Hitler had appointed Müller's chief enemy within the Nazi party, Alfred Rosenberg (the author of the anti-Christian *Myth of the 20th Century*), as his 'personal representative to supervise the entire spiritual and ideological education of the NSDAP'.[10]

At the end of 1934 Hitler finally decided to drop Müller. There seem to have been three main reasons: increased opposition from within the church, since having failed to gain acceptance he had attempted to impose his rule by force; threats from Bishop Bell of Chichester and the Archbishop of Canterbury that the international ecumenical movement would break off relations with Müller's Reichskirche; and the adverse effect which Müller's campaign for a 'German church independent of Rome' was having on the Catholic population of the Saar (where a plebiscite was to be held in January 1935 to decide whether the province should rejoin the German Reich).[11]

Hitler was now in a dilemma. He had probably supported Müller in the belief that *Gleichschaltung* (integration) of the Protestant church could be achieved by agreement or at least with only the minimum of force. This belief had proved false: the Protestant church was divided and Müller had been unable to persuade or to bully his opponents into submission.

    8. A. Zoller, *Hitler Privat. Erlebnisbericht seiner Geheimsekretärin* (Düsseldorf, 1949), pp. 191–2. Rauschning, *Hitler Speaks*, p. 59.

    9. Scholder, 'Die evangelische Kirche in der Sicht der nationalsozialistischen Führung', pp. 19–21.

    10. R. Bollmus, *Das Amt Rosenberg und seine Gegner. Zum Machtkampf im nationalsozialistischen Herrschaftssystem* (Stuttgart, 1970), pp. 54–9. Bollmus shows that the coincidence of Rosenberg's appointment and Hitler's renewed support for Müller was not deliberate. For Rosenberg's view of Müller, see Seraphim, *Das politische Tagebuch Alfred Rosenbergs*, pp. 55–6.

    11. A. Boyens, *Kirchenkampf und Ökumene 1933–1939*, (Munich, 1969) pp. 112–15.

Hitler was not prepared to embark on outright persecution. Not only did he not want an open conflict, but the Protestant church enjoyed strong support in military circles and within the civil service[12] and it might create difficulties in foreign policy. The last was particularly important with regard to England, where Hitler was keen to maintain good relations.[13] On the other hand, he was not willing to accept a policy of non-interference. Having sided with Müller and the German Christians this would be seen as a personal defeat and an independent church might develop into a centre of opposition to the regime.[14] All the policies represented by his subordinates were therefore unacceptable. He could not endorse Rosenberg's ideology because that would mean a *Kulturkampf*. The same applied to Göring's plan for a Staatskirche supported by police terror. On the other hand, a policy of non-interference recommended by Heß and Frick was too weak.[15]

At the end of January 1935 Hitler received a memorandum from a young Nazi lawyer and former official in the Prussian Ministry of Education, Wilhelm Stuckart.[16] Stuckart discussed three ways by which the churches could be brought into line with Nazi policy. He rejected working through a church movement like the German Christians which had already failed. He also rejected the old idea of separation of church and state since although it would reduce

12. M. Broszat, *Der Staat Hitlers* (Munich, 1969), pp. 293–8. The *Bekennende Kirche* commanded considerable sympathy in the judiciary for instance. For an account of a notable case, see F. Gollert, *Dibelius vor Gericht* (Munich, 1959).

13. The Anglo-German naval agreement was concluded in June 1935.

14. A report by Heydrich's *Sicherheitshauptamt* in Feb.–March 1935 alleged that the enemies of the Third Reich were exploiting the church conflict. H. Boberach, *Berichte des SD und der Gestapo über Kirchen und Kirchenvolk in Deutschland 1934–1944* (Mainz, 1971), pp. 66–9.

15. Scholder, 'Die evangelische Kirche in der Sicht der nationalsozialistischen Führung', pp. 20–2. J. Glenthøj, 'Hindenburg, Göring und die evangelischen Kirchenführer' in *Arbeiten zur Geschichte des Kirchenkampfes* (Göttingen, 1965), xv. 54–5.

16. J. S. Conway, *The Nazi Persecution of the Churches 1933–45* (London, 1968), pp. 116–21. L. Wenschkewitz, 'Zur Geschichte des Reichskirchenministeriums und seines Ministers' in *Tutzinger Texte, Sonderband I, Kirchenkampf* (Munich, 1969), pp. 188–94. Weneschkewitz points out the similarity between the ideas behind Stuckart's programme and the Nuremberg Laws for which he was also responsible.

the status and wealth of the churches, it might unite them in opposition and it would also free them from state control. Instead he recommended that the state should exert pressure on the churches by controlling their finances and appointments to church offices through a government department. Hitler appeared to endorse this policy and appointed Hans Kerrl[17] (a senior party member and former Prussian Minister of Justice) to take over the departments for church affairs from the relevant Reich and Prussian Ministries.[18]

However, Kerrl saw his task as to persuade the church to integrate itself into the Third Reich rather than to put pressure on it (in the way Stuckart had suggested). This approach suited Kerrl's personal convictions: at his death Hitler commented, 'Kerrl, with the noblest of intentions, wanted to attempt a synthesis between National Socialism and Christianity'.[19] But there were also political reasons. Stuckart's memorandum had concealed the basic problem facing anyone who tried to implement Hitler's policy. As we have seen, he would neither tolerate an independent church nor authorize its coercion. This meant there was no alternative, any more than there had been for Müller, to trying to win over the church by persuasion. Kerrl's only advantage was that he was not committed to the German Christians and could therefore negotiate with representatives of all sections within the church.[20]

During the course of 1936 it became obvious that Kerrl had failed. No compromise could be found which was

17. L. Wenschkewitz, 'Zur Geschichte des Reichskirchenministeriums und seines Ministers', pp. 194–206; L. Wenschkewitz, 'Politische Versuche einer Ordnung der Deutschen Evangelischen Kirche durch den Reichskirchenminister 1937 bis 1939' in *Arbeiten zur Geschichte des Kirchenkampfes* (Göttingen, 1971), xxvi. 121–38. J. Schmidt, *Martin Niemöller im Kirchenkampf*, pp. 306–8. Schwerin von Krosigk, *Es geschah in Deutschland*, pp. 254–60.

18. According to a Reichskanzlei official, Hitler had not meant to create a new Ministry by this decree (16 July 1935). However, Kerrl styled himself Reich Minister for Church Affairs and this was accepted. E. N. Peterson, *The Limits of Hitler's Power* (Princeton, 1969), p. 55.

19. H. R. Trevor-Roper, *Hitler's Table Talk 1941–1944* (2nd edn., London, 1973), p. 145.

20. See Kerrl's speech to the *Wirtschaftsrat der deutschen Akademie*, 16 Oct. 1935, in P. Meier-Benneckenstein, *Dokumente der deutschen Politik*, Bd. 3 (Berlin, 1937), pp. 267–70, and minutes of a meeting between Kerrl and representatives of the *Länder*, 8 Aug. 1935, in H. Michaelis, E. Schraepler, *Ursachen und Folgen* (Berlin, n.d.), xi. 213–21.

generally acceptable and like Müller, Kerrl began to rely
increasingly on force. On 15 February 1937 Hitler intervened
again and announced new elections. The reasons for this step
are unknown. It was apparently a repudiation of Kerrl's new
tough tactics and a decision at last for non-intervention.
Presumably Hitler decided to break free of the tiresome
burden of church politics. He may have hoped that the
church would break up into warring factions and that its
public influence would be weakened.[21] However, in March he
hesitated and deferred a decision on the election date; he
then postponed this decision indefinitely so that the elections
were never held.[22] There is a suggestion that he decided that
the Protestant opposition was strong enough for the election
to be interpreted as a defeat for the Third Reich.[23] Once
again the fact of previous intervention made a policy of
disengagement difficult. As his plans for a more aggressive
foreign policy matured in 1937, Hitler also had an interest in
avoiding domestic division such as the election campaign
might cause.[24]

The period from March 1937 until the outbreak of war in
September 1939 was the most dangerous time. Two
attempts, Müller's and Kerrl's, to establish a partnership
between the church and the Third Reich had collapsed. In
1938, Hitler's domestic position was strengthened when he
assumed control over the German army. The church had
cause to fear that its relatively sheltered existence would no
longer be allowed. But, although from 1937 until 1940 police
activity against Protestant clergy was at a higher level than
previously, it remained a selective deterrent.[25] Nor was there

21. Rosenberg noted in his diary that the church might fall apart;
Wenschkewitz, 'Politische Versuche einer Ordnung der Deutschen Evangelischen
Kirche durch den Reichskirchenminister', pp. 122-3.
22. On this period, see H. Brunotte, 'Die kirchenpolitische Kurs der
Deutschen Evangelischen Kirchenkanzlei von 1937 bis 1945' in *Arbeiten zur
Geschichte des Kirchenkampfes* (Göttingen, 1965), xv. 95-145.
23. Ibid., pp. 100-1.
24. Kerrl is reported to have referred in July 1937 to the importance for
reasons of foreign policy of avoiding conflict with the churches. For this as an
explanation of Hitler's changes of tactics towards the Catholic church in this
period, see H. G. Hockerts, *Die Sittlichkeitsprozeße gegen katholische Ordensangehörige und Priester 1936/1937* (Mainz, 1971), pp. 75-7.
25. F. Zipfel, *Kirchenkampf in Deutschland 1933-1945* (Berlin, 1965), p.
124.

any change of religious policy: Hitler neither enforced integration on the church as Kerrl wished, nor separation as the
Nazi radicals would have liked.[26] The church was probably
again protected by the dangers of Hitler's foreign policy
which made national unity a first priority. On 19 January
1940 Rosenberg recorded a conversation of a few days before
about religious policy, during which: 'The Führer said tough,
political action was naturally also thinkable; but only when
Germany's international position was completely secure.
Otherwise the domestic political strife which would break
out could ruin us'.[27] The nearest Hitler came to a change of
policy was in his Reichstag speech of 30 January 1939 when
he threatened the churches with separation of church and
state if their existing, privileged position did not content
them.[28]

This uneasy *modus vivendi* continued within the pre-1939
German Reich during the war. Hitler ordered that no
measures were to be taken which would upset relations with
the churches.[29] This did not apply, however, to the area of
occupied Poland, known as the Warthegau, where the Nazi
radicals were given a free hand to produce a model Nazi
society. This included a new system of church–state relations
which could be described without qualification as persecution. The aim was to reduce church influence to the minimum by destroying its legal and financial security and its
place in education, and by prohibiting any activity (such as
welfare work) outside the church. Only adults were allowed
to be church members and no government official, party

---

26. On the increasing influence of Bormann and the attitude of Himmler and
Heydrich, see K. Scholder, 'Die Kirchen im Dritten Reich' in *aus politik und zeit
geschichte, beilage zur wochen zeitung das parlament* B 15 (1971), 27–9. On
Himmler, also J. Ackermann, *Heinrich Himmler als Ideologe* (Göttingen, 1970),
pp. 88–96.

27. Seraphim, *Das politische Tagebuch Alfred Rosenbergs*, p. 118.

28. M. Domarus, *Hitler, Reden und Proklamationen 1932–1945* (Würzburg,
1962-3), ii. 1058-60.

29. H. Mohr, *Katholische Orden und deutscher Imperialismus* (Berlin, 1965),
pp. 315, 316-7, 328-9. This order was, however, incompletely observed. See the
memorandum from Bishop Wurm to Kerrl, December 1941, in R. Fischer, G.
Schäfer, *Landesbischof D. Wurm und der nationalsozialistische Staat 1940–1945.
Eine Dokumentation.* (Stuttgart, 1968), pp. 279–86.

member, or school teacher was allowed to belong to a church.[30]

It is possible that Hitler intended to implement this programme throughout Germany once the war was over[31] but his comments during the war do not suggest that he had committed himself. Sometimes he repeated the views he had expressed in April 1933. On 14 October 1941, for instance, he declared, 'The best thing is to let Christianity die a natural death' and on 13 December 1941 he said that when the war was over, 'I shall then consider that my life's final task will be to solve the religious problem'. He went on, 'When I was younger, I thought it was necessary to set about matters with dynamite. I've since realised that there's room for a little subtlety. The rotten branch falls of itself'. Perhaps thinking of his support in the past for Müller's and Kerrl's Reichskirche, he added, 'Against a Church that identifies itself with the State, as in England, I have nothing to say. But, even so, it's impossible eternally to hold humanity in bondage with lies.'.[32] On 8 February 1942 he adopted a more threatening tone:

The evil that's gnawing out vitals is our priests, of both creeds. I can't at present give them the answer they've been asking for, but it will cost them nothing to wait. It's all written down in my big book. The time will come when I'll settle my account with them, and I'll go straight to the point . . . I shan't let myself by hampered by juridical scruples. Only necessity has legal force. In less than ten years from now, things with have quite another look, I can promise them.[33]

30. Conway, *The Nazi Persecution of the Churches,* pp. 311–22. The churches involved were German churches, (the area was formerly the Prussian province of Posen). Polish Catholics were the victims of much more brutal persecution.

31. Nazi radicals certainly expected that the influence of the churches would be eliminated as soon as Hitler was free to deal with them. See Schäfer and Fischer, *Landesbischof D. Wurm und der nationalsozialistische Staat,* pp. 19–23.

32. *Hitler's Table Talk,* pp. 59, 142–3.

33. Ibid., p. 304. A similar remark, recorded by Rosenberg, is quoted in H. Buchheim, 'War die katholische Kirche eine vom nationalsozialistischen Regime verfolgte Organization?' in *Gutachten des Instituts für Zeitgeschichte* (Munich, 1958), p. 45. Goebbels too recorded that Hitler had decided 'inexorably' to destroy the Christian churches after victory; Bollmus, *Das Amt Rosenberg und seine Gegner,* p. 117.

However, according to Albert Speer,

Even after 1942 Hitler went on maintaining that he regarded the church as indispensable in political life. He would be happy, he said . . . if someday a prominent churchman turned up who was suited to lead one of the churches—or if possible both the Catholic and Protestant churches reunited. He still regretted that Reich Bishop Müller was not the right man to carry out his far-reaching plans.

Speer adds that Hitler 'sharply condemned the campaign against the church',

Undoubtedly, he continued, the church would learn to adapt to the political goals of National Socialism in the long run, as it had always adapted in the course of history. A new party religion would only bring about a relapse into the mysticism of the Middle Ages. The growing SS myth showed that clearly enough, as did Rosenberg's unreadable *Myth of the Twentieth Century*.[34]

The most probable explanation of this conflicting evidence is that the confusion, which had characterized Hitler's attitude towards the churches from the start, remained unresolved.[35]

ii. The Reaction of the Protestant Church

a. *Conflict within the church*

The uncertainty of Nazi policy placed the Protestant church in an unusual position. If it had been persecuted as an enemy of the state, it would have had no choice but resistance. If the separation of church and state had been enforced, it would have been bitterly opposed as it was in the Warthegau in 1941 and as it had been previously in Prussia in 1918. Equally, if the church had been made to conform to Nazi ideology, those Protestants who believed this to be irreconcilable with Christianity would have been forced into opposition.

---

34. Speer, *Inside the Third Reich*, p. 95.

35. There seems no reason to discount Speer's record which, he says, is based on notes made during his first years of imprisonment (p. 94). It is, however, in direct conflict with the *Table Talk* where Hitler, for instance, said he was glad that the Reich bishop experiment had failed (see above, p. 149). This contradiction cannot simply be explained by Bormann's eagerness to record deprecating comments on the church (noted by Speer, p. 95) because the other source for the *Table Talk*, the text of Dr. H. Picker, gives essentially the same picture of Hitler's views despite some differences of detail. Picker, *Hitlers Tischgespräche im Führerhauptquartier 1941–1942*, especially pp. 154–6, 176, 393–6.

But (with the exception of the Warthegau) the church was faced with none of these. At times, it seemed as though compulsory separation or integration might occur and, indeed, the two main attempts at integration (by Müller and Kerrl) were known to have Hitler's support and were able to call upon some assistance from the police. However, when put to the test, Hitler drew back from full-scale terror. Instead, the main aim of Nazi policy until 1937 was to win the voluntary integration of the Protestant church, and when stalemate had been reached in 1937, Hitler shelved the problem. This meant that the main question for the church was not how it should resist persecution, but whether it would agree to do the state's bidding. The Kirchenkampf was, in the first place, a conflict within the church about what its answer should be.

The first stage of this conflict ended in the election of Müller as the first Reich bishop in September 1933.[36] His victory was made possible by strong support for the German Christians in the parishes, the division of the church leadership and the help of Hitler. Nevertheless, by 1935 it was clear that Müller's attempt to reorganize the church on Nazi principles had miscarried. Müller himself, deserted by his friends, was pushed aside. How did this change of fortunes occur?

The most important reason was that the opposition within the Protestant church was strong enough to prevent voluntary integration. On 21 September 1933 Martin Niemöller launched the Pastor's Emergency League as an organization for clergymen who were being harassed by the German Christians. Members promised to stand by the Gospel and the Reformation creeds and they affirmed that the introduction of an 'Aryan paragraph' into the church would violate the creed.[37] At the National Synod in Wittenberg on 27 September 1933 at which Müller was elected Reich bishop, a declaration was posted in the name of 2,000 members of the Pastors' Emergency League protesting against the suppression

36. See above, p. 141.
37. This forbade Jews to hold church office, on the model of Nazi legislation for the civil service. It had been introduced into the Old Prussian Union on 6 Sept. 1933. *Kirchliches Jahrbuch,* 60.-71. Jg. (1933-44), 24.

of the views of the opposition and proclaiming that the church was in fact deeply divided. By January 1934 over 7,000 pastors, nearly half the total number, had joined the League.[38]

The opposition to Müller was greatly assisted by a crisis within the German Christian movement at the end of 1933. The radical German Christians were dissatisfied with Müller. To become Reich bishop, he had presented himself as a sensible, moderate man whom the old church leadership could trust and, at the same time, as the man who could keep the German Christians under control. After the German Christian victory in the parish elections of July 1933, the radicals were no longer ready to accept this approach. Müller, however, realized that he still needed wider support than the German Christians. He was prepared to share power in the Reichskirche with the Lutheran bishops who had mostly supported his candidacy to the Reich bishopric and he did not introduce an Aryan paragraph for the whole Reichskirche into the National Synod. The radicals tried to force a break at a meeting of the Berlin section of the German Christians. A resolution was passed condemning a 'hollow truce' and demanding the dismissal of clergy who were unable to work 'in the spirit of National Socialism'. The criteria by which this was to be judged were indicated by the further demands for the introduction of an Aryan paragraph, the rejection of the Old Testament and 'oriental distortion' of the Gospel in favour of a heroic picture of Christ. This meeting discredited the movement among many of those who had voted for it in July 1933. Müller felt it necessary to dissociate himself by giving up his title of 'Protector'. The remaining German Christians split into three separate organizations. Their potential as a mass movement for the conquest of the church had been destroyed.[39]

This was an opportune moment for the Protestant opposition. Its main objective was to secure Müller's resignation from the Reich bishopric. When Müller tried to suppress criticism by a decree which became known as the 'muzzle

38. W. Niemöller, *Texte zur Geschichte des Pfarrernotbundes* (Berlin, 1958), p. 10.

39. K. Meier, *Die Deutschen Christen* (Göttingen, 1964), pp. 35–56.

decree', the Pastors' Emergency League issued a protest to be
read from the pulpits. It criticized Müller for not taking more
energetic action against paganism in the church and for
threatening to coerce those who stuck to the creed; the
League declared that they had lost confidence in Müller and
would not obey his decree. Müller's position was, however,
temporarily strengthened by Hitler. At a meeting with Protestant leaders on 25 January 1934, he succeeded in isolating
Niemöller and winning the renewed support of the Lutheran
bishops for Müller's leadership.[40]

Müller proceeded to waste this advantage by attempting to
enforce the subordination of the individual Landeskirchen
into the central Reichskirche. In north Germany, where the
German Christians had in most cases established a strong hold
over the official church leadership, this was not difficult.
However, the move was bitterly resisted by the Protestant
opposition which started to organize its own separate
synods.[41] Müller tried to suppress the opposition by suspend-
ing the clergy concerned. The one official synod (in Westphalia) where the opposition to the German Christians was in
the majority was closed by the police. In April 1934 Müller
summoned to his assistance August Jäger whose ruthless
methods the church had already experienced in June 1933.[42]

By threatening the independence of the Landeskirchen,
however, Müller forfeited the support of the Lutheran
bishops, three of whom remained in office—Marahrens of
Hanover, Wurm of Württemberg, and Meiser of Bavaria. They
now joined the Protestant opposition around Niemöller in a
united front against Müller's Reichskirche. In two famous
synods at Barmen and Berlin-Dahlem in May and October
1934, they condemned the Reichskirche as heretical and
declared that they, the 'Confessing Church',[43] constituted

40. W. Niemöller, *Hitler und die evangelischen Kirchenführer* (Bielefeld,
1959); H. Baier, 'Das Verhalten der lutherischen Bischöfe gegenüber dem
nationalsozialistischen Staat 1933/34' in *Tutzinger Texte, Sonderband I, Kirchenkampf* (Munich, 1969), pp. 87–116.
41. *Kirchliches Jahrbuch*, 60.–71. Jg. (1933–44), 45.
42. See above, pp. 137–9.
43. The term was derived from the German word for creed, *Bekenntnis*. The
'Confessing' (German, *Bekennende*) Church means the church which confessed
the creed.

the rightful church; they set up their own organization in competition with the Reichskirche. The Barmen synod rejected 'the false doctrine that the state could and should exercise single and total control over human life including the church'.[44] When, in October 1934, Müller and Jäger attempted to enforce the submission of the Württemberg and Bavarian Landeskirchen and had the bishops put under house arrest, they were met by popular demonstrations of support for the bishops.[45] The opposition had now become embarrassing to Hitler and Müller was forced to withdraw. He attempted to save his position by annulling the legislation incorporating the Landeskirchen into the Reichskirche, but he no longer exercised any authority although he continued to carry the title of Reich bishop.[46]

Confessing Church leaders proposed that the state should recognize their claim to the leadership of the whole church.[47] Instead, Hitler appointed Hans Kerrl to administer church affairs. At first Kerrl was conciliatory towards the Confessing Church and admitted that the state had made mistakes. However, he was not prepared to reverse Nazi policy and side with the Confessing Church against the German Christians. Instead, he set up a new organization which was committed to neither side. It consisted of a Reich Church committee of clergymen who had not taken part in the conflict. The task of the committee was to administer the so-called 'disrupted' Landeskirchen where both the German Christians and the Confessing Church were strongly represented for a transitional period of two years. During this time, the committee was to find a platform which both sides could accept and which would meet the interests of the Third Reich. The state would then withdraw from church politics. On 17 October 1935, the Reich Church committee issued its first public declaration which affirmed that the 'inalienable basis' of the German Protestant church was the Gospel and

44. *Kirchliches Jahrbuch*, 60.–71. Jg. (1933–44), 65.

45. A comprehensive account of the events in Bavaria is given in H. Baier, *Die Deutschen Christen Bayerns im Rahmen des bayerischen Kirchenkampfes* (Nuremberg, 1968), pp. 128–72.

46. H. Hermelink, *Kirche im Kampf* (Tübingen, 1950), pp. 83–191.

47. K. D. Schmidt, *Dokumente des Kirchenkampfes II, Die Zeit des Reichskirchenausschusses 1935–1937* (Göttingen, 1964–5), i. 3–7.

the Reformation creeds but went on to say that it approved
of the National Socialist principles of 'race, blood, and
soil'.[48]

The committee put the Confessing Church in a difficult
position. It was a defeat for the German Christians in so far
as their title to the official church leadership had not been
recognized but the claim of the Confessing Church had not
been accepted either. What confidence could they have in an
attempt to find agreement with the German Christians whom
they had condemned as heretics? The fact that the attempt
originated with the government made it particularly suspect.
The Confessing Church leaders in most of the 'disrupted'
areas therefore refused to co-operate with the Reich Church
committee. When Kerrl prohibited their organization they
declared they would not obey him.[49]

However, the churches which had not been split by the
German Christians, the so-called 'intact' churches, judged the
situation differently although they were also members of the
Confessing Church. They, (the most important were
Württemberg and Bavaria) did not come under the Reich
Church committee and they did not believe that the attempt
to restore unity to the 'disrupted' churches was to be
condemned outright. The Lutheran Hanover Landeskirche
adopted the same policy although it was not completely
'intact'. (Its organization was reformed in agreement with the
Minister for Church Affairs but its bishop, Marahrens, was
left in control.)[50] This difference led to a bitter split within
the Confessing Church as a result of which two separate
leaderships, one for the 'disrupted' churches and one for the
'intact' churches with Hanover, were formed.[51]

The opposition in the 'disrupted' churches, however, was
enough to ensure the failure of the Reich Church committee.
The committee's object had been to find a common plat-

48. *Kirchliches Jahrbuch,* 60.–71. Jg. (1933–44), 104. See, further, K. D.
Schmidt, *Dokumente des Kirchenkampfes II,* particularly the meetings of
Confessing Church leaders with Kerrl on 23 Aug. and 27 Nov. 1935, ibid. ii.
1372–7, and i. 83–90.

49. *Kirchliches Jahrbuch,* ibid., 105–9.

50. E. Klügel, *Die lutherische Landeskirche Hannovers und ihr Bischof
1933–1945* (Berlin and Hamburg, 1964–5), i. 283–9.

51. K. D. Schmidt, *Dokumente des Kirchenkampfes II,* i. XXIII–IV.

form. Instead, it won only the rather reluctant support of the more moderate of the German Christians and the co-operation of the 'intact' churches. It resigned when it tried to extend its authority to the Landeskirchen of Thuringia, Mecklenburg, and Lübeck, which were under the control of a radical German Christian group, but was prevented by Kerrl.[52]

The second major attempt to achieve the voluntary integration of the Protestant church had failed. Both experiments raised the fundamental question of whether the church attached the same importance to race as did the Third Reich. This was bound to arise whoever tried to implement Hitler's policy. Despite attempts to evade the issue, the controversy over the Aryan paragraph showed that a significant group within the church was not, in this instance, prepared to adopt Nazi principles. Hitler, like Frederick William III, found that by interfering with the creed he had overreached himself.[53]

The resignation of the Reich Church committee was followed by a period of confusion. Hitler announced elections but then postponed them indefinitely. The fact that Hitler dared not risk new elections which the Confessing Church threatened to boycott, showed the progress it had made since the German Christian victory in July 1933.[54] Kerrl took a number of measures to increase the pressure against the Confessing Church.[55] Particularly important were his powers to control church expenditure, which could be used to starve the Confessing Church of funds, and which were extended in June 1937 to include collections taken from church congregations.

The failure to reach agreement with Kerrl also left the Confessing Church more exposed to the enmity of the anti-Christian group in the Nazi party. In 1937 some 805 pastors including Martin Niemöller were arrested; most were

52. *Kirchliches Jahrbuch,* 60.–71. Jg. (1933–44), 140–53; K. D. Schmidt, *Dokumente des Kirchenkampfes II,* ii. 1347–55. See also Meier, *Die Deutschen Christen* pp. 110–44, 209–15.

53. See above, pp. 1–2.

54. On the attitude of the Confessing Church to the election, see J. Schmidt, *Martin Niemöller im Kirchenkampf,* pp. 416–32.

55. *Kirchliches Jahrbuch,* 60.–71. Jg. (1933–44), 165–6, 188–90, 201, 224–5.

detained only for short periods, but Niemöller, whose attacks on Nazi church policy had been particularly sharp, was held in concentration camps until 1945 despite a verdict in his favour by the court;[56] others suffered from restrictions such as being forbidden to speak in public or expulsion from their parishes. In October 1937 Himmler prohibited the theological schools set up by the Confessing Church.[57] At the same time Rosenberg, whose influence had caused the church concern before, published a new attack on the church.[58]

In October 1938 partly in order to resist the growing strength of the anti-Christian group in the party, Kerrl presented new proposals for ending the conflict but this initiative had even less success than the Reich Church committee.[59] The leaders of the 'intact' churches put forward counter-proposals which had the support of 67 per cent of Protestant clergy, but which did not go far enough for Kerrl.[60] When he tried instead to secure acceptance of a number of basic principles, only Bishop Marahrens from among the Confessing Church leaders was prepared to agree and he was mainly motivated by the hope that Kerrl would be able to restrain the Rosenberg group and ease the pressure on the Confessing Church.[61] By the summer of 1939 it was clear that this last attempt at agreement had failed.

b. *Conflict with the state*

Interference by the state in church affairs and the violation of moral standards by the Nazi party provoked a number of important protests from the Confessing Church. This gave the

56. Zipfel, *Kirchenkampf in Deutschland*, p. 124. J. Schmidt, *Martin Niemöller im Kirchenkampf*, pp. 425–47.

57. *Kirchliches Jahrbuch*, 60.–71. Jg. (1933–44), 209.

58. A. Rosenberg, *Protestantische Rompilger*, (Munich, 1937). In the introduction Rosenberg explained that he had completed the book in 1935 but had delayed publication in the hope that 'a great part of Protestant orthodoxy would find its way back to the nation'. But the tolerance of the state had, he said, only made church leaders more provocative and he had therefore decided to publish.

59. *Kirchliches Jahrbuch*, 60.–71. Jg. (1933–44), 278–9. Wenschkewitz, 'Politische Versuche einer Ordnung der Deutschen Evangelischen Kirche durch den Reichskirchenminister', pp. 125–38.

60. *Kirchliches Jahrbuch*, ibid., 279–80, 283–90. Klügel, *Die lutherische Landeskirche Hannovers and ihr Bischof*, i. 362.

61. *Kirchliches Jahrbuch*, ibid., 299–301; Klügel, op. cit., i. 363–70.

Kirchenkampf a second dimension as a conflict not simply within the church but between the Confessing Church and the Third Reich. By its policies, the Nazi party forced the Confessing Church to become what has been described as a 'reluctant resistance movement'.[62] The protests took the form of declarations by synods, appeals to Hitler and to Kerrl, and announcements to be read from the pulpits including prayers for clergymen who had been arrested.

The memorandum from the leaders of the Confessing Church in the 'disrupted' Landeskirchen to Hitler, dated 28 May 1936, is the most impressive example.[63] The authors declared that attacks on the church were more pronounced than at any time since 1918. Important people in the state and the Nazi party were involved; was it to become official policy? The church was never given the opportunity to reply (a reference to press and radio censorship). A deliberate policy of undermining the church was being pursued under cover of promises to respect its integrity. Clergy had been imprisoned and even interned in concentration camps. Their public influence was being reduced under the pretext of 'overcoming denominational divisions'. The church was discredited by the Hitler Youth and other Nazi organizations and parents were put under pressure not to send their children to denominational schools. Religious education was often perverted by the exclusion of the Old Testament and the inclusion of Germanic paganism and in theological faculties preference was given to those who taught false doctrine (the German Christians). Items of Christian interest were increasingly excluded from the mass media. The Christian could not accept that blood and race were eternal truths; the glorification of the Aryan race was in conflict with the doctrine that all men were sinners and anti-Semitism in the form of hatred of the Jews was in conflict with the principle of loving one's neighbour. The new morality put national expediency above respect for truth or the individual conscience. Particular mention was made of arbitrary justice, the concentration camps, and the Gestapo. All this amounted to

62. E. Wolf, 'Political and Moral Motives behind the Resistance in H. Graml, H. Mommsen, H-J. Reichhardt, E. Wolf, *The German Resistance to Hitler* (Engl. edn., London, 1970), p. 209.
63. K. D. Schmidt, *Dokumente des Kirchenkampfes II*, i. 695–719.

a campaign of de-christianization which would lead the nation to destruction. Hitler himself was frequently honoured in a way which was appropriate only to God.

The memorandum was delivered to the Reich Chancellery on 4 June 1936.[64] Against the wishes of its authors, who had intended to keep it secret until they saw what effect it would have, the text was made available to the foreign press in July by members of the church. Its publication abroad forced the authors to take responsibility for it.[65] They issued an address to be read from the pulpits, a course which had already been considered in case they were met by official silence. The address, circulated for Sunday 23 August, contained a summary of the memorandum, though it was less specific on certain matters including arbitrary justice and anti-Semitism.[66] It gave church members a formula for 'reluctant resistance' by reminding them that 'the Protestant Christian should be loyal to his state and nation always and in all circumstances. Loyalty includes resistance by a Christian against an order that is contrary to God's Word, thereby recalling the state to obedience to God'. It is estimated that about 1,000,000 copies of the address were circulated and that about three-quarters of the Confessing Church pastors in the 'disrupted' Landeskirchen read it from the pulpit. It did not have the support of the leaders of the 'intact' churches although they were responsible for other statements which were not as detailed and direct.

In the years after 1936 the Confessing Church reasserted its principles on several important occasions. In September 1938 when it seemed that war was imminent over Czechoslovakia, they issued an order of prayer which was in marked contrast to the nationalist tone hitherto characteristic of wartime religious pronouncements. It included the following confession:

We confess before you the sins of our nation. Your Name is blasphemed, Your Word is opposed, Your Truth is suppressed. Much

64. For the following events see W. Niemöller, *Die bekennende Kirche sagt Hitler die Wahrheit* (Bielefeld, 1954).

65. They did not, however, attempt to protect those involved in its release to the press. One of these, Dr. Weissler, died in 1937 in a concentration camp as a result of maltreatment.

66. K. D. Schmidt, *Dokumente des Kirchenkampfes II*, ii. 984-9.

injustice has happened in public and in secret. Parents and masters are scorned, life is injured and destroyed, marriage broken, property robbed and the honour of the neighbour violated.

The prayer was in fact never used because of the Munich agreement. The Nazis, nevertheless, reacted angrily to it, perhaps because they were already sensitive to popular fears of war.[67] Kerrl accused the Confessing Church leaders concerned of treason and threatened to have them sent to concentration camps. He succeeded once again in splitting the opposition by securing a statement from the leaders of the 'intact' churches that they disapproved of the prayers 'for religious and patriotic reasons'.[68]

Despite its assertion of moral principles, the Confessing Church was slow to take up the cause of Jewish persecution. From the outset it recognized that within the church there could be no racial distinctions, and after 1939, when this again became an issue, it renewed its opposition to measures like the Aryan paragraph in the church. It did not, however, dispute the right of the state to enforce a system of total discrimination against Jews in secular life. This was partly because of fear of exposing the church on a political issue on which the Nazis would brook no opposition but it was also due to the widespread belief that there was a 'Jewish problem' which required some action. The Confessing Church did recognize dangers in anti-Semitism and it tried to offer humanitarian assistance to the victims. The 1936 memorandum rejected 'anti-Semitism in the form of hatred of the Jews' and in September 1938 an organization was set up under Pastor Grüber to offer relief and to arrange emigration.[69] The pogrom of November 1938, however, passed without public condemnation though there were individual protests. A conference in Berlin in December 1938 expressed solidarity with those pastors who had been victimized because 'in face of the action against the Jews they had preached the ten commandments in earnest, and it also

---

67. Cf. Boberach, *Berichte des SD und der Gestapo über Kirchen und Kirchenvolk*, p. 298.

68. *Kirchliches Jahrbuch*, 60.-71. Jg. (1933–44), 263–72.

69. H. Grüber, *Erinnerungen aus sieben Jahrzehnten* (Cologne and Berlin, 1968), pp. 103–45.

expressed sympathy for Jewish Christians. However, in May 1939, during Kerrl's last attempt at integration, the leaders of the 'intact' churches were still prepared to agree that 'a serious and responsible racial policy for maintaining the purity of our people is necessary' though they refused Kerrl's formulation approving a 'relentless campaign' against Jewish influence.[70]

The programme of extermination from 1941 forced the Confessing Church to take a new stand. Church leaders had already been alerted to the Nazi method of mass killing by the euthanasia programme against the mentally and incurably sick. A member of the staff of the Inner Mission, Pastor Braune, prepared a detailed memorandum exposing the programme which the Nazis had attempted to keep secret.[71] Bishop Wurm of Württemberg in a letter to the Reich Minister of the Interior, which was copied and widely circulated, condemned it and on 16 July 1943 he wrote again to Hitler on behalf of the Jews and other victims of Nazi persecution in occupied countries.[72] In October 1943 the synod of the Confessing Church in the Old Prussian Union declared:

It is not given to the state to wield the sword beyond killing the criminal and the enemy in war. Whoever does so notwithstanding kills wilfully and to his own detriment . . . Concepts such as 'extermination', 'liquidation', and 'useless life' are unknown in the divine order. The annihilation of people merely because they are related to a criminal, or because they are old or mentally sick, or because they belong to another race, is a wielding of the sword that is not given to the state by God . . .

Man's life belongs to God alone. It is sacred to Him, as are the lives of the People of Israel.[73]

The protests of the Confessing Church against the Third Reich were made because the church believed it had a duty

---

70. K. Meier, *Kirche und Judentum. Die Haltung der evangelischen Kirche zur Judenpolitik des Dritten Reiches* (Göttingen, 1968).

71. H. C. von Hase, *Evangelische Dokumente zur Ermordung der "unheilbar Kranken" unter der nationalsozialistischen Herrschaft in den Jahren 1939–1945* (Stuttgart, 1964), pp. 14–22, 108–16.

72. For these and other statements by Wurm on the same topics, see Schäfer and Fischer, *Landesbischof D. Wurm und der nationalsozialistische Staat*, pp. 113–71.

73. *Kirchliches Jahrbuch*, 60.–71. Jg. (1933–44), 401.

to uphold certain basic moral principles, if necessary against the state. It was never the aim of the Confessing Church, however, to be a political resistance movement, working to overthrow the Third Reich.[74] In the first years of the Kirchenkampf, the Confessing Church repeatedly affirmed its loyalty to the state.[75] Martin Niemöller sent Hitler a telegram of congratulations when Germany left the League of Nations in 1933 and the Confessing church leadership again congratulated Hitler on the result of the Saar plebiscite in 1935 (though by this time Niemöller disapproved of the gesture).[76] The memorandum of 1936 and the address to the parishes showed that the church was becoming more critical. Its language betrayed, however, the dismay it felt at going over to opposition. The address to the parishes referred to the welcome given by Protestants to the 'new beginning' three years before and declared that they found it 'almost inconceivable' that representatives of the German state should turn against the Gospel.[77] Martin Niemöller at his trial in 1938 did not attack the Third Reich, but rather defended himself against the accusation of disloyalty by referring to his past career as a naval officer and the fact that he had voted for the NSDAP from 1924.[78] In the same year the Confessing Church agreed to allow its clergy to take an oath of loyalty to Hitler, provided it was made clear that this could not infringe their primary loyalty to God.[79] When, at the time of the Sudeten crisis, Karl Barth wrote that every Czech soldier would be fighting for the Christian church, the Confessing Church accused him of speaking as a politician and not as a theologian.[80]

74. W. Niemöller, *Die evangelische Kirche im dritten Reich*, (Bielefeld, 1956), p. 396.

75. See for instance *Kirchliches Jahrbuch*, 60.–71. Jg. (1933–44), 93, 112.

76. Zipfel, *Kirchenkampf in Deutschland*, p. 87.

77. K. D. Schmidt, *Dokumente des Kirchenkampfes II*, ii. 985.

78. Zipfel, *Kirchenkampf in Deutschland*, pp. 101–2.

79. A. Gerlach-Praetorius, *Die Kirche vor der Eidesfrage* (Göttingen, 1967), pp. 115–16.

80. *Kirchliches Jahrbuch*, 60.–71. Jg. (1933–44), 265. Karl Barth, a leading Protestant theologian, had a major influence on the Barmen declaration of 1934. In 1935 he was forced to give up his chair in Bonn by the Nazis and left Germany for his native Switzerland.

The reasons why the Confessing Church accepted an opposition role only slowly and incompletely are complex. Part of the explanation is theological doctrine, including the Lutheran tradition of obedience to the state. The belief that the church should be free of politics was also important. The main attack on the German Christians had been precisely because they were attempting to make the church conform to a political model. Confessing Church leaders were also influenced by tactical considerations. Hitler warned repeatedly that, while he would protect religious freedom, he would not tolerate political priests.[81] Confessing Church leaders naturally sought to use the guarantee of religious freedom against harassment by the anti-Christian group in the Nazi party and coercion by the German Christians, without incurring the charge of political disloyalty.

Confessing Church leaders were also only gradually alienated from the Third Reich. This remains an inadequately explored subject but it seems that only in exceptional cases had a position of total rejection of the Nazi state been reached before the Second World War. Karl Barth had reached this position from outside Germany in 1938. He condemned Nazism as an utterly destructive, inhumane, totalitarian dictatorship against which the church should pray as it had once prayed for the downfall of Islam.[82] Another theologian, Dietrich Bonhoeffer, expressed a similar view in June 1939:

Christians in Germany will face the terrible alternative of either willing the defeat of their nation in order that Christian civilization may survive, or willing the victory of their nation and thereby destroying our civilization. I know which of these alternatives I must choose . . .

This attitude led Bonhoeffer to involvement with the conspiracy against Hitler which cost him his life.[83]

---

81. In his speech to the Reichstag of 30 Jan. 1939 for instance, he declared, 'We will protect the German priest as a servant of God, but we will destroy the priest as a political enemy of the German Reich'. M. Domarus, *Hitler, Reden und Proklamationen*, ii. 1061.

82. K. Barth, 'Die Kirche und die politische Frage von heute' (1938) in K. Barth, *Eine Schweizer Stimme, 1938–1945* (Zurich, 1945), pp. 69–107.

83. E. Bethge, *Dietrich Bonhoeffer. Theologian, Christian, Contemporary* (Engl. edn., London, 1970), p. 559.

This was not the view of the Confessing Church as a whole. It remained trapped by the attitudes which had led the Protestant leadership to applaud the 'national revolution' of 1933. The belief that the Third Reich was a natural reaction to the national humiliation of the years 1918–33 made it very difficult to admit that Nazism was irreparably perverted and that Germans had a duty to destroy it. Perhaps, in addition to fear of Nazi reprisals, this is the explanation of the psychological block which Bishop Wurm noted in his memoirs. Referring to the failure of the Confessing Church to react to the pogrom of November 1938, he wrote: 'In those years whether one was gathered in a large or small group—it was as if there was a spell over us, as if our mouths were closed by an invisible power.'[84] Even during the Second World War when disillusion with the Third Reich became intense, a Confessing Church report (from the Winter of 1941–2) noted:

A desperate conflict is going on between having confidence in the Führer and recognizing reality. Even among the Confessing Church parishes of the Wuppertal there was recently a rumour abroad that Hitler had experienced conversion and now confesses the Christian faith and like Bismarck of old is reading the daily watchwords of the Moravian Brethren.[85]

In October 1945 the Confessing Church leaders acknowledged their failure. They declared to representatives of the ecumenical movement,

With great pain we say: through us endless suffering has been brought over many nations and countries . . . We certainly fought through long

84. T. Wurm, *Erinnerungen aus meinem Leben* (Stuttgart, 1953), p. 148. Wurm's attitude hardened during the war with the experience of Nazi mass murder and because he came to the conclusion that the Nazis intended to destroy Christianity. In addition to his many protests to government and party leaders, he also tried to convince other church leaders of the futility of concessions. Although he was in contact with resistance circles, however, he does not seem to have played a major part within them. Nor did he look forward to Germany's defeat by the Allies. Schäfer and Fischer, *Landesbischof D. Wurm und der nationalsozialistische Staat*, pp. 270, 318–65.

85. *Kirchliches Jahrbuch*, 60.-71. Jg. (1933–44), 386. The Moravian Brethren are a Protestant sect. Their 'watchwords', biblical extracts and prayers for daily use, were widely read by German Protestants.

years in the Name of Jesus Christ against the spirit which found terrible expression in the National Socialist regime of violence but we blame ourselves for not confessing more courageously, praying more truly, believing more joyfully and loving more ardently.[86]

Martin Niemöller was more specific. To German audiences, he said,

In 1933 and the following years there were in Germany 14,000 Protestant clergy and nearly as many parishes. If we had then recognized that in the Communists who were thrown into concentration camps, the Lord Jesus Christ Himself lay imprisoned and looked for our love and help, if we had seen that at the beginning of the persecution of the Jews it was the Lord Christ in the person of the least of our human brethren who was being persecuted and beaten and killed, if we had stood by him and identified ourselves with him, I do not know whether God would not then have stood by us and whether the whole thing would not then have had to take a different course.[87]

iii. Conclusion

The record of the Protestant church under the Third Reich compares favourably with that of secular institutions. This was partly because Hitler supported a policy of voluntary integration which allowed the church more freedom than institutions like the press and the universities.[88] However, had Hitler decided on more determined coercion, this would have aroused stronger resistance than occurred in secular institutions and Hitler's fear of a conflict was one reason for his relative moderation.

Protestant opposition existed because, despite the appeal of Nazism, a substantial body of church members including between a third and a half of all Protestant clergy found in loyalty to their creed an independent standard of

86. *Kirchliches Jahrbuch*, 72.–75. Jg. (1945–1948), 26. A. Boyens,'Das Stuttgarter Schuldbekenntnis vom 19. Oktober 1945' in *Vierteljahrshefte für Zeitgeschichte*, 19. Jg. (1971), 374–97.
87. *Kirchliches Jahrbuch*, ibid., 34.
88. For a description of the press and education, see K. D. Bracher, *The German Dictatorship*, (Engl. edn., London, 1971), pp. 247–72. The Roman Catholic church requires separate treatment. It did not face the problem of integration in the same way as the Protestant church; on the other hand it suffered worse persecution. See Lewy, *The Catholic Church and Nazi Germany* and the series of monographs and documents in course of publication by the *Kommission für Zeitgeschichte bei der Katholischen Akademie in Bayern*.

behaviour.[89] At first they did not believe this need involve them in conflict with the Third Reich but only with the German Christians' attempt to adapt the creed to Nazi ideology. Gradually, because of official support for the programme of integration and attacks on the church by Nazi radicals, and also because of an increasing awareness of the moral corruption of the Third Reich, the Confessing Church was forced unwillingly into resistance. This became most pronounced among the Confessing Church 'radicals' in the 'disrupted' Landeskirchen. Even here, however, with a few exceptions, disillusion with the Third Reich fell short of total condemnation of it before the Second World War. It required the atrocities of the war and the devastation of 1945 to shock church leaders into recognition of the character of National Socialism and of the inadequacy of their opposition.

The stand taken by the Christian churches did contribute to the defeat of one Nazi programme, the main euthanasia action—*Aktion T 4*—launched secretly in October 1939 and cancelled by Hitler in August 1941.[90] In this case the churches had strong public support and wartime morale was at risk.[91] It is natural to ask whether the churches could have led a successful opposition on other issues like arbitrary justice, the persecution of the Jews, and foreign policy. Without more knowledge of the development of public opinion during the Third Reich, it is impossible to judge what would have happened if the church opposition had set out to force the Third Reich to change its policies. We can only

89. As a Sicherheitshauptamt report noted in 1935, referring to the German Christians and the Confessing Church, 'It must be admitted that, at least as far as genuine members are concerned, neither faction is against the state. Nevertheless, there are undoubtedly a large number of inward opponents of National Socialism within the Confessing Church, simply because the church is more important to them than the state.' Boberach, *Berichte des SD und der Gestapo über Kirchen und Kirchenvolk*, p. 64.

90. Conway, *The Nazi Persecution of the Churches*, pp. 267–72; L. Gruchmann, 'Euthanasie und Justiz im Dritten Reich' in *Vierteljahrshefte für Zeitgeschichte*, 20. Jg. (1972), 235–79.

91. Hitler had also made the mistake—not repeated with the extermination of the Jews—of attempting to carry out the programme within Germany. It provoked persistent criticism from the state judicial machinery. Gruchmann, ibid.

conclude that Hitler had to accept a stalemate in church affairs for fear of the damage which a conflict would do to his other policies; but with the exception of euthanasia, he succeeded in implementing the rest of his programme without making concessions to the churches.

BIBLIOGRAPHICAL NOTE

This book relies mainly on manuscript sources. The most important collections are those of the Kirchenbund, in the archive of the *Evangelische Kirche in Deutschland* in Hanover, and of the Old Prussian Union, in the archive of the *Evangelische Kirche der Union* in West Berlin. Both these are comprehensive and intact. The files of other Landeskirchen and the private collection of Friedrich von Bodelschwingh provided further material for the Reich bishop crisis. The policy of Republican governments towards the church is less well documented. At Reich level, the appropriate files of the Reichskanzlei are useful and help to fill the gap caused by the loss of the records of the Reich Ministry of the Interior. They also contain references to important disputes at *Land* level. The records of the *Auswärtiges Amt* complement the Kirchenbund collection on foreign affairs in the archive of the *Kirchliches Außenamt* in Frankfurt-am-Main. The most important state collection for this subject, however, was the surviving records of the ecclesiastical section of the Prussian Kultusministerium (later incorporated in Hitler's *Reich Ministerium für die kirchlichen Angelegenheiten*) in the *Deutsches Zentralarchiv* at Potsdam and Merseburg. The files of the Prussian Staatsministerium in the *Geheimes Staatsarchiv* in West Berlin were also valuable.

The newspaper references in the text, other than those from publications cited in the bibliography, were taken from press cuttings in the archives. The church archives, in particular, contain a large collection of press cuttings.

A number of people involved in the events described in these pages were kind enough to grant me interviews.

BIBLIOGRAPHY

A. MANUSCRIPT SOURCES

Church Archives

1. Archiv der Evangelischen Kirche in Deutschland (E.K.D.)
   A 1. Eisenacher Konferenz
   A 2. Deutscher Evangelischer Kirchenausschuß 1918–33
      Kirche und staatspolitisches Leben
      Repräsentation und Apologetik der Kirche
      Schulakten
      Okumenische Arbeit
   A 3. Deutscher Evangelischer Kirchenbund 1922–33
   A 4. Deutsche Evangelische Kirche–Kirchenkanzlei 1933
   B 3. Kirchenbundesamt
   Miscellaneous files including Nachlaß Hundt

2. Archiv der Evangelischen Kirche der Union (E.K.U.) (formerly Old Prussian Union)
   Generalia
      Trennung von Kirche und Staat
      Konkordat und Kirchenvertrag
      Miscellaneous files on political topics
   Präsidialia
   General Synode
   Kirchensenat

3. Archiv des kirchlichen Außenamts (A.k.A)
   Stockholmer Weltkirchenkonferenz
   Kriegsschuldfrage

4. Archiv der Evangelisch-lutherischen Kirche im Hamburgischen Staate
   Miscellaneous files on the Deutsche Christen and the policy of the Landeskirche in 1933

5. Bielefelder Archiv des Kirchenkampfes im Dritten Reich
   Sammlungen Hesse, W. Niemöller, L. Müller

6. Hauptarchiv Bethel
   Reichsbischof files

7. Landeskirchliches Archiv, Nuremberg
   Nachlaß Meiser
   Miscellaneous files on the policy of the Landeskirche in 1933

8. Landeskirchliches Archiv, Stuttgart
    Nachlaß Wurm
    Miscellaneous files on the policy of the Landeskirche in 1933

9. Landeskirchliches Archiv, Hanover
    Nachlaß Marahrens
    Newspaper archive

10. Archiv des Evangelischen Konsistoriums Berlin- Brandenburg
    Nachlaß Wienecke

11. Nachlaß Kapler, in possession of Pfarrer A. Kapler, West Berlin

State Archives

1. Deutsches Zentralarchiv, Potsdam (D.Z.A.)
    Reichsministerium für die kirchlichen Angelegenheiten—
    Miscellaneous files including Trennung von Staat und Kirche,
    Neuregelung des Kirchenregiments, Deutsche Christen,
    Neuordnung der evangelischen Landeskirchen (Reichskirche)
    Evangelischer Reichsausschuß der DNVP
    Präsidialkanzlei
    Reichsinnenministerium
    Reichsjustizministerium

2. Deutsches Zentralarchiv, Merseburg (D.Z.A.)
    Rep. 76. Preußisches Ministerium für Wissenchaft Kunst und
    Volksbildung
    Rep. 77. Preußisches Ministerium des Innern
    Rep. 90a. Staatsministerialprotokolle

3. Bundesarchiv, Koblenz
    R 431. Reichskanzlei
    R 135. Preußisches Justizministerium
    Nachlaß Traub

4. Das politische Archiv des Auswärtigen Amtes (A.A.)
    Kulturpolitische Abteilung VI A-B
    Schuldreferat

5. Geheimes Staatsarchiv, West Berlin (G.St.A.)
    Rep. 90. Preußisches Staatsministerium

6. Nachlaß Becker, in possession of Professor H. Becker, West Berlin

7. NSDAP Hauptarchiv (Film)
    Reel 53, Folder 1240 Verschiedenes
    Reel 23, Folder 487 Evangelische Kirche

B. PRINTED SOURCES

(1) Primary Sources

Allgemeines Kirchenblatt für das evangelische Deutschland (Berlin, 1918-33).

Althaus, P., *Staatsgedanke und Reich Gottes* (3rd edn., Langensalza, 1926).

——, *Die deutsche Stunde der Kirche* (3rd edn., Göttingen, 1934).

Asmussen, H., *Reichskirche* (Hamburg, n.d., 1933).

——, *Zur jüngsten Kirchengeschichte* (Stuttgart, 1961).

Baier, H., Wright, J. R. C., 'Ein neues Dokument Zum Staatseingriff in Preußen 1933' in *Zeitschrift für Kirchengeschichte*, (forthcoming).

Barth, K., 'Quousque tandem' in *Zwischen den Zeiten*, 8. Jg. (Munich, 1930).

——, *Eine Schweizer Stimme, 1938-1945* (Zurich, 1945).

Baumgarten, O., *Mein Lebensgeschichte* (Tübingen, 1929).

Bell, G. K. A., *The Stockholm Conference, 1925* (London, 1926).

Berner, M., *Das Kirchenregiment in der altpreußischen Landeskirche* (Berlin, 1919).

Beyer, H., 'Volk, Staat und Kirche in der Übergangs—und Krisenzeit 1932-1934' in G. Kretschmar, B. Lohse, *Ecclesia und Res Publica* (Göttingen, 1961).

Boberach, H., *Berichte des SD und der Gestapo über Kirchen und Kirchenvolk in Deutschland 1934-1944* (Mainz, 1971).

Braun, O., *Von Weimar zu Hitler* (New York, 1940).

Brecht, A., *Aus Nächster Nähe. Lebenserinnerungen 1884-1927* (Stuttgart, 1966).

Bredt, J. V., *Die Rechte des Summus Episcopus* (Berlin, 1919).

——, *Neues evangelisches Kirchenrecht für Preußen* (Berlin, 1921-7).

Breucker, W., *Die Tragik Ludendorffs* (Oldenburg, 1953).

Brüning, H., *Memoiren 1918-1934* (Stuttgart, 1970).

Die Christliche Welt (Marburg, 1919-21; Gotha, 1922-32).

Conrad, W., *Der Kampf um die Kanzeln* (Berlin, 1957).

Dehn, G., *Die alte Zeit, Die vorigen Jahre* (Munich, 1962).

Denkschrift der Jungreformatorischen Bewegung über ihre Stellung zur Reichsbischofsfrage (Göttingen, 1933).

Deutscher Reichsanzeiger und Preußischer Staatsanzeiger (Berlin, 1918).

Dibelius, O., *Das Jahrhundert der Kirche* (1st edn., Berlin, 1927).

——, *Nachspiel* (Berlin, 1928).

——, *Friede auf Erden?* (Berlin, 1930).

——, *Ein Christ ist immer im Dienst* (Stuttgart, 1961). English translation, *In the Service of the Lord* (London, 1964).

Documenta. Unsere Pfälzische Landeskirche innerhalb der Deutschen Evangelischen Kirche in den Jahren 1930-1944 (Speyer, 1960), vol. 1.

Domarus, M., *Hitler, Reden und Proklamationen 1932-1945* (Würzburg, 1962-3).

Ebers, G. J., *Reichs- und preußisches Staatskirchenrecht* (Munich, 1932).

——, *Evangelisches Kirchenrecht in Preußen* (Munich, 1932).

Entscheidungen des Reichsgerichts in Zivilsachen (Berlin, 1921-9).

Fleisch, P., *Erlebte Kirchengeschichte. Erfahrungen in und mit der hannoverschen Landeskirche* (Hanover, 1952).

Friedrich, O., *Der evangelische Kirchenvertrag mit dem Freistaat Baden* (Lahr, 1933).

Gauger, J., *Gotthard Briefe. Chronik der Kirchenwirren* (Elberfeld, 1934).

Gerber, H., *Die Idee des Staates in der neueren evangelichen theologischen Ethik* (Berlin, 1930).

Gesetzes und Verordnungsblatt für die Vereinigte Evangelisch-protestantische Kirche Badens (Karlsruhe, 1919, 1932).

Giese, F., Hosemann, J., *Die Verfassungen der Deutschen Evangelischen Landeskirchen* (Berlin, 1927).

——, ——, *Das Wahlrecht der Deutschen Evangelischen Landeskirchen* (Berlin, 1929).

Göbell, W., *Kirche, Recht und Theologie in vier Jahrzehnten. Der Briefwechsel der Brüder Theodor und Julius Kaftan, ii. 1910-1926* (Munich, 1967).

Gogarten, F., *Politische Ethik* (Jena, 1932).

——, *Wider die Achtung der Autorität* (Jena, n.d.).

Gollert, F., *Dibelius vor Gericht* (Munich, 1959).

Grüber, H., *Erinnerungen aus sieben Jahrzehnten* (Cologne and Berlin, 1968).

Haenisch, K., *Neue Bahnen der Kulturpolitik* (Stuttgart and Berlin, 1921).

Handbuch des Landtags des Volkstaates Hessen, I.-III. Landtag 1919-1927 (Darmstadt, 1926).

Handbuch über den Preußischen Staat (Berlin, 1928, 1929).

Hase, H. C. von, *Evangelische Dokumente zur Ermordung der 'unheilbar Kranken' unter der nationalsozialistischen Herrschaft in den Jahren 1939-1945* (Stuttgart, 1964).

Heine, L., *Geschichte des Kirchenkampfes in der Grenzmark Posen-Westpreußen 1930-1940* (Göttingen, 1961).

Hermelink, H., *Kirche im Kampf* (Tübingen, 1950).

Heydt, F. von der, *Gute Wehr, Werden, Wirken und Wollen des Evangelischen Bundes* (Berlin, 1936).

Hier spricht Dibelius (Berlin, 1960).

Hirsch, E., *Staat und Kirche im 19. und 20. Jahrhundert* (Gottingen, 1929).

——, *Deutschlands Schicksal* (3rd edn., Gottingen, 1925).

——, *Das kirchliche Wollen der Deutschen Christen* (Berlin, 1933).

Hitler, A., *Mein Kampf* (Munich, 1925, 1927).

Hitler's Official Programme and its Fundamental Ideas (Engl. edn., London, 1938).

Hosemann, J., *Der Deutsche Evangelische Kirchenbund* (2nd. edn., Berlin, 1932).

Hossenfelder, J., *Die Richtlinien der Deutschen Christen* (Berlin, 1932).

——, *Volk und Kirche* (Berlin, 1933).

——, *Unser Kampf* (Berlin, 1933).

Jäger, A., *Kirche im Volk* (Berlin, 1937).

Kahl, W., *Lehrsystem des Kirchenrechts und der Kirchenpolitik* (Freiburg, 1894).

Kahl-Furthmann, G., *Hans Schemm spricht. Seine Reden und sein Werk* (8th edn., Bayreuth, 1936).

Kempner, R. M. W., 'Der Kampf gegen die Kirche. Aus unveröffentlichten Tagebüchern Alfred Rosenbergs' in *Der Monat*, 1. Jg. (1949).

Kirchliches Gesetz- und Verordnungsblatt (Berlin, 1918-33).

Kirchliches Jahrbuch für die evangelischen Landeskirchen Deutschlands, 44.-75. Jg. (Gütersloh, 1917-48).

Kirchliche Wegweisung, No. 1 (Berlin, 1933).

Kleist-Schmenzin, von, *Der Nationalsozialismus eine Gefahr* (Berlin, 1932).

Klotz, L., *Die Kirche und das dritte Reich* (Gotha, 1932).

Köhler, W., *Ernst Troeltsch* (Tübingen, 1941).

Kolb, E., *Der Zentralrat der Deutschen Sozialistischen Republik* (Leiden, 1968).

Kretschmar, G., Nicolaisen, C., *Dokumente zur Kirchenpolitik des Dritten Reiches*, Bd. 1, *Das Jahr 1933* (Munich, 1971).

Kübel, J., 'Die politische Einstellung der evangelischen Kirche' in *Der Zusammenschluß*, 1. Jg. (Berlin, 1926-7).

——, *Der Vertrag der evangelischen Landeskirchen mit dem Freistaat Preußen* (Berlin, 1931).

Künneth, W., Wilm, Pf., Schemm, H., *Was haben wir als evangelische Christen zum Rufe des Nationalsozialismus zu sagen?* (Dresden, 1931).

Künneth, W., Schreiner, H., *Die Nation vor Gott* (3rd edn., Berlin, 1934).

Kulturpolitische Aufgaben ed. by *Arbeitsgemeinschaft für staatsbürgerliche und wirtschaftliche Bildung* (Berlin, 1919).

Landé, W., *Die Schule in der Reichsverfassung* (Berlin, 1929).

Meier, K., *Kirche und Judentum. Die Haltung der evangelischen Kirche zur Judenpolitik des Dritten Reiches* (Göttingen, 1968).

Meier-Benneckenstein, P., *Dokumente der deutschen Politik*, Bd. 3 (Berlin, 1937).

Michael, H., Lohmann, K., *Der Reichspräsident ist Obrigkeit* (Hamburg, 1932).

Michaelis, H., Schraepler, E., *Ursachen und Folgen. Vom deutschen Zusammenbruch 1918 und 1945 bis zur staatlichen Neuordnung in der Gegenwart*, Bde. ix, xi (Berlin, n.d.).

Miller, S., *Die Regierung der Volksbeauftragten 1918/1919* (Düsseldorf, 1969).

Mirbt, C., 'Das bayerische Konkordat vom 29. März 1924' in *Neue kirchliche Zeitschrift*, 36. Jg. (Leipzig, 1925).

Mitteilungen aus der Arbeit der dem Evangelischen Oberkirchenrat und dem Generalsynodalvorstand beigeordneten Vertrauensmänner der Evangelischen Landeskirche, Nos. 1-12 (Berlin, 1918-19).

Mulert, H., 'Die politische Haltung der deutschen evangelischen Landeskirchen', in *Der Zusammenschluß*, 1. Jg. (Berlin, 1926-7).

Mumm, R., *Der christlich-soziale Gedanke. Bericht über eine Lebensarbeit in schwerer Zeit* (Berlin, 1933).

Niemöller, W., *Die bekennende Kirche sagt Hitler die Wahrheit* (Bielefeld, 1954).

——, *Hitler und die evangelischen Kirchenführer* (Bielefeld, 1959).

——, *Texte zur Geschichte des Pfarrernotbundes* (Berlin, 1958).

Papen, F. von, *Memoirs* (Engl. edn., London, 1952).

Picker, H., *Hitlers Tischgespräche im Führerhauptquartier 1941-1942* (2nd edn., Stuttgart, 1965).

Prater, G., *Kämpfer wider Willen. Erinnerungen des Landesbischofs von Sachsen D. Hugo Hahn* (Metzingen, 1969).

Preußische Gesetzsammlung (Berlin, 1919).

Quervain, A. de, *Die theologischen Voraussetzungen der Politik* (Berlin, 1931).

——, *Theologie und politische Gestaltung* (Berlin, n.d.).

Rauschning, H., *Hitler Speaks* (Engl. edn., London, 1939).

——, *Germany's Revolution of Destruction* (Engl. edn., London, 1939).

Ringwald, C., *Offener Brief an Seine Exzellenz Dr. Adolf von Harnack (Berlin) von einem badischen Laien* (Freiburg, 1925).

Rosenberg, A., *Wesen, Grundsätze und Ziele der Nationalsozialistischen Deutschen Arbeiterpartei* (Munich, 1923).

——, *Der Mythus des 20. Jahrhunderts* (1st edn., Munich, 1930).

——, *Protestantische Rompilger* (Munich, 1937).

Schäfer, G., *Die evangelische Landeskirche in Württemberg und der Nationalsozialismus. Eine Dokumentation zum Kirchenkampf*. Bd. 1. *Um das politische Engagement der Kirche 1932-1933*. Bd. 2. *Um eine deutsche Reichskirche 1933* (Stuttgart, 1971-2).

——, Fischer, R., *Landesbischof D. Wurm und der nationalsozialistische Staat 1940-1945. Eine Dokumentation* (Stuttgart, 1968).

Schian, M., *Die deutsche evangelische Kirche im Weltkriege* (Berlin, 1921, 1925).

Schiffer, E., *Ein Leben für den Liberalismus* (Berlin, 1951).

Schmidt, K. D., *Die Bekenntnisse des Jahres 1933* (2nd edn., Göttingen, 1937).

——, *Dokumente des Kirchenkampfes II, Die Zeit des Reichskirchenausschusses 1935-1937*, 2 vols. (Göttingen, 1964-5).

Schmitt, C., *Legalität und Legitimität* (Munich and Leipzig, 1932).

Schoen, P., *Das neue Verfassungsrecht der evangelischen Landeskirchen in Preußen* (Berlin, 1929).

Schotte, W., *Das Kabinett Papen Schleicher Gayl* (Leipzig, 1932).

Schreiner, H., *Der Nationalsozialismus vor der Gottesfrage* (Berlin, 1931).

Schwerin von Krosigk, L. Graf, *Es geschah in Deutschland* (3rd edn., Stuttgart, 1952).

Seraphim, H-G., *Das politische Tagebuch Alfred Rosenbergs, 1934/5 und 1939/40* (Munich, 1964).

Severing, C., *Mein Lebensweg* (Cologne, 1950).

Silbergleit, H., *Die Bevölkerungs-und Berufsverhältnisse der Juden im Deutschen Reich* (Berlin, 1930).

Sitzungsberichte der Verfassunggebenden Preußischen Landesversammlung, –des Preußischen Landtags (Berlin, 1919–32).

Smend, R., 'Protestantismus und Demokratie' (1932), reprinted in *Staatsrechtliche Abhandlungen und andere Aufsätze* (Berlin, 1955).

Speer, A., *Inside the Third Reich* (Engl. edn., London, 1970).

Stapel, W., *Sechs Kapitel über Christentum und Nationalsozialismus* (Hamburg, 1931).

——, *Der christliche Staatsmann* (Hamburg, 1932).

Stark, J., *Nationalsozialismus und katholische Kirche* (Munich, 1931).

Statistisches Jahrbuch für den Preußischen Staat (Berlin, 1920), ——*für den Freistaat Preußen* (Berlin, 1929).

Stehkämpfer, H., *Der Nachlaß des Reichskanzlers Wilhelm Marx* (Cologne, 1968).

Stenographische Berichte des Hauptausschusses des Preußischen Landtags (Berlin, 1928–9).

Strathmann, H., *Nationalsozialistische Weltanschauung?* (Nuremberg, 1931).

Stresemann, G., *Vermächtnis*, vol. 2 (Berlin, 1932).

Thimme, F., Rolffs, E., *Revolution und Kirche* (Berlin, 1919).

Traub, G., *Das bayerische Konkordat und was es für Volk und Staat bedeutet* (Munich, 1925).

Traub, G., *Erinnerungen* (Munich, 1949).

Trevor-Roper, H. R., *Hitler's Table Talk 1941-1944* (2nd edn., London, 1973).

Troeltsch, E., *Spektatorbriefe* (Tübingen, 1924).

Tyrell, A., *Führer Befiehl . . . Selbstzeugnisse aus der 'Kampfzeit' der NSDAP. Dokumentation und Analyse.* (Düsseldorf, 1969).

Ullmenried, W., *Die Reihe der deutschen Führer, Heft 6, Hossenfelder* (Berlin, 1933), *Heft 7, Müller* (Berlin, 1933).

Verhandlungen des Deutschen Evangelischen Kirchentags 1919, 1921, 1924, 1927, 1930 (Berlin, 1920, 1921, 1925, 1928, 1931).

Verhandlungen der außerordentlichen Kirchenversammlung, –der Generalsynode der evangelischen Landeskirche Preußens 1920, 1921-1922, 1925, 1927, 1929, 1930, 1931 (Berlin, 1920-31).

Verhandlungen der Landessynode der Evangelisch-Lutherischen Kirche im Bayern r. des Rheins, 1930-1936, Außerordentliche Tagung in Bayreuth 3.-5. Mai 1933 (Bayreuth, n.d.).

Verhandlungen der verfassunggebenden Nationalversammlung (Berlin, 1920).

Verhandlungen des Reichstags. III. Wahlperiode 1924 (Berlin, 1924).

182   BIBLIOGRAPHY

Wienecke, F., *Christentum und Nationalsozialismus* (2nd edn., Küstrin, 1931).
——, *Die Glaubensbewegung 'Deutsche Christen'* (6th edn., Soldin, 1933).
——, *Die Kampf- und Glaubensbewegung 'Deutsche Christen'* (Soldin, 1936).
Wolff, W., 'Die deutschen evangelischen Kirchen' in H. Müller, G. Stresemann, *Zehn Jahre Deutsche Geschichte 1918-1928* (Berlin, 1928).
Wünsch, G., *Reich Gottes, Marxismus, Nationalsozialismus* (Tübingen, 1931).
Wurm, T., *Erinnerungen aus meinem Leben* (Stuttgart, 1953).
Zahn-Harnack, A. von, *Adolf von Harnack* (Berlin, 1936).
Zentralblatt für die gesamte Unterrichtsverwaltung in Preußen 1918, 1919 (Berlin, 1918-19).
Zoellner, D. W., *Die ökumenische Arbeit des Deutschen evangelischen Kirchenausschusses und die Kriegsschuldfrage* (Berlin, 1931).
Zoller, A., *Hitler privat. Erlebnisbericht seiner Geheimsekretärin* (Düsseldorf, 1949).

(2) Secondary Sources

Ackermann, J., *Heinrich Himmler als Ideologe* (Göttingen, 1970).
Arndt, I., 'Die Judenfrage im Licht der evangelischen Sonntagsblätter von 1918-1933' (unpublished Diss. Phil., Tübingen, 1960, microfilm in Bodleian Library, Oxford).
Bahne, S., 'Die Kommunistische Partei Deutschlands' in E. Matthias, R. Morsey, *Das Ende der Parteien* (Düsseldorf, 1960).
Baier, H., *Die Deutschen Christen Bayerns im Rahmen des bayerischen Kirchenkampfes* (Nuremberg, 1968).
——, 'Das Verhalten der lutherischen Bischöfe gegenüber dem nationalsozialistischen Staat 1933/34' in P. Rieger, J. Strauss, *Tutzinger Texte, Sonderband I* (Munich, 1969).
Bethge, E., *Dietrich Bonhoeffer. Theologian, Christian, Contemporary* (Engl. edn., London, 1970).
Bigler, R. M., *The Politics of German Protestantism. The rise of the Protestant church elite in Prussia, 1815-1848* (Berkeley and London, 1972).
Bizer, E., 'Der Fall Dehn' in W. Schneemelcher, *Festschrift für Günther Dehn* (Neukirchen, 1957).
Bollmus, R., *Das Amt Rosenberg und seine Gegner. Zum Machtkampf im nationalsozialistischen Herrschaftssystem* (Stuttgart, 1970).
Borg, D. R., 'Volkskirche, Christian State, and the Weimar Republic' in *Church History*, 35 (1966).
Boyens, A., *Kirchenkampf und Ökumene 1933-1939* (Munich, 1969).
——, 'Das Stuttgarter Schuldbekenntnis vom 19. Oktober 1945' in *Vierteljahrshefte für Zeitgeschichte*, 19. Jg. (1971).

Bracher, K. D., *Die Auflösung der Weimarer Republik* (4th edn., Villingen, 1964).

——, *The German Dictatorship* (Engl. edn., London, 1971).

——, Sauer, W., Schulz, G., *Die nationalsozialistische Machtergreifung* (Cologne and Opladen, 1962).

Brandt, W., *Friedrich von Bodelschwingh 1877–1946* (Bethel, 1967).

Bremen, E. von, *Die Preußische Volksschule* (Stuttgart, 1905).

Broszat, M., *Der Staat Hitlers* (Munich, 1969).

Brunotte, H., 'Die kirchenpolitische Kurs der Deutschen Evangelischen Kirchenkanzlei von 1937 bis 1945' in *Arbeiten zur Geschichte des Kirchenkampfes*, xv (Göttingen, 1965).

Buchheim, H., *Glaubenskrise im Dritten Reich* (Stuttgart, 1953).

——, 'Die organisatorische Entwicklung der Ludendorff-Bewegung und ihr Verhältnis zum Nationalsozialismus' and 'War die katholische Kirche eine vom nationalsozialistischen Regime verfolgte Organisation?' in *Gutachten des Instituts für Zeitgeschichte* (Munich, 1958).

Buchheim, K., *Geschichte der christlichen Parteien in Deutschland* (Munich, 1953).

Bullock, A., *Hitler, a study in tyranny* (Revised edn., London, 1967).

Carsten, F. L., *The Reichswehr and Politics 1918–1933* (Oxford, 1966).

Cecil, R., *The Myth of the Master Race. Alfred Rosenberg and Nazi ideology* (London, 1972).

Chadwick, O., 'The present stage of the "Kirchenkampf" enquiry' in *Journal of Ecclesiastical History*, 24 (1973).

Chanady, A., 'The disintegration of the German National Peoples' Party 1924–1930' in *Journal of Modern History*, 39 (1967).

Christ, H., *Der politische Protestantismus in der Weimarer Republik. Eine Studie über die politische Meinungsbildung durch die evangelischen Kirchen im Spiegel der Literatur und der Presse* (Diss. Phil., Bonn, 1967).

Conway, J. S., *The Nazi Persecution of the Churches 1933–1945* (London, 1968).

Conze, W., Raupach, H., *Die Staats- und Wirtschaftskrise des Deutschen Reichs 1929/33* (Stuttgart, 1967).

Cordes, C., 'Hannoversche Pfarrer und Politik 1918–1929' in *Hannoversches Pfarrerblatt*, 74. Jg. (Hanover, 1967).

Dahm, K-W., *Pfarrer und Politik. Soziale Position und politische Mentalität des deutschen evangelischen Pfarrerstandes zwischen 1918 und 1933* (Cologne, 1965).

Deuerlein, E., *Das Reichskonkordat* (Düsseldorf, 1956).

Deutsch, H. C., *The Conspiracy against Hitler in the twilight war* (Minnesota and London, 1968).

Doetsch, W. J., *Württembergs Katholiken unterm Hakenkreuz 1930–1935* (Stuttgart, 1969).

Dorpalen, A., *Hindenburg and the Weimar Republic* (Princeton, 1964).

Elben, W., *Das Problem der Kontinuität in der deutschen Revolution* (Düsseldorf, 1965).

Elliger, W., *Die Evangelische Kirche der Union* (Witten, 1967).

Erger, J., *Der Kapp-Lüttwitz-Putsch* (Düsseldorf, 1967).

Eyck, E., *A history of the Weimar Republic* (Engl. edn., London, 1962-4).

Fischer, F., 'Der deutsche Protestantismus und die Politik im 19. Jahrhundert' in *Historische Zeitschrift*, 171 (Munich, 1951).

Förster, E., *Adalbert Falk* (Gotha, 1927).

Frank, W., *Hofprediger Adolf Stoecker* (2nd edn., Hamburg, 1935).

Friedrich, O., *Einführung in das Kirchenrecht unter besonderer Berücksichtigung des Rechts der Evangelischen Landeskirche in Baden* (Göttingen, 1961).

Gerlach-Praetorius, A., *Die Kirche vor der Eidesfrage* (Göttingen, 1967).

Giese, F., *Deutsches Kirchensteuerrecht* (Stuttgart, 1919).

Giesecke, H., 'Zur Schulpolitik der Sozialdemokraten in Preußen und im Reich 1918/19' in *Vierteljahrshefte für Zeitgeschichte*, 13. Jg. (1965).

Glees, P. A., 'Albert Grzesinski and the politics of Prussia 1926-1930' (B. Phil. thesis, Oxford, 1972).

Glenthøj, J., 'Unterredung im Vestibül. Das Gespräch zwischen Pfarrer Backhaus und Hitler am 28. Juni 1933' in *Kirche in der Zeit*, 17. Jg. (1962).

——, 'Hindenburg, Göring und die evangelischen Kirchenführer' in *Arbeiten zur Geschichte des Kirchenkampfes*, xv (Göttingen, 1965).

Götte, K. H., *Die Propaganda der Glaubensbewegung 'Deutsche Christen' und ihre Beurteilung in der deutschen Tagespresse* (Diss. Phil., Münster, 1957).

Golombek, D., *Die politische Vorgeschichte des Preußenkonkordats (1929)* (Mainz, 1970).

Goyau, G., *L'Allemagne religieuse. Le Protestantisme* (Paris, 1898).

Goodspeed, D. J., *Ludendorff* (London, 1966).

Gruchmann, L., 'Euthanasie und Justiz im Dritten Reich' in *Vierteljahrshefte für Zeitgeschichte*, 20. Jg. (1972).

Grünthal, G., *Reichsschulgesetz und Zentrumspartei in der Weimarer Republik* (Düsseldorf, 1968).

Gurian, W., *Der Kampf um die Kirche im Dritten Reich* (Lucerne, 1936).

Hartenstein, W., *Die Anfänge der Deutschen Volkspartei 1918-1920* (Düsseldorf, 1962).

Herberle, R., *Landbevölkerung und Nationalsozialismus. Eine soziologische Untersuchung der politischen Willensbildung in Schleswig Holstein 1918-1932* (Stuttgart, 1963).

Hermelink, H., *Geschichte der evangelischen Kirche in Württemberg von der Reformation bis zur Gegenwart* (Stuttgart and Tübingen, 1949).

Hertzman, L., *DNVP. Right-Wing Opposition in the Weimar Republic, 1918-1924* (Lincoln, 1963).

Heuss, T., *Friedrich Naumann* (2nd edn., Stuttgart, 1949).

Hockerts, H. G., *Die Sittlichkeitsprozeße gegen Katholische Ordensangehörige und Priester 1936/1937* (Mainz, 1971).

Huber, E. R., *Dokumente zur deutschen Verfassungsgeschichte* (Stuttgart, 1966).

Hudson, D., *The Ecumenical Movement and World Affairs* (London, 1969).

Jacobson, J., *Locarno Diplomacy. Germany and the West 1925-1929* (Princeton, 1972).

Jasper, R., *George Bell. Bishop of Chichester* (London, 1967).

Jochmann, W., 'Die Ausbreitung des Antisemitismus' in W. E. Mosse, *Deutsches Judentum in Krieg und Revolution 1916-1923* (Tübingen, 1971).

Jonas, E., *Die Volkskonservativen 1928-1933* (Düsseldorf, 1965).

Karg, T., *Von der Eisenacher Kirchenkonferenz zum Deutschen Evangelischen Kirchenbund* (Diss. Recht, Freiburg, 1961).

Karlström, N., 'Movements for International Friendship and Life and Work, 1910-1925' in R. Rouse, S. C. Neill, *A History of the Ecumenical Movement 1517-1948* (London, 1954).

Kater, H., *Die Deutsche Evangelische Kirche in den Jahren 1933 und 1934* (Göttingen, 1970).

Kent, G., Pope Pius XII and Germany in *American Historical Review*, 70 (1964).

Kimmich, C. M., *The Free City. Danzig and German Foreign Policy 1919-1934* (New Haven and London, 1968).

Klemperer, K. von, *Germany's New Conservatism* (2nd edn., Princeton, 1968).

Klügel, E., *Die lutherische Landeskirche Hannovers und ihr Bischof 1933-1945* (Berlin and Hamburg, 1964-1965).

Köhler, G., *Die Auswirkungen der Novemberrevolution von 1918 auf die altpreußische evangelische Landeskirche* (Diss. theol., Berlin, 1967).

Kolb, E., *Die Arbeiterräte in der deutschen Innenpolitik 1918-1919* (Düsseldorf, 1962).

Kressel, H., *Simon Schöffel* (Schweinefurt, 1964).

Kretschmar, G., Lohse, B., *Ecclesia und ResPublica* (Göttingen, 1961).

Kupisch, K., *Zwischen Idealismus und Massendemokratie. Eine Geschichte der evangelischen Kirche in Deutschland von 1815-1945* (Berlin, 1955).

——, *Die deutschen Landeskirchen im 19. und 20. Jahrhundert* (Göttingen, 1966).

Lewy, G., *The Catholic Church and Nazi Germany* (London, 1964).

Mehnert, G., *Evangelische Kirche und Politik 1917-1919* (Düsseldorf, 1959).

Meier, K., *Die Deutschen Christen* (Göttingen, 1964).

——, 'Kirche und Nationalsozialismus' in K. D. Schmidt, *Arbeiten zur Geschichte des Kirchenkampfes*, xv. (Göttingen, 1965).

Milatz, A., *Wähler und Wahlen in der Weimarer Republik* (Bonn, 1965).

Mohr, H., *Katholische Orden und deutscher Imperialismus* (Berlin, 1965).

Morsey, R., *Die Deutsche Zentrumspartei 1917-1923* (Düsseldorf, 1966).

Mosse, W., *Entscheidungsjahr 1932. Zur Judenfrage in der Endphase der Weimarer Republik* (Tübingen, 1965).

Motschmann, C., *Evangelische Kirche und preußischer Staat in den Anfängen der Weimarer Republik* (Lübeck, 1969).

Neumann P., *Die Jungreformatorische Bewegung* (Göttingen, 1971).

Niedner, J., *Die Ausgaben des preußischen Staats für die evangelische Landeskirche der älteren Provinzen* (Stuttgart, 1904).

Niemöller, W., *Die evangelische Kirche im Dritten Reich* (Bielefeld, 1956).

——, *Karl Koch. Präses der Bekenntnissynoden* (Bethel, 1956).

Noakes, J., *The Nazi Party in Lower Saxony 1921-1933* (Oxford, 1971).

Norden, G. van, *Kirche in der Krise: Die Stellung der evangelischen Kirche zum nationalsozialistischen Staat im Jahre 1933* (Düsseldorf, 1963).

Opitz, G., *Der christlich-soziale Volksdienst* (Düsseldorf, 1969).

Oxenius, H. G., *Die Entstehung der Verfassung der Evangelischen Kirche der altpreußischen Union von 1922* (Diss. Phil., Cologne, 1959).

Peterson, E. N., *The Limits of Hitler's Power* (Princeton, 1969).

Plewnia, M., *Auf dem Weg zu Hitler. Der völkische Publizist Dietrich Eckart* (Bremen, 1970).

Pressel, W., *Die Kriegspredigt 1914-1919 in der evangelischen Kirche Deutschlands* (Göttingen, 1967).

Pridham, G., *Hitler's Rise to Power. The Nazi Movement in Bavaria 1923-1933* (London, 1973).

Rathje, J., *Die Welt des freien Protestantismus* (Stuttgart, 1952).

Die Religion in Geschichte und Gegenwart (3rd edn., Tübingen, 1957-1965).

Rittberg, E. von, *Der Preußische Kirchenvertrag von 1931. Seine Entstehung und seine Bedeutung für das Verhältnis von Staat und Kirche in der Weimarer Republik* (Diss. Phil., Bonn, 1960).

Rothenbücher, K., *Die Trennung von Staat und Kirche* (Munich, 1908).

Runge, W., *Politik und Beamtentum im Parteienstaat* (Stuttgart, 1965).

Schieder, J., *D. Hans Meiser* (Munich, 1956).

Schieder, T., *Hermann Rauschning's 'Gespräche mit Hitler' als Geschichtsquelle*, Rheinisch-Westfälische Akademie der Wissenschaften, Vorträge G 178 (Opladen, 1972).

Schmid, H., *Apokalyptisches Wetterleuchten* (Munich, 1947).

Schmidt, K. D., 'Eine folgenreiche Episode' in *Evangelische Theologie*, 22. Jg. (1967).

Schmidt, J., *Martin Niemöller im Kirchenkampf* (Hamburg, 1971).

——, 'Die Erforschung des Kirchenkampfes. Die Entwicklung und der gegenwärtige Stand der Erkenntnis' in *Theologische Existenz heute*, 149 (1968).

——, 'Studien zur Vorgeschichte des Pfarrernotbundes' in *Zeitschrift für Kirchengeschichte*, 79 (1968).

Scholder, K., 'Die evangelische Kirche in der Sicht der national-sozialistischen Führung' in *Vierteljahrshefte für Zeitgeschichte*, 16. Jg. (1968).

——, 'Die Kapitulation der evangelischen Kirche vor dem national-sozialistischen Staat' in *Zeitschrift für Kirchengeschichte*, 81 (1970).

——, 'Die Kirchen im Dritten Reich' in *aus politik und zeit geschichte, beilage zur wochenzeitung das parlament*, 15 (1971).

Schwarz, W., *August Hinderer* (Stuttgart, 1951).

Schwend, K., 'Die Bayerische Volkspartei' in E. Matthias, R. Morsey, *Das Ende der Parteien* (Düsseldorf, 1960).

Siegmund-Schultze, F., *Ekklesia, v, Die evangelischen Kirchen in Polen* (Leipzig, 1938).

Söhngen, O., *Hundert Jahre Evangelischer Oberkirchenrat der Altpreußischen Union* (Berlin, 1950).

——, 'Der 2. Juli 1933, der "Sonntag der Kirche" ' in *Evangelisch-lutherische Kirchenzeitung. Festausgabe zum 60. Geburtstag von Präsident D. Heinz Brunotte*, 11 June 1956, Nr. 12.

——, 'Wie es anfing. Die Einsetzung des Staatskommissars und die Usurpierung des Evangelischen Oberkirchenrates in Berlin im Juni 1933' in H. Kruska, *Gestalten und Wege der Kirche im Osten* (Ulm, 1958).

——, 'Hindenburgs Eingreifen in den Kirchenkampf 1933' in *Arbeiten zur Geschichte des Kirchenkampfes*, xv (Göttingen, 1965).

——, 'Die Reaktion der "amtlichen" Kirche auf die Einsetzung eines Staatskommissars durch den nationalsozialistischen Staat' in *Arbeiten zur Geschichte des Kirchenkampfes*, xxvi (Göttingen, 1971).

Sontheimer, K., *Antidemokratisches Denken in der Weimarer Republik* (Munich, 1962).

Southern, D. B., 'Political and Legal Aspects of *Aufwertung*' (B. Phil. thesis, Oxford, 1972).

Stoll, G. E., *Die evangelische Zeitschriftenpresse im Jahre 1933* (Witten, 1963).

Stoltenberg, G., *Politische Strömungen im schleswig-holsteinischen Landvolk 1918-1933* (Düsseldorf, 1962).

Stribrny, W., 'Evangelische Kirche und Staat in der Weimarer Republik' in H. J. Schoeps, ed., *Zeitgeist im Wandel*, vol. 2: *Zeitgeist der Weimarer Republik* (Stuttgart, 1968).

Stürmer, M., *Koalition und Opposition in der Weimarer Republik 1924-1928* (Düsseldorf, 1967).

Suck, E. A., 'Der religiöse Sozialismus in der Weimarer Republik' (unpublished Diss. Phil., Marburg, 1953).

Sundkler, B., *Nathan Söderblom* (London, 1968).

Toaspern, P., *Arbeiter in Gottes Ernte. Heinrich Rendtorff. Leben und Werk* (Berlin, 1963).

Treue, W., *Deutsche Parteiprogramme 1861-1961* (3rd edn., Göttingen, 1961).

Turner, H. A., *Stresemann and the Politics of the Weimar Republic* (Princeton, 1963).

Tyrell, A., 'Der Mann, der Hitlers Kreise störte' in *Publik* (16 Jan. 1970).

Vierhaus, R., 'Die politische Mitte in der Weimarer Republik' in *Geschichte in Wissenschaft und Unterricht*, 15. Jg. (1964).

Vogelsang, T., *Reichswehr, Staat und NSDAP* (Stuttgart, 1962).

Volk, L., *Der Bayerische Episkopat und der Nationalsozialismus 1930-1934* (Mainz, 1965).

Weller, K., *Die Staatsumwälzung in Württemberg 1918-1920* (Stuttgart, 1930).

Wende, E., *C. H. Becker* (Stuttgart, 1958).

Wenschkewitz, L., 'Zur Geschichte des Reichskirchenministeriums und seines Ministers' in *Tutzinger Texte, Sonderband I* (Munich, 1969).

——, 'Politische Versuche einer Ordnung der Deutschen Evangelischen Kirche durch den Reichskirchenminister 1937 bis 1939' in *Arbeiten zur Geschichte des Kirchenkampfes*, xxvi (Göttingen, 1971).

Wer ist's? (10th edn., Berlin, 1935).

Wer ist Wer (14th edn., Berlin, 1965).

Westermanns Atlas zur Weltgeschichte (Berlin, 1956).

Wheeler-Bennett, J. W., *The Nemesis of Power* (2nd edn., London, 1967).

Wolf, E., 'Political and Moral Motives behind the Resistance' in H. Graml, H. Mommsen, H-J. Reichardt, E. Wolf, *The German Resistance to Hitler* (Engl. edn., London, 1970).

Wright, J. R. C., 'The political attitudes of the German Protestant church leadership, November 1918-July 1933' (D. Phil. thesis, Oxford, 1969).

Zipfel, F., *Kirchenkampf in Deutschland 1933-1945* (Berlin, 1965).

C. INTERVIEWS

(Personal details refer first to the time of the interview and then to the period covered by the book.)

O. Dibelius, Bishop of Berlin; member of the Oberkirchenrat 1921-5, Generalsuperintendent 1925-33; Berlin, 23 Oct. 1965, 19 Aug. 1966.

J. Hossenfelder, Pastor; *Reichsleiter der Deutschen Christen* 1932-3; Ratekau (nr. Lübeck), 16 Jan. 1968.

M. Niemöller, *Kirchenpräsident i. R.*; member of Bodelschwingh's staff 1933; Wiesbaden, 18 Jan. 1968.

G. Stratenwerth, *Vizepräsident i. R.*; member of Bodelschwingh's staff 1933; Frankfurt, 15 Sept. 1966.

A. Kapler, *Pfarrer i. R.*; son of President Kapler; Berlin, 13 Oct. 1965.

W. Conrad, *Oberregierungsrat a.D.*; senior official in Reich Ministry of the Interior with responsibility for church affairs; Berlin, 24 May 1966.

T. Heckel, *Dekan*; member of theological staff of Kirchenbundesamt; Munich, 2 May 1966.

B. Karnatz, *Oberkonsistorialrat i. R.*; member of Berlin Oberkirchenrat, 1919-33; Berlin, 20 Oct. 1965.

O. Söhngen, *Vizepräsident der Kanzlei der Evangelischen Kirche der Union*; junior member of Oberkirchenrat 1932-33; Berlin, 16 Aug. 1968.

R. Smend, Professor Emeritus, Göttingen; member of executive committee of the middle party in the General Synod of the Old Prussian Union; Göttingen, 3 Dec. 1966.

H. Lilje, Bishop of Hanover; member of *Jungreformatorische Bewegung* 1933; Hanover, 2 Dec. 1965.

INDEX

Allgemeine Evangelisch-Lutherische Kirchenzeitung, 83, 84 fn. 46
Althaus, P., 54–5, 74–5, 78, 108 fn. 39
Altona, 100; declaration, 100 fn. 6
Angriff, Der, 84–5
Anhalt, 2, 77, 87, 100 fn. 6
Anti-Republican Right, v, 24, 33, 48; and Protestant leadership, 57–9, 61, 63–5, 67, 74–98, 145–6; contribution of church to, 104–5
Anti-Semitism, 77, 86, 104; Protestant leadership and, 54–5, 75, 90, 114–7; in Nazi programme, 79–83; in German Christian programme, 93–4; Confessing Church and, 157–8, 164–7
Army, v, 11, 151, 153
Arnim-Kröchlendorff, W. von, 44, 46
Austria, 72

Baden, 2, 27, 32, 51–2, 56, 77
Barth, K., 85, 168–9
Bavaria, 1–2, 27, 77–8, 102–3, 132, 136 fn. 113; concordat and church treaties in, 32, 34–6
Beamte, xvi, 5, 9
Becker, C. H., 26, 36 fn. 19, 176; and concordat and church treaty, 37–8, 42–3
Bekennende Kirche, see Confessing Church
Bell, G., 150
Bierschwale, A., 113 fn. 11, 121
Bismarck, O. von, 2, 8, 55
Blomberg, W. von, 123
Bodelschwingh, F. von, 118, 127–8, 130–8, 142, 174; nominated Reich bishop, 134–5; resigns, 137
Bonhoeffer, D., 169
Bormann, M., 154 fn. 26, 156 fn. 35
Bracht, F., 107
Braun, O., 38–42, 46, 47 fn. 87, 62, 65 fn. 76
Braune, P-G., 167
Bremen, 27, 100 fn. 6
Brüning, H., 41 fn. 45, 91 fn. 73, 99, 109 fn. 40
Brunswick, 27, 56, 87; Bishop

Brunswick—*contd.*
Bernewitz of, 87 fn. 59, 100, 108 fn. 38
Burghart, G., 96, 102 fn. 16, 105 fn. 28, 114 fn. 19
Buttmann, R., 84, 110, 133
BVP, xiv, 80

Calvinist churches, *see* Reformed churches
Centre party, 17–18, 20–2, 24, 50, 53, 105, 113; and concordat, 33, 38, 41; Protestants think unprincipled 54; and Reich School Law, 56; attacked by NSDAP, 85; and von Papen, 109 fn. 40
Christian state, 8, 106, 108–10, 145
Christian Social *Volksdienst*, 83
Christlich-Deutsche Bewegung, 89
Christliche Welt, 7, 35
Church elections, to constituent assembly of the Old Prussian Union, 23; parish elections, 1931–2, 91–8; parish elections 1933, 131, 140–1; proposal for in 1937, 153, 162
Church liberals, 7–8, 11, 21, 23–5, 59
Church parties, 7–8, 92, 120
Church tax, 5
Civil service, v, 11, 112, 151
Civil war, 99–100, 109, 147
Confessing Church, 142, 159–73; memorandum of, 164–5; order of prayer 1938, 165–6; 'intact' churches in, 161–2, 165–7; Prussian synod 1943, 167; and resistance, 163–73
Conrad, W., 110 fn. 1, 189

Dehn, G., 105 fn. 26
Deutsche Zeitung, 24, 62
DDP, 18, 20–1, 55; and church treaty, 38 fn. 31, 41–2
Deutschkirche, 77–8
Dibelius, O., 25, 97 fn. 94, 151 fn. 12, 189; biog., 17 fn. 30; and election campaign 1919, 17; and church treaty, 47–8; and revolu-

Dibelius, O.—*contd.*
 tion of 1918, 50; and propaganda
 for Protestants abroad, 68; and
 Vaterländische Verbände, 71,
 76–7; and NSDAP, 84; and constitutional reform, 107 fn. 35;
 and restoration of the monarchy,
 146 fn. 2; in 1933, 112–3, 115
Dieterich, A., 12–13, 17, 24
Dinter, A., 80–1, 142
DNVP, xiv, 18, 60, 71, 85, 89, 94 fn.
 78, 104 fn. 25, 176; and church
 treaty, 33–4, 38, 41–3, 46; allies
 of Protestant church, 17, 49, 51,
 57–8; and Reich School Law, 56;
 and Young plan, 63
DVP, xiv, 17–18, 55–7, 60; and
 church treaty, 38 fn. 31, 41–2, 46

Ebert, F., 59
Eckert, E., 52
Economic crisis (1930–2), 67, 71–4,
 99–100, 147
Ecumenical movement, 67–72,
 115–6, 150, 170–1
Eisenacher Kirchenkonferenz, 3
Erzberger, M., 58
Euthanasia, 167, 172–3
Evangelischer Bund, xvi, 35, 79 fn.
 19
Evangelischer Oberkirchenrat, *see*
 Oberkirchenrat
Expropriation of royal houses, 53

Falk, A., 6
Fezer, K., 125–6, 136
Frederick William III, 1–2, 4, 162
Frederick William IV, 3–4
Free-masons, 75–7
Frick, W., 86–7, 110, 119, 122, fn.
 49, 138–9, 151, 167

Generalsuperintendenten, xvi, 5–6,
 23, 45, 51, 119, 138, 141
General Synod of the Old Prussian
 Union, xvi; origin of, 6; church
 parties in, 7–8; and constitution
 of 1922, 20–1, 25; President of,
 25; and church treaty, 36–8,
 41–2, 44, 46, 48, 146; and war
 guilt, 70; and Müller, 141
Gerber, H., 108 fn. 39
German Christians, 25, 85, 89, 111,

German Christians—*contd.*
 144, 146, 148, 151–2; in parish
 elections, 91–8, 140–1; in east
 Prussia, 94, 97, 125–6; Reich
 conference of, 113, 117, 119,
 121; conflict with Protestant
 leadership, 117–42; differences
 between Müller and Hossenfelder
 groups, 124–6; campaign for
 Müller as Reich bishop, 129–30,
 135–7; less threatening in provinces than in Berlin, 134; Hitler
 and, 149; in Third Reich, 157–62,
 164, 169, 172
German Empire, Protestant leadership identified with, v, 66;
 position of church in, 4–5, 54
German paganism, 75, 79, 84 fn. 45,
 156, 159, 164
Goebbels, J., 83, 84 fn. 47, 89,
 155 fn. 33
Göring, H., 83, 143–4, 151
Gogarten, F., 108 fn. 39
Grimme, A., 43–5, 107
Groener, W., 100, 123 fn. 53
Grüber, H., 166
Grzesinski, A., 102

Haenisch, K., 12, 15–17, 21, 24–5
Hamburg, 27, 132
Hanover, 2, 62, 65 fn. 75, 66
Harnack, A. von, 8 fn. 17, 18–19
Heckel, J., 107, 143 fn. 1
Heckel, T., 189
Heß, R., 151
Hesse, H., 122, 123 fn. 55, 124, 135
 fn. 110, 175
Hessen, 2, 27, 53, 56; Hessen-Nassau,
 92; Hesse-Kessel, 100
Heydrich, R., 151 fn. 14, 154 fn. 26
Himmler, H., 154 fn. 26, 156, 163
Hindenburg, P. von, 62, 112 fn. 8,
 138; Reich Presidential election
 1925, 50, 59; Reich Presidential
 election 1932, 105–6; intervenes
 in 1933, 139
Hirsch, E., 120–1, 130 fn. 83
Hitler, A., 24, 85–6, 91, 99, 105,
 109, 116, 138, 141–2, 146,
 164–5, 167–8, 170; claim to be a
 friend of the church, 78–80, 83;
 described as gift of God, 85;

Hitler, A.—*contd.*
  difference between Rosenberg and, 88-9, 156; support of church members for, 106; religious policy of, 92, 110, 124, 128, 148-57, 160, 162, 169, 171-3; promises to respect rights of church, 113, 122; celebrations for birthday of, 114; and Müller, 118, 126, 130, 135, 148-51, 156, 159; alleged to favour Protestant bloc, 119; and Mecklenburg Staatskommissar, 122; and Reich bishop, 127-31, 149; and Prussian Staatskommissar, 139, 144; broadcasts in support of German Christians, 140

Hoffmann, A., 12-16
Hohenzollern dynasty, 39, 146
Hossenfelder, J., 87 fn. 61, 189; Reich leader of the German Christians, 92-4, 96, 119, 148; demands German Christian representation on church bodies, 121, 122 fn. 48; and Müller, 123-6, 142; radical demands of, 124-5; proposes Müller as Reich bishop, 129; vice-president of the Oberkirchenrat, 138-9, 141; and appointment of the Staatskommissar, 144 fn. 3

Hugenberg, A., 57, 63, 71, 99
Hundt, E., 111, 143-4, 175

Inner Mission, 7, 54, 89, 91, 94, 118, 134, 167

Jäger, A., 110, 137-9, 142-4, 159-60

Kaftan, J., 51
Kahl, W., 16, 18, 41 fn. 43, 51, 60
Kapler, A., 50 fn. 4, 122 fn. 50, 176, 189
Kapler, H., 81, 91, 108, 176; President of the Oberkirchenrat, 25-6; and church treaty, 34-48; and Weimar Republic, 39, 50, 145-6; and Reich School Law, 57; and Hindenburg, 59, 105-6; and Young Plan, 63-4, 93; and ecumenical movement, 69-72; and 'national movement', 76-7;

Kapler, H.—*contd.*
  and NSDAP, 89-90, 101-2; and political violence, 100, 112; and Nazi pastors, 101; policy in 1933 of, 111-42; resists intervention in the church, 113-14, 121-2, 142; and Hitler's birthday, 114; and persecution of the Jews, 114-17; and reform of church organization, 118-20, 124-35, 140; and Müller, 128-32; resignation of, 132, 135 fn. 110; and appointment of the Staatskommissar, 143-4

Kapp *Putsch,* 58
Karnatz, B., 57 fn. 38, 143 fn. 1, 189
Kerrl, H., 152-5, 157, 160-4, 166-7
Kirchenausschuß, xvi; origin of, 3; President of, 3, 30; and Kirchenbund, 28-30; membership of, 29-30; and church treaty, 33-5; and *Kultur,* 51-2; and Communism, 52; and expropriation of royal houses, 53; and Reich School Law, 56-7; and anniversary of the Weimar constitution, 61-2; protests against Allies, 67, 71; and 'national movement', 76; and NSDAP, 100-1; and constitutional reform, 107-8; and 'national revolution' 111; and persecution of the Jews, 116; and church reform, 124; in June 1933, 136-7

Kirchenbund, vii, 3, 174-5; formation of, 28-30; organization of, *see* Diagram B, p. 29; government support for, 67-8; reform of, 117-27, 139-40
Kirchenbundesamt, xvi; set up, 30; *Oberkonsistorialrat* Scholz, official of, 52, 81-2, 88 fn. 62; memorandum on Jewish question, 116-17; occupied by S.A., 139; Hosemann, J., director of, 112 fns. 8, 9

Kirchenbundesrat, xvi; set up, 29; and Deutschkirche, 78
Kirchenkampf, 111, 141-2, 148, 156-73
Kirchenkommissar, *see* Staatskommissar
Kirchensenat, xvi, 121; creation of,

Kirchensenat—*contd.*
  23; President of, 23, 25; and
  church treaty, 37, 40–41, 44–6;
  and Müller, 141; and the Staatskommissar, 143–4
Kirchentag, xvi; in 1848, 3; in
  Weimar Republic, 28–30, 50–2,
  54, 100; *Vaterländische Kundgebung* of, 60–1, 75, 77, 146; protests against Allies, 67; and war
  guilt, 70; and 'national movement', 74–5
*Körperschaft des öffentlichen
  Rechts,* xvi, 4, 19, 23, 47
Konsistorium, xvi, 5
KPD, xiv, 52–3, 74, 84 fn. 46, 88,
  90, 99, 148, 171; and church
  treaty, 38 fn. 31, 43 fn. 64, 46
Kübel, J., 43 fn. 64
Kube, W., 91–3, 113
Kulturkampf, xvi, 8, 24, 138, 151
Kultusministerium, xvi, 4; *see*
  Prussian Kultusministerium

Land, xvi; church within jurisdiction
  of, 3–5
Landesherrliches Kirchenregiment,
  xvi, 5, 10
Landeskirche, vii, xvi; history of, 2;
  position of before 1918, 3–7;
  independence of, 29–30
Landtag, xvi, 8, 10; and church
  treaty, 38, 40–44, 46–7
Ley, R., 130–1
Liebknecht, K., 14
Lilje, H., 189
Locarno, Treaty of, 72
Ludendorff, E., 75–80
Lübeck, 27, 103, 162
Luther, M., 60, 62, 93, 102 fn. 15,
  107 fn. 35, 112, 123 fn. 55, 169
Lutheran churches, 1–3, 7–8; and
  Bodelschwingh, 132–4, 136–9,
  141; in Third Reich, 159–60; *see*
  Confessing Church, 'intact'
  churches in
Luxemburg, R., 14

Marahrens, A., 122, 124, 140, 176;
  and Bodelschwingh, 132, 135–6; in
  Third Reich, 159, 161, 163
Marx, W., 59
Maurenbrecher, M., 24

Mecklenburg, 27, 132, 162; Staats-
  kommissar in, 117–18, 121–2
Meiser, H., 132 fn. 95, 133, 138,
  140, 159–60, 175
Mittelstand, 65, 105
Moeller, R., 25 fn. 71, 34, 36, 50, 61
Müller L., 118–19, 152–3, 175; biog.,
  123; Hitler's representative for
  Protestant affairs, 123–4; and
  Hitler, 110, 123, 148–51, 155–6;
  as a moderate, 94, 121 fn. 40,
  123–4, 142, 158; co-operates with
  Kapler's committee, 124–5; and
  German Christians, 124–6, 158;
  and Reich bishopric, 128–37,
  140–2, 157–60; takes over
  Kirchenbund, 138–9
Münchmeyer, L., 104
Mumm, R., 18, 33–4, 43 fn. 64, 57
  fn. 39

National Constituent Assembly,
  15–16, 18–19
Naumann, F., 4 fn. 6, 18 fn. 39
'New' Prussian churches, 2, 26; and
  church treaty, 36, 40, 47
Niemöller, M., 132, 142, 157, 159,
  162–3, 168, 171, 189
NSDAP, xiv, 104 fn. 25, 109 fn. 41,
  134, 144, 146–7, 168; and church
  treaty, 38 fn. 31, 43 fn. 64, 46;
  and Young Plan, 63; and education, 81, 83, 113, 164; membership of by clergy, 85–7, 103;
  exploitation of church by, 102–5;
  religious policy of, 74, 77–91,
  110–11, 119, 148–56; and Müller,
  131, 135–6; and parish elections,
  91–5, 97, 140

National Socialist *Pastorenbund,*
  85–6, 92

Oberkirchenrat, xvi; creation of, 6;
  attitude to state, 8–10; President
  of, 9, 23, 30, 141; and constitution of 1922, 20–4; and Kultusministerium, 25–6; and church
  treaty, 33, 36–8, 40–3; and
  Deutschkirche, 77; and NSDAP,
  82, 90, 105–6; and German
  Christians, 95–6; and desecration

Oberkirchenrat—*contd.*
    of Jewish cemeteries, 101; and
    exploitation of church by pol-
    itical groups, 101–4; and religious
    education, 107; address of, in
    April 1933, 114; members dis-
    missed, 138, 143
Oldenburg, 27, 87, 103
Old Prussian Union, vii, 174–5; origin
    of, 2; degree of self-government
    before 1918, 7–8; constitution of
    1922, 20–25; survives revolution
    intact, 24; organization of, *see*
    Diagram A, p. 22; maintains con-
    nection with lost provinces, 67;
    and Bodelschwingh, 132; and
    Müller, 141; and Staatskommissar,
    143–4

Pacelli, E., 37
Papen, F. von, 99, 106–9, 113 fn. 15
Parity, principle of, 8, 33, 37, 41
Pastors' Emergency League, 142 fn.
    141, 157–9
Pechmann, W. von, 35, 51, 115–16,
    122 fn. 50
Piechowski, P., 52 fn. 14, 53, 63
Poland, 67, 72
Positive Christianity, 79, 84, 89, 93
Protestant church, membership of, vi,
    120 fn. 39; idea of uniting im-
    practicable, 2; demand for more
    independence for, 8; difficulty of
    reforming, 11–12, 24–5; repre-
    sented by Kirchenausschuß,
    29–30; in First World War, 66;
    and NSDAP, 88–90, 103; ex-
    ploitation by political groups of,
    101–5; support for Hitler from,
    106; revolution within in 1933,
    117–42; desire for reform, 120–1;
    police measures against, 153, 159,
    162–3; in Third Reich, 156–73
Protestant leadership, membership
    of, vi, 25–6; conservative group, v;
    appointment to, 5, and *see*
    Prussian church treaty, political
    clause; and democracy, 55, 99;
    condemns Rathenau's assassina-
    tion, 58; unlikely to have been
    appeased, 72–3; and NSDAP,
    87–91, 98, 105, 146–7; and Third
    Reich in 1933, 111–17; criticism
    of, 120; disunity of, 131–7;

Protestant leadership—*contd.*
    141–2; and Weimar Republic,
    145–6; *see* also Kirchenausschuß
Prussian church treaty, 32–48, 60,
    63, 86, 93; political clause, 33,
    37–8, 43–8; and NSDAP, 43,
    113, 121; and the Staats-
    kommissar, 143–4
Prussian Constituent Assembly, 17,
    20–1
Prussian constitution, 6, 13, 19
Prussian Kultusministerium, 6, 174;
    departmental officials of, 16,
    21–4; and constitution of Old
    Prussian Union, 20–24; and Ober-
    kirchenrat, 25–6; and church
    treaty, 36–8, 40, 42–5; and Nazi
    pastors, 101–2, 104; in 1933,
    110, 118, 138–9; and Hossen-
    felder, 121; and the Staats-
    kommissar, 143–4
Prussian *Land*, provisional govern-
    ment of, 12–16; Three Ministers
    of, 20–2; Ministry of the Interior,
    123

Quervain, A. de, 108 fn. 39

Rade, M., 7
Rathenau, W., 58
Rauschning, H., 110, 148–50
Reformed churches, 1–2, 120, 122
Reich government, 3, 12, 22, 28–30
Reich bishop, 111, 118, 125, 127,
    140, 144, 160
Reich Minister of the Interior, 27,
    35, 100, 103, 174; W. von Gayl
    as, 108 fn. 36; in 1933, 110, 133,
    139
Reichsbanner, xvii, 82 fn. 32
Reichsbote, Der, 62
Reichsgericht, 27–8
Reichskirche, 28, 91, 93, 119,
    123–4, 127, 155, 159–60
Religious education, 13, 15, 17–19,
    27, 107; Nazi policy towards, 81,
    164
Religious Socialists, 43, 52 fn. 14,
    53, 103, 105, 112 fn. 7; criticism
    of NSDAP by, 82–3
Rendtorff, H., 89, 100, 106, 122 fn.
    49, 133
Revolution of 1918, 9–11, 50–1

Roman Catholic church, 1, 4, 8, 28, 30, 50, 66; and concordats, 31–41, 46; Protestant objections to, 54; and Young Plan, 63; and NSDAP, 84, 88 fn. 63, 148, 150, 153 fn. 24, 171 fn. 88; and persecution of the Jews, 116 fn. 30

Rosenberg, A., 78, 80, 83, 86, 88–9, 149 fn. 5, 150–1, 153 fn. 21, 154, 155 fn. 33, 156, 163

Rust, B., 43, 110, 125, 137, 143–4

S.A., 85, 93, 139

Saxony, 27–8; Bishop Ihmels of, 100

Schemm, H., 86, 91 fn. 71, 92, 133–4

Schleswig-Holstein, 2, 55 fn. 29, 77, 103, 136 fn. 113; Bishop Mordhorst of, 78, 138

Schmitt, C., 107 fn. 35

Schöffel, S., 133, 134 fn. 103, 140

Schools, supervision of, 7, 13; in Weimar constitution, 19; Reich School Law, 19, 55–7; in concordats, 34–7; Nazi policy towards, 81, 86–7, 113, 164

Schreiner, H., 89

Schwerin von Krosigk, L. Graf, 131 fn. 90, 149 fn. 7

Separation of church and state, 4, 9, 11–15, 19, 151–2, 154, 156

Severing, C., 63, 123

Smend, R., 48, 189

Söderblom, N., 69

Söhngen, O., 189

Soviet Union, 52, 85

SPD, xiv, 20, 24, 102, 105–6; religious policy of, 11–12, 18; and church treaty, 33, 38, 42–3, 46; and Protestant church, 30–1, 52–4, 64–5, 90; NSDAP criticism of, 85

Speer, A., 149 fn. 6, 156

Staatsgerichtshof, 45, 138

Staatshoheitsrechte, xvii, 5–6

Staatskirche, 8–9, 19, 83, 127 fn. 75, 142, 151

Staatskommissar, xvii, 117–19, 121–2, 124 fn. 57, 137–44

Stahlhelm, xvii, 63, 77, 89, 101–3

Stapel, W., 108 fn. 39

Stark, J., 84

State subsidies, 6–7, 11, 13, 16, 19, 27, 152; and church treaty, 35, 37, 46; attacked by SPD, 53; NSDAP and, 86, 113

Stoecker, A., 9 fn. 21, 66

Stöhr, F., 81–2

Stoltenhoff, E., 144

Strasser, G., 80, 92–3, 148

Stratenwerth, G., 131 fn. 90, 137 fn. 118, 189

Streicher, J., 149

Stresemann, G., 39 fn. 33, 60, 65, 70, 72

Stuckart, W., 151–2

Summus Episcopus, xvii, 5, 39

Synods, vi, 3–6; conservative majority in, 8; Prussian provincial synods, 20, 36; National Synod, 127, 140–1, 157–8; Barmen synod, 159–60, 168 fn. 80; Prussian synod 1943, 167

Tägliche Rundschau, 121–2, 126

Tannenbergbund, 75–8

Thuringia, 56, 80, 100, 102–3, 136 fn. 113; NSDAP in, 86–7; German Christians in, 92, 162

Traub, G., 18, 35, 58 fn. 43, 83–4, 176

Trendelenburg, F., 36–8, 40, 44, 101, 110 fn. 1

Troeltsch, E., 21, 22 fn. 59, 24–5

United Prussian Church, 1–3, 7

Vaterländische Verbände, 71, 76–7

Vernunftrepublikaner, 16 fn. 26, 55, 60, 63–5, 106, 145–6; ambivalence of, 90, 108

Versailles, Treaty of, 59, 66–7, 70–2, 85 fn. 51; and reparations, 59, 147

Vertrauensrat, xvii, 13, 17, 20, 58 fn. 43

Völkischer Beobachter, 80, 85, 87

Vorwärts, 53 fn. 20, 63

Vossische Zeitung, 63–4

War guilt, 68–70, 72

Warthegau, 154–7

Weichert, L., 125–6

Weimar constitution, 3, 10, 20–1, 24, 27–8, 45, 50, 106; religious

Weimar constitution—*contd.*
    provisions of, 18–19; celebration
    of the anniversary of, 50, 61–3;
    limits of Protestant leadership's
    commitment to, 107–8; and
    Enabling Law, 112
Weimar Republic, studies of Prot-
    estant church in, vi–vii;
    rapprochement of church with,
    10, 25–6, 30–1, 49, 64–5; signifi-
    cance of church treaty for, 48
Weismann, R., 39
Wessel, L., 14–16
Westphalia, 1, 138 fn. 120, 140, 159
Wienecke, F., 85–6, 89 fn. 65, 176
William I, 55

William II, 9, 50, 67
Winckler, F., 25, 39, 45–6, 57 fn. 39
Wirth, J., 58
Wirtschaftspartei, 38 fn. 31, 41–3
Workers' and soldiers' councils,
    14–15, 27
Württemberg, 1, 27, 100 fn. 6,
    102–3, 132
Wurm, T., 57 fn. 39, 103–4, 108–9,
    133, 154 fn. 29, 159–60, 167,
    170, 176

Young Plan, 42, 63–4, 71, 93
Young Reformer Movement, 121,
    127–8, 135, 140